TOPPING THE DOME

Art and Politics During the Construction of the Capitol Dome

An historic novel based on the actual events as they unfolded from 1835 to 1863

Richard F. Novak

To my wife Rose and family

Table of Contents

Prologue

On March 6, 1805, Benjamin Henry Latrobe, the architect for the United States Capitol, sent a letter to the American Consul in Leghorn, Italy, for Phillip Mazzei, a close friend of President Thomas Jefferson. The letter began,

> Phillip Mazzei, Esq.
>
> Sir: By direction of the President of the United States I take the liberty to apply to you for your assistance in procuring for us the services of a good sculptor in the erection of the public buildings in this city, especially the Capitol. The Capitol was begun at a time when the country was entirely destitute of artists, and even of good workmen in the branches of architecture, upon which the superiority of public buildings depends.[1]

The letter goes on to describe the terms of employment as well as the wages. It also asks Mazzei to see if Antonio Canova, the leading sculptor at the time in Rome, would do a sculpture of a nine foot (sitting) figure of Liberty.

The Capitol plan had been submitted in 1791 to President George Washington by Pierre Charles L'Enfant for the seat of the new government on land ceded by Maryland. The plan included a site but no drawings for the building when L'Enfant was fired. Secretary of State Thomas Jefferson was eager to begin the building and suggested a competition with an award of $500 plus a city lot for the design of a Capitol.

Seventeen entries were received, but none satisfied the commissioners appointed by the President. More likely, they did not please Jefferson, one of the commissioners, a man with a passion for architecture. After the competition was over, Dr. William Thornton submitted some drawings in the classical style, which was admired by Jefferson. President Washington gave final approval for the Thornton plan April 15, 1793.

Progress was slow. For 12 years the construction of the Capitol suffered through revisions, stoppages and oversight by men not trained as architects. In 1803, Jefferson, now president, appointed Benjamin Henry Latrobe surveyor of public buildings. Latrobe was a successful architect, and Jefferson wanted him to oversee the work, expedite the construction, and develop further architectural and ornamental details for the building. The lack of experienced, skilled American craftsmen frustrated Latrobe. Thorton's original proposal divided the Capitol into three sections, aligned north and south, with the central area covered by a low dome inspired by the Pantheon in Rome. In 1805, only the North Wing had been completed.

Mazzei received Latrobe's letter while in Pisa, Italy. In September, he wrote Jefferson that two sculptors were on their way to Baltimore. When Mazzei visited Rome, he found Canova old and unenthusiastic, but then he met Bertel Thorvaldsen, a protégé of Canova, who expressed interest in the project. Mazzei also suggested Thorvaldsen was a better sculptor.

The two Italian sculptors leaving for America were Giuseppe Franzoni, son of the President of the Academy of Fine Arts in Carrara, and Giovanni Andrei.[2] They arrived in February, 1806. Soon other Italian sculptors and artisans followed to work on the Capitol.

Latrobe began reworking the infrastructure of the North Wing, already in poor repair. By 1809, he had completed the North Wing which would house the Senate, Supreme Court, and the Library of Congress. The central area of the building was an unfinished shell. He complained of the slow work of the Italian sculptors, but they had completed the decoration in the North Wing, seat of the House of Representatives.

Jefferson did not hesitate to provide changes to the plans, leaving Latrobe to deal with both the Jefferson's architectural preferences and appropriation of funds by the Congress which expressed their displeasure about the lack of work for American artists. In 1810, Jefferson's successor, President James Madison, and the Congress, did not show much interest in the construction of the Capitol. They were concentrating on preparations for an impending war with the British.

Congress declared war against Great Britain August 18, 1812. On August 24, 1814, a large force of British troops stormed an inadequate American army defending Washington D.C., sacked and burned the Capitol, gutting the interior of the North and South Wings including the work of the Italian sculptors.

After 21 years of construction, the Capitol had not been completed, but the Italian sculptors would now have more work. Perhaps a similar pace of construction might give American sculptors an opportunity to participate in its final development, but the Italians in Washington, eager to maintain their jobs, were unwilling to train any American sculptors. Artists from all over the world traveled to Italy to train in painting and sculpture, and now it was time for Americans to make their pilgrimage to the land of creativity and the Renaissance.

Part I

Thomas Crawford's first transatlantic trip had been as anticipated, difficult. A rough crossing kept him seasick for all 20 days from New York to Gibraltar. Crawford was 20, strong, and accustomed to long hours of hard work carving stone, but he knew early in the trip he would not win his struggle with the undulating ocean. He welcomed disembarking for three days in Gibraltar which gave him time to recuperate. From Gibraltar to Leghorn, his first stop in Italy, the calmer Mediterranean Sea allowed him to relax and enjoy the cool sea breeze. After a period of quarantine at Leghorn, an overnight sail took the ship along the western shore of Italy to the port of Civita Vecchia.

The appearance of this port of entry to Rome could only be described as chaotic. Loud, rude harbor workers rushed about in every direction. Only the Italians aboard were at ease in the confusion on the dock. Crawford was the only American on the ship, the other foreigners were English. Getting to this point had been difficult and tiring, but if this was what he could expect in Rome, he worried that he would accomplish little.

When his trip began, he had enough money to last a year, but already there had been unanticipated expenses. After a long wait, he found and identified his two trunks. A porter was soon at his side, hovering over the trunks repeating in Italian, "Permesso, permesso." With no other option apparent, he nodded, assuming this would get him to the customs house.

He was not yet free of the ship. A deckhand, who may or may not have carried the trunks off the ship, stepped in front of them. His facial expression, loud remarks in Italian, and uninhibited body gestures made it clear he felt entitled to some payment for his dubious labor. Crawford had already left money with the purser and considered his gratuity obligations to the crew completed. Looking around, he noted the English passengers were in a similar situation and equally confounded. He gave the man a coin, received a scowl in return, and replied to the scowl by turning his back and began to deal with the next problem.

The porter attempted to move the first trunk, but it would not move easily. Crawford knew it must be the trunk which contained his metal sculpture tools. The porter decided to try the other trunk and, finding it lighter, placed it on the heavier trunk and set his handcart in place beneath the two. "Andiamo, andiamo," he said, and with an arm gesture, the porter motioned toward a building at the end of the dock. The English tourists were already moving in that direction and they followed.

Idlers were standing in front of the one and two-story stone buildings lining the dock or sitting on cargo scattered in no particular order. A few sat outside a trattoria sipping coffee and assessing the newly arrived tourists. Barefooted children in ragged clothes thrust their hands forward, begging for a coin as the line of arrivals continued toward the customs house.

The day was sunny and clear. In spite of all the confusion, he enjoyed the cool crisp air of early fall and marveled at the sky with brilliant blue hues which he had never seen before. There were five ships docked either loading or unloading. Everyone was rushing. The mayhem on the dock and the anticipation of finally reaching Rome only increased the anxiety of the travelers.

The line slowed at a large building at the end of the dock with an official-looking coat of arms carved in stone above the wide doorway. Crawford followed the porter into a large room where the line split, each prong heading to a wooden table. The room, lit by two small windows, had dirty floors and bare walls. Behind each of the tables stood two uniformed customs officers with fancy gold-fringed hats in much better condition than their coats, trousers, and boots. Each had a sword on his belt. Beyond this, toward the rear of the room, were two desks with a customs officer behind each. Another door, at the rear of the building, was flanked by two soldiers with muskets at their sides.

Silence pervaded the room. The only sound was from barked orders. Crawford watched as each porter took the luggage and placed it on the table. When the trunks were opened for inspection, a senior customs official would begin speaking rapid Italian in a harsh tone as he tossed the trunk contents randomly, much to the consternation of the travelers. The officer would pick up something in the trunk, look seriously at the traveler, and his tirade would transform into a suspicious operatic tone while the second officer reviewed the passports and reported the payment due for the trunks. The traveler would pay the fee and extend his hand to accept the customs' documents, but they were not forthcoming. The documents would not be stamped until the traveler realized it might be a good idea to give the officer additional money. If this was done, the other officer's tirade and inspection suddenly ceased; the documents would be stamped, and the traveler could move to the next station.

Crawford now understood the procedure, and after tipping the first customs officer, his trunks were cleared. He moved to the next station to obtain a visa for the Pontifical State of Rome and again, there was a fee plus the unspoken fee. Crawford's visa was obtained without delay compared to some of the English travelers. Later, he was told by the American Consul in Rome this was no accident or luck, since America and Americans were new friends of Italy. There were no historical disagreements between the two countries. England and Italy had a history and English travelers, a terrible reputation. Now, already late in the afternoon, he had his passport stamped by an official of the Papal State: 10 September, 1835.

Just beyond the exit of the customs house, he was stopped by a local policeman who reviewed his passport and customs clearance. This superficial review, of course, required another payment, after which he indicated Crawford was free to continue. There were several inns across the street and to the right, a group of carriages. Rome was still hours away. An overnight stay before continuing would be another expense; money was disappearing at a rapid pace in Civita Vecchia. At one of the carriages he noticed two Englishmen he recognized from the boat, negotiating with a driver. Perhaps this was his chance. Three in a carriage should be cheaper then two, and he could get away from Civita Vecchia.

As he approached the three, it was hard to tell which side was the rudest. Negotiation did not seem the proper word for this disagreeable discussion. He pulled one of the Englishmen aside and explained his desire to get to Rome that night. The Englishman agreed it was a good idea, his friend agreed, and a new dimension was added to the shouting. Eventually, a price was determined and the Englishmen assured him it was the best they could do. They could leave after the trunks were loaded and be in Rome before midnight.

The porter, who had been with him all afternoon had to be paid, which was a difficult decision. He calculated several amounts in his head, chose the one in the middle and handed the money to the porter. He was prepared for a scowl and perhaps worse, but there was only a semi-scowl and a "Grazie." This made him think he had given the porter too much. Crawford had not eaten all day. He bought bread, cheese, and a bottle of wine at a nearby trattoria. The price seemed reasonable but again, because this was Civita Vecchia, he could only believe he overpaid.

After more confusion and shouting during the loading of the trunks, the carriage at last began to move. Crawford sat back, took a sip of wine, and tried to relax and think of Rome. Difficult as the day had been, he was sure the introductory letter he carried to the sculpture studio of Bertel Thorvaldsen would also introduce him to a studio assistant who could help him find affordable accommodations. An intermediary, fluent in Italian, would be essential. The little Italian he had been able learn before the trip was, so far, of no use. Everyone spoke rapidly, and words blended incomprehensibly one into another.

Crawford thought he could now put this unpleasant experience behind him, but Civita Vecchia had one more surprise for him. At the city gate the carriage was stopped, the door opened, and a policeman made it clear a fee must be paid by all leaving the city. The Englishmen protested to no avail. A fee was paid by all, and only then could the carriage leave Civita Vecchia.

∽

Gazing out the coach window at the landscape of the Campagna, Crawford sipped more wine. In America, wine was a drink of the wealthy, and his experience with it was limited. The taste was pleasant enough, possibly any drink would have been welcome as he tried to relax. The English companions, weary of the turmoils of the day, dozed.

He thought of America and his friends Robert Launitz and John Frazee, who taught him marble carving. Before working for them, he spent two years as an apprentice woodcarver where his natural artistic talent was ignited. Launitz recognized his talent and for five years taught him the basics of working with stone. If he had continued working with Launitz, his future would have been financially secure, but ornamental work, fireplace mantels and gravestones, did not satisfy him. Detecting a restlessness and clear signs of a passion for art in the talented young man, Launitz surprised him, in fact caught him completely off guard, when he offered Crawford a small stipend to study in Rome with Bertel Thorvaldsen, Launitz's former mentor.

As a youth, Crawford enjoyed sketching. After work, he attended drawing classes at the National Academy of Art and spent hours in its library looking at engravings of works of art, particularly sculpture. Two of the drawing instructors had studied in Rome. They constantly lamented the fact their classes were limited to working with plaster casts of Ancient Greek and Roman figures and reliefs. In Rome they drew from live models, nude, from all angles and poses, an impossibility when studying art in puritan America. Sculpture, apart from woodcarving, was rare in America. There were many painters, excellent wood-carvers, but few Americans working as sculptors. John Frazees's portrait busts were the closest thing to sculpture Crawford ever saw. Launitz told him many tales of working in Rome and Crawford knew he had to be more than just a carver which came naturally to him. It was time to become a sculptor and study in Rome.

After stopping only once, midway to rest the horses, a fog began covering the countryside and by the time they reached the outer walls of Rome, about ten in the evening, it was quite dense. They entered at the Porta Cavalleggierri where another fee had to be paid.

The darkness and fog made it difficult to see anything. Crossing a bridge, he knew it must be the Ponte Sant' Angelo, but he could barely make out the outlines of sculptures along the balustrade. Rome was all around him, but not visible in the darkness and fog. The Englishmen, now awake, told Crawford they had instructed the driver to go directly to their hotel near the Piazza di Spagna, the area where foreigners stayed. The promise of a bed on stable ground sounded perfect, so after the commotion of unloading, paying the driver, and getting into his room, Crawford fell into bed and a sound sleep.

His first day in Rome, he awoke to the noise and activity in the narrow street below. His large, clean room cost more than he could continue to pay. After dressing, he went downstairs expecting to find a dining room. To his sur-prise, there was none and was told guests took meals in their rooms which were ordered from a trattoria down the street. The staff of the hotel understood and spoke English, a pleasant surprise, but this was the 'foreigner' area of Rome. Breakfast, coffee, and bread, were brought to his room. The tiny cup gave no warning of the potent bitter taste, stronger than he had ever experienced from such a small amount of liquid.

He needed directions to Thorvaldsen's studio. The proprietor suggested sending a young boy with him to help find it. He agreed, and letter in hand, he finally began his Rome adventure. Everyone on the street seemed to be in a hurry, most were delivering food and bread, the latter carried in large bas-kets young boys balanced on their heads. The stone buildings were three to four stories high, many upper floor windows were open on this warm Septem-ber day. Washed clothes hung from windows, the streets were dirty, and shop owners were opening their doors. The boy moved quickly and as they approached a wider street, Crawford noted the name of the hotel street carved into a stone above the first floor of the corner building, Via dei Condotti.

Directly in front of him, at the end of Via dei Condotti, he was startled by the massive staircase, the Spanish Steps or Scalinata della Trinita dei Monti. He motioned for the boy to stop. The engravings he had studied in America had not done the stairs justice. They were much wider. At the bottom of the stairs was a fountain, an odd shaped boat filled with flowing water. He could not remember the name but he did remember it was by Bernini. Tourists strolled on and below the stairs studded with vendors. Beggars moved among the tourists as Italians moved to and fro.

The top of the stairs framed a view of a large church with two bell towers, Trinita dei Monti. Crawford had never seen anything like this and stood staring. The combination of architecture and sculpture took his breath away. It took a while for him to regain his composure and continue.

The boy motioned to the right and they started down the street. At the next intersection with one of the narrow streets, he noticed the street name, Via Sistina. His eyes were moving every which way, attempting to take in as much as possible, causing him to stumble on the uneven stone streets or bump into others. This slowed their progress. He also noted the clothes of the Italian men. They only had to look at Crawford's boots, coat, or hat to know he was a foreigner, making him feel self-conscious.

They came to a large Piazza with a fountain in its center, a Triton surrounded by dolphins. The Triton blew water through a large conch shell. Now, somewhat calmer, he remembered, this would be the Fontana del Triton, again by Bernini. Adjusting to these sharp contrasts of unkempt streets intermixed with dazzling fountains and piazzas would take time. As they moved farther from the Piazza di Spagna, no English could be heard. He sensed he was easing into a different world.

They walked across the Piazza, and stopped in front of three large buildings at the corner of Via delle Colonette and the Piazza. To his right was a larger and grander building, and he wondered if is this was what they meant by a Pallazo (he would soon learn it was the Palazzo Barberini on the Piazza Barberini). They walked to the end of the Pallazo to a building across the street, stopped at a door, where the boy pointed and said, "Ecco." A number on the door was the only identifying feature. Crawford stood, not knowing what to do next. The boy walked to the side of the door, pulled a string set in the wall, and a bell could be heard ringing inside.

෴

After a few minutes the door opened and a young woman greeted him with "Buon giorno." Flustered by the situation and his lack of experience with speaking the little Italian he knew, Crawford mumbled a few incoherent words, then defensively pulled the letter from Launitz out of his pocket, pushed it toward the young woman, and said, "Is Thorvaldsen here?" The woman looked him over, took the letter, and replied "Prego," motioning for him to enter. He looked back and the boy was already gone. Pointing to a chair with a "Momento," she turned, opened a door to another room, and left.

The room contained two small marble sculptures on pedestals, classic female figures, done in white marble. Running his fingers over the surfaces of the figures sparked a moment of anxiety. The finale of this journey had been reached; would he be welcome? He did not lack confidence, but from what he had seen so far during the short walk through Rome and in this room, expectations would be high. He had worked on some portrait busts and copied a relief of Thorvaldsen's from an engraving, but he had never carved a full figure.

The inner door opened, and a man of about 50 entered, greeting Crawford with, "Buon giorno. Welcome to Rome, I have not read the letter but my guess is that you are not from this country. Perhaps America? I am the foreman, Vincenzo. Maestro Thorvaldsen is here and working. Please look around the studio and I will give him the letter." Opening the door wider, Vincenzo led him into the next room.

Leaving Crawford to himself he hurried off. This room contained at least ten completed pieces, varying in size. They were stunning, marble, yet appearing soft. He moved from piece to piece first standing back to take in the whole figure, then moving closer to check the details. He was impressed by the depths of the under cuts. The surfaces were smooth, no unevenness, always flowing correctly. Work like this did not exist in New York.

The next room was larger. He took a quick step back, stunned by the sight. The light from the windows, reflecting on at least 50 white plaster pieces scattered throughout the room, shocked the eye. So these were the bozzette or models Launitz talked about with tiny holes scattered over the surfaces which guided the carvers. The variety and size of subjects was impressive. In the corners, half hidden, were forgotten pieces covered with a thicker layer of dust, some with broken fingers or chips. Spider webs that extended to the wall were covered with dirty plaster dust.

Mold making and plaster casting were taking place in the next area. A group of men worked together applying plaster over a clay model crisscrossed with multiple small strips of thin metal, used to delineate the different segments of a future mold. They paid little attention to his presence.

As he moved on the noise and the number of workers increased. Carvers were at work ahead. Crawford marveled at how effortlessly they worked each marble block.

Entering a larger room, he found a group of men working on an equestrian sculpture. One man directed the others and he assumed it was Thorvaldsen since he held a letter in his hand. He was a large man, about the same size as Crawford with deep blue eyes and flowing yellow gray hair resting on broad shoulders. The bones of the face, cheeks and jaw were prominent. As he came closer, Crawford noticed the large hands. Smiling warmly the man introduced himself, "I am Bertel Thorvaldson, welcome to Rome," his English was slow and had a Scandinavian accent. Since the death of Canova he was Rome's leading sculptor. "Your friend Launitz recommends you highly. I remember Launitz well. So you wish to work in my studio?"

"Yes,...yes," replied Crawford. "I would be honored to work here. I have been carving marble and studying drawing for the past five years and felt it was time to come to Italy and learn from the master."

"Another American, Greenough, stayed in Rome briefly but went on to Florence to work. Do you plan to stay in Rome or are you also planning to go north?" asked Thorvaldsen.

Crawford quickly answered, "No, I was given money to study here and intend to do so."

"Fine, then with this excellent recommendation, I would be pleased to have you study here. You realize, of course, there will be no salary and you will have to find your own housing. We may not have enough for you to learn in one year," Thorvaldsen said with a laugh. "Vincenzo can show you around and introduce you." He turned to his foreman and said, "Vincenzo, be certain Mr. Crawford meets our other young student." Turning back to the assistants, he resumed pointing to areas on the horse which needed reworking.

∽

Vincenzo motioned for Crawford to follow him. Leaving the building, they passed through a courtyard with raw marble blocks stacked in one corner. Entering another building, they came to a small room where a young man was modeling a clay figure, copying a plaster reproduction of an ancient Roman Sculpture. Vincenzo interrupted him, "Paolo, this is a new student from America. uh, uh...."

"Thomas," interjected Crawford, extending his hand to Paolo who clumsily tried to wipe the clay from his hands with his apron.

"Piacere," replied Paolo, "America, America, io non conosco... I niente... never know American."

Paolo obviously spoke as little English as Crawford spoke Italian, but the expression on his face said welcome. He was smaller, Italian small, had a handsome Roman face, dark, dark black hair and looked younger. Vincenzo left the two, each happy to meet a fellow student but unable, or at least hesitant, to begin a conversation.

Crawford moved to the clay, inspected it from all sides, and introduced his Italian, "Bene, bene, qui..qui... fecit...who did the clay?" He knew his Italian was incorrect, but he had to begin sometime. The clay was good, very good. Seeing this sophisticated work by a fellow student made it clear he had much to learn and this was the place. Rome, the studio, the sculptures he saw, everything so far had excited him.

Just then, Thorvaldsen walked in and studied Paolo's clay. Speaking in Italian to Paolo, with his hands and a simple tool he subtly reshaped the clay. The critique involved all sides, areas Crawford had thought were good. The small changes made by the master resulted in dramatic improvements and gave the piece a new look. His constructive and non-intimidating manner suggested the master was a gentle giant, a welcome relief. As quickly as he came, Thorvaldsen left, leaving the two to review the changes. In silence, they now understood each other perfectly as they studied the changes. These critiques continued on a daily basis the entire time Crawford was with Thorvaldsen.

Crawford studied the room. Empty sculpture stands and high stools were scattered about and Paolo seemed to be the only one working here. The light was sufficient, but not the best. He noted a large covered bin against the wall and assumed it contained clay. Soft gray dust covered the floor and windows. Paolo, looked around the room, spread his arms wide, and broke the silence, "Per noi,.....for us." Crawford grinned as he began to feel welcome in Rome.

Without tools and too excited to begin working, he decided to continue his exploration of the atelier. Adjacent rooms contained more workers. As he walked around, the Italian studio system became clearer.

From what he could tell, the sculptor, after completing his drawings, prepared a clay model less than a meter high, a beginning no different from New York. Mold makers took over, first making a thin plaster waste mold over the clay, which when dry, easily separated from the moist clay. Into this mold, they poured plaster and then chipped the outer plaster mold away ('waste mold') giving the sculptor a plaster casting of his clay model. This plaster cast could be revised further by the sculptor. These were things he had done before at home. From this point forward, he noted a difference.

The plaster sculpture or model could be left the same size, enlarged, or even reduced in size by the craftsmen. Before beginning the carving, a wooden frame was built around both the plaster model and the marble block. The top of each frame was divided into the identical number of marks. With the plaster model as a point of reference, the carvers used a system similar to navigating by sighting stars, and with calipers used the points in the plaster where nails had been inserted as a reference to the marks on the two frames.

They could enlarge the carving by doubling or tripling these distances. When the carving was completed, the surface of the plaster model would be covered with the multiple holes from the nails.[3] In New York, Crawford did all his own carving and had not worked with this method. All these workers or assistants were skilled craftsmen.

Now, he not only understood the reason most marble sculpture came from Italy, but why it was the best. Both marble and the highly skilled craftsman were available; Launitz had not exaggerated. After many centuries, it was in their blood.

∾

Crawford returned to the room where he would be working but Paolo was gone, his clay was covered with a damp cloth to keep it from drying. He sat down and thought about all he had seen his first day in Rome. It was, on one hand overwhelming, but, on the other, better and more than he had hoped for or imagined. The only thing he ever wanted to do was be an artist, a sculptor, and good fortune found him in the perfect spot. The uneasiness of being far from home, family, and friends began to fade.

Using the Piazza di Spagna as a landmark, he had no trouble finding his hotel, but he needed to locate a less expensive room. Over the next few days, with the help of Paolo, he found a room just off the Piazza Barbarini, not as comfortable as the hotel, by far, but affordable. Now he could unpack, write some letters home and let family and friends know he was settled in Rome.

At the atelier, Paolo helped him find the materials for armatures, the support structure of the soft, wet clay, and he began his first clay model. Thorvaldsen had purchased plaster copies of many ancient Roman and Greek sculptures to be copied by his students. From the daily critiques, Crawford soon learned he would not be allowed to move on to any detailed work on a piece until the master was satisfied with the proportions of the body or distribution of mass related to the height and an appropriate line of motion in the piece. The first few weeks were difficult for Crawford since he liked to work fast, and Thorvaldsen's daily review always set him back. The master wished to make his point clear.

The approximately 40 workers in the studio gave little acknowledgment to Crawford's presence. No smiles, no pleasant greetings, just cold looks when he moved around the rooms. This bothered him until Paolo explained that this should be expected from these proud craftsmen. First, they had to see if his talent measured up to the excellent quality of work in the studio. When they decided he had potential, then, he would be welcome, but not until then.

Adjusting to the daily routine, he began to make some progress with his clays, destroying them after Thorvaldsen gave his final approval and immediately beginning another. He started in the morning before the others arrived, and, in the late afternoon, he began to explore Rome and its art treasures. Two museums captured his interest because of their collections of sculptures, the Capitoline and the Vatican Museum.

He studied each of the works from as many angles as possible and sketched many. It was even possible to visit the Vatican Museum on certain nights and view the works by torchlight which accentuated the shadows of the undercuts and exaggerated highlighted surfaces. This helped him better understand how the sculptor took advantage or made the most out of the compact space available in a marble block. His days were long but enjoyable and allowed little time for any other activities.

One evening on his way home, he remembered Launitz telling him about Caffe Greco, where the artists of Rome congregated.[4] He thought some hot coffee might alleviate the evening's fall chill. He had seen the sign on the Via dei Condotti near the hotel where he first stayed. Paolo had also suggested it because there, he might meet some artists who spoke English.

He found it, Caffe Greco, Via dei Condotti 86. When he opened the door, thick cigar smoke filled his nostrils. In the first room, men were clustered around a noisy bar, engaged in animated discussions in several different languages. High arches separated the long, narrow space into three rooms. In the other rooms, he saw men sitting at small wooden tables, cups or wine glasses in hand. Not many seemed to be eating, and no one paid much attention to his presence. He went to the bar and ordered a coffee. His American accent was noted by some.

As he warmed his hands around the cup of coffee, someone at the other end of the bar looked toward him. He was a large man with red cheeks and a full beard wearing a velvet jacket and a colorful cravat. He wore a stove-pipe or high crowned conical hat similar to the hats of many in the Caffe. With a glass of wine in one hand, the man approached him and extending the other hand said, "Welcome, I have not seen you here before. It sounds as though you are an American? Been here long? Allow me to introduce myself, Frederick Philip, Pennsylvania."

"Accepting Philip's hand he replied. "Thomas Crawford, New York. I've been here only about three weeks."

"I assume you are an artist, since no respectable tourist or Italian would visit this place," said Philip with a chuckle.

"I'm a sculptor studying with Thorvadlsen. Are you a sculptor?"

"No, a painter. I haven't met any sculptors from America in Rome; you're the first. There are a few painters, but no sculptors. You came to the right place and found the right teacher. Sculptors are hard to find back home."

"Yes, most exist as decorative carvers either in wood or marble. There was an American sculptor, Greenough, here in Rome a few years ago, but he moved to Florence. I've been working hard and getting used to Rome, and it's time to meet other artists."

"Well, this would be the place. There are hundreds of painters and sculptors in Rome, and sooner or later they all come here for a drink, and more often to talk because most have little money. See that box in the corner? That's the mailbox. Many use this as their mailing address, so you will always see someone checking it when they first arrive. The food's no good, but the coffee and wine are cheap, and the conversation the best part of the evening, after working alone all day. If you want something to eat, stop at the ristorante across the street, Lepre. The food is decent. Then come here for a drink."

"How long have you been in Rome?"

"Three years, finish your coffee and let me show you the rest of the place."

Philip led him into the next room. Small tables were surrounded by groups of colorfully dressed younger men who were drinking and deep in conversation. Benches set against the wall handled the overflow. Every seat was taken, some men stood. As they passed between the tables, Philip exchanged greetings with many, and announced a new arrival, an American sculptor. They greeted him in many different languages.

Moving to the back room the tables were occupied by older men talking in more subdued tones. Pointing to some tables in the rear, Philip explained, "Those are current residents of the French Academy in the Villa Medici, purchased by Napoleon. The French government gives them a stipend, room and board, as well as a studio for two years to study in Rome. It has been said that when Hector Berlioz, the French composer, spent his time at the Villa, he called all the French artists in the Caffe Greco not from the Villa 'men from down below.' It's quite a place. You can join drawing classes there and share the cost of a model. I don't know if you have used any yet; they cost less than a dollar a day. Models are plentiful because of the lack of work, but the younger ones may bring their mother for protection. There's even a group of Russians on the other side of the room, also sent by their government."

"Thanks for the tour. I'd liked to visit your studio. Where is it?" Crawford asked. Philip gave him directions and told him he could come anytime during the day. At night, more often than not, he could be found at the Caffe Greco.

◌⌇

The superb quality of the work at Thorvaldsen's atelier, the availability of so many works of the past to study, and now this introduction to the artistic life in Rome at the Caffe Greco, all took Crawford's passion for sculpture to another level. Yet, he knew the future problem would be finding enough money to stay in Rome and the location was essential for developing his reputation.

After copying many plaster reproductions at the atelier in clay, he decided to carve a marble piece. Apprehensive, he thought about this carefully because there were many master carvers in the studio, and he knew they would be judging his ability with skepticism. Could this American carve?

Taking one of his drawings from the Vatican Museum, he made a rough clay sketch and found a large piece of scrap marble suitable for carving a relief of the clay model. He had worked with Italian marble in New York but this piece of 'bianco puro' (pure white) had a much softer feel with the chisel and worked with minimal effort.

As the details emerged, some of the Italian craftsmen surprised him with a smile and "buon giorno." Paolo told him he had passed his first major test and would now be treated as a colleague. Paolo also liked what he saw and Thorvaldsen on his daily rounds had few comments for Crawford, an indication of his approval. This lack of critical comment by the master was noticed by the craftsmen, a further confirmation of his progress.

Crawford needed no external motivation, nor approval, and continued to work harder than anyone else. Even from noon to three or four, the siesta time for the Italians, he would be the only one at the studio. As the workers left for home and lunch he could hear an occasional "e pazzo," (he's crazy), muttered by one of the men.

The stone buildings of Rome brought the cold of winter inside both the studio and his room. The winter of New York might have been colder, but the homes had more efficient fireplaces and kitchen stoves which always provided a warm refuge. There were no fireplaces in the studios.

Besides studying sculpture, he observed how Thorvaldsen sold his work. Once a week he opened his studio to visitors, and because of his reputation, many came to Rome just to see his work. The royalty that came from different countries were welcome any day.

Thorvaldsen's confident and exuberant manner discussing his work enthralled visitors and he made all questions seem important. Women were charmed by his rugged handsomeness and romantic descriptions of works either finished or unfinished. While the gentlemen made the final decisions, he directed much of his conversation to the accompanying spouse, knowing she could make or break the final decision.

Crawford began to see that talent produced the art, but reputation, connections, and salesmanship helped sell it. Without these commodities, no matter how good or how much his friends praised it, work would never leave the studio without a patron or customer to buy the art. Since Crawford had never sold anything, he needed to learn more about this aspect of being an artist. It was an eye opener.

Crawford's hectic pace continued throughout the winter when he joined some of the evening drawing sessions at the French Academy of Art. The training the French artists had before they came to Rome must have been good, because they all produced excellent drawings. This made him work even harder. Drawing from live models introduced a new perspective of the human form and he saw more as he drew. A French painter, looking at one of Crawford's drawings, said, "Interesting how we all look but do not see. My friend, you are beginning to see." These sessions prompted him to take a course in human anatomy in a hospital morgue that featured dissection and drawing.

Among the artists of Rome, he became known as the driven American, the one who had invented a headpiece which held a candle allowing him to work into the night. He enjoyed his visits to the Caffe Greco, but there were long intervals between them. Perhaps this made him even more interesting. In any case, Crawford and the excellent quality of his work began to become a topic of their conversations at the Caffe Greco.

∞

Crawford's apprenticeship continued throughout the summer of 1837, which became dangerous due to an outbreak of cholera killing hundreds of people in Rome. Tourists disappeared and a special permit was required for anyone wishing to enter the city. Even Thorvaldsen had few visitors to his studio. Those who could afford it, left to escape the heat and disease. Crawford had little choice, so he remained in Rome throughout the summer.

Working in the studio where large projects or monuments took shape from drawings to their full size, fascinated him. As many as 40 assistants worked on various stages of Thorvaldsen's commissions. Crawford studied the drawings and spent many hours watching the assistants as they constructed the armatures or support structures of the large monuments. He dreamed of the time when he could create such works. The studio craftsmen watched and wondered if the young American might be a possible successor to the master.

Overseeing all the projects in different stages of completion kept Thorvaldsen busy throughout the day. Crawford noted he still found enough time to develop new ideas in his private working area, answer his correspondence, and deal with the visitors to the studio. He warmly welcomed everyone because, one could never predict which visitor might become the patron of a new work.

The months Crawford spent at the studio resulted in the accumulation of a number of marble reliefs, plaster busts, and many ideas or rough sketches in clay. He realized it was time for him to find his own studio or go broke. He could not sell out of Thorvaldsen's studio, and returning to New York at this time did not seem to be an option. One evening at the Caffe Greco, a German sculptor told him about a vacant studio on the Via del Orto di Napoli. Crawford decided to take a look. This would be a major step forward in his career, an exciting and expensive step.

The street with the vacant space was near Thorvaldsen's studio. That would make it possible for him to continue studying in the mornings and work at his studio in the afternoon and evening. The unimpressive building with the vacant space blended with others on the street. Getting the owner to answer the bell took awhile, but eventually, a small, cranky old man led Crawford to the space on the first floor.

Although the bare room was larger than the space he used at Thorvaldsen's studio, it certainly was not the space of his dreams with its unpainted rough walls and mediocre lighting. It looked better after he was told the price; a dollar a week. Two smaller adjacent rooms could be used for sleeping and storage.

He decided to take it, gave the man the first month's rent and then spent the next hour walking around the main room, marveling at the changes in his life since he left America two years ago. From marble yard apprentice in New York, to sculptor in Rome about to begin work on his own terms and in his own studio, he was quite full of himself.

༄

Late one afternoon in the fall of 1837, Crawford was missing a much needed transfer of money from his sister. He decided to visit the American Consul in Rome to see if he could move things along. The office and residence of the American Consul was near the Piazza Barbarini, a short distance from the studio of Thorvaldsen. Crawford climbed the steps to the first floor, and stood before the traditional Italian double doors which always amused him. They had no handles or knobs on the outside, because Italians preferred to look through a small peephole in the doors to view a visitor before responding. He rang the bell.

An older women who spoke broken English greeted him and asked his business. When he said he wished to see the Consul, she led him into a small entry room which opened into a long hall lined by doors. She knocked on the first door on the right and opened it after she heard a muffled "avanti."

George Washington Greene, grandson of Nathanael Greene, an important general in the Revolutionary Army and close friend of George Washington, greeted him. Greene had recently arrived in Rome. He had left a teaching job in America, visited London, Paris, southern France, and Florence before accepting the job as Consul. His office was filled with books and a desk covered with papers. It looked like a library.

The appointment of Consul included no salary and the appointee either had to have another source of income or sustain himself by collecting fees for the services he performed for American visitors to Rome. Greene, took the position as an opportunity to pursue his real interest, studying Italian culture and history. At the time, there were about 150,000 citizens of Rome and at least 500 American ex-patriots. However, 400 to 500 Americans passed through the city each year. Since there were no formal relations between America and the Papal State, and no American Embassy, many called on the Consul for various services.

Greene had already heard of Crawford, "that American sculptor," but had not yet met him. Greene 25, and Crawford 23, were immediately drawn to one another even with their different backgrounds and physical features. Greene was short, with delicate facial features, and a handsome scholarly look, Crawford, taller, and muscular. Greene had spent 3 years at Bowdoin College and 2 years as principal of an academy in Connecticut. One was well educated and passionate about scholarship, the other had little formal education other than serving an extensive apprenticeship in his area of passion, sculpture. Nevertheless, they were two young men who knew they wanted to become important in their fields.

After listening to Crawford's problem and assuring him he probably could get an answer for him from the bank, Greene asked, "Would you like to go for a coffee or drink?"

"I had planned to work this evening, but, yes, that sounds good," replied Crawford.

Leaving the Consular office, they walked to a nearby tratorria familiar to Greene and took a table inside to escape the chill of the fall evening. Greene wanted to know more about this lone American sculptor in Rome, and after ordering some wine he began, "Did you have any trouble finding a studio?"

"Finding a studio in Rome is no problem. They say there are as many artist studios in Rome as there are churches and there must be 100 of those. I found a studio close to Thorvaldsen's, hoping the overflow of his many visitors might be directed my way. He has referred clients to me for portrait busts. I do the clay models, which are then carved by his studio assistants and I receive a portion of the fee. I am certain they will identify them as works from his studio, not by the still unknown Crawford."

"It's a beginning and he may continue sending clients?"

"Not for long, he's going to Denmark and may be gone at least a year. I am able to afford only a small studio and even that will be difficult without selling works on my own. I am very concerned about my future finances. I could go back to New York and find plenty of decorative work, but it would not be the type of work that interests me."

"So you are committed to staying in Rome?"

"Yes, America needs monuments and sculpture for its Capitol. To do larger works, you must have a studio complete with different artistic craftsmen and they are not available in America. Here, sculpture assistants with different skills are plentiful and the best marble comes from north of here.

"I need to have visitors to the studio, where I can show them my work and persuade them to have a portrait bust made or buy something I have on hand. Then I could stay in Rome and develop a reputation. I'm confident my work is good. That plan is working in Florence for Hiram Powers. Some of the painters at the Caffe Greco who have stopped in Florence on their way to Rome say a visit to his studio is a popular stop for American travelers and he has many commissions."

"Well," said Greene, "there are many American travelers passing through Rome, but as you say, attracting them to your studio is another matter. When do you think your studio will be ready?"

"Next week."

"Good, I'll visit after you get settled. Just let me know when."

"How about next week Monday?" Crawford replied.

"I'll be there late in the morning," said Greene who then turned to a waiter and told him they were ready to order.

During dinner, they discussed each other's backgrounds in America and, as they left, promised to meet on Monday. On his way back to his room, Crawford felt euphoric. Although it could have been the wine, he knew finding this new friend who might help him meet the many American tourists visiting Rome was the real cause. For the moment, the financial future did not look as bleak.

∾

Greene, late because of unexpected Consular business, reached Crawford's studio just after noon on Monday. The drab room would have been of little interest to any visitor were it not for the contents, sculptures scattered about the room. Crawford gave Greene a few minutes to look around before beginning to explain his work.

As Crawford moved from one piece to another, the influence of Thorvaldsen on the artist's neoclassical style was evident. As they moved from the clay models to his marble busts, reliefs, and plasters, Greene realized he was seeing the work of a first-rate sculptor, and an American at that. When he was shown the numerous drawings which Crawford had accumulated, Greene was surprised with the extent of his knowledge of the classics. He had visited other sculptors in Rome as well as Powers and Greenough in Florence. This work not only compared favorably to what he had seen, it had a quality which drew the viewer into the work. There would be no problem recommending American tourists to visit this studio.

"I'm impressed," said Greene, looking around the room, "you have quite a bit of work for only two years in Rome. However, getting people to see it may, as you have said, be a problem. Word of mouth always helps, but being mentioned in the newspapers and some of the periodicals in America will also be necessary. Tourists preparing for their trips are always looking for ideas. You mentioned you have sold nothing on your own?"

"No, nothing. Not knowing where to begin I'm frustrated and open to any ideas. I can't afford to buy marble or hire studio assistants until I get some work," replied Crawford.

"Let me think about this. I'm a writer, with no experience selling paintings or sculpture, but I do know what it took to develop a sufficient reputation to get published in newspapers and periodicals at home. There must be some similarities. Talent is the driving force, but a little luck and meeting the right people is also necessary."

It was already after three when Greene suggested they take a walk in the Pincio Gardens. Crawford hesitated, even though he had no project or deadline.

Such impromptu nonproductive periods were not on the daily agenda of this intense artist, but Greene was an important new friend and he agreed.

As they walked, Greene led the conversation, it was a chance for him to discuss in depth the background for some of the drawings he had seen. Quite the raconteur as well as a classical scholar he felt close to this talented fellow American. As they approached the Gardens, Greene said, "I wish I could have seen these gardens in Roman times. They were magnificent, but nothing was done to maintain them after the fall of the Empire. When the French occupied Rome, they began the restoration we now see."

Pointing to an obelisk, Greene said, "Did you know that Napoleon brought that obelisk to these gardens? Hadrian originally erected it in memory of his favorite slave, Antonius. Rome is certainly the obelisk capital of the world. The view from up here of the obelisk in the Piazza del Popolo below is particularly striking. It's amazing how the Romans shipped and hauled these heavy obelisks to Rome. The ancient Romans sacked Egypt, taking away the obelisks. When the Huns sacked Rome, it never occurred to them to struggle with these slabs of granite. They were satisfied with raping the women and taking all the gold. Thus you have a definition of 'a difference in cultures.' The more Italian history I read, the more fascinated I become."

"Have you been inside the Villa Medici, the French Academy of Art?" asked Crawford.

"Yes, the outside appearance is unimposing and does not prepare you for the large salons, inner facade, and gardens."

"The stonework carving of the facade facing the courtyard is probably my favorite in Rome."

"And my favorite view overlooking Rome is from the courtyard gardens," said Greene. "The French treat their prized artists like royalty while in residence at the Villa. Do you realize they not only have painters and sculptors in residence but also writers, poets, and musicians? Writers, I'm envious. They stay one to two years, all expenses paid by the French government. Our new Capitol, in Washington, can't compete with the boulevards, parks, and palaces of Paris, which have been evolving for over 1000 years. Our Capitol is still incomplete. We are just getting over our growing pains, let alone financing Villas for our artists."

"The French government doesn't know about the other wing of the Villa, the Caffe Greco. The French, residents and nonresidents, of the Academy, are nightly patrons, always boasting about their country and critical of everyone else's. If I were a resident of the Villa, I suppose I also would. Do you ever go to the Caffe Greco George?"

"Indeed I do and find it very stimulating intellectually, as well as just a good place to occasionally drink a little too much."

After a while, they agreed to meet again the following week. Walks such as these would become frequent, and as time passed, dinner, and a visit to Caffe Greco often followed.

༶

Americans on the Grand Tour visiting Rome did not rush to visit Crawford's studio. His reputation as a good carver helped him get work copying Roman and Greek sculptures. This paid a little, but he barely made enough to pay the rent and eat. The winter of 1838-39 tested his determination to stay in Rome.

Greene mentioned Crawford's studio to everyone visiting his office. He wrote his friend, Henry Wadsworth Longfellow who had taught at Bowdoin College during Greene's tenure from 1824 to 1827. Longfellow had left to travel through Europe and study the continent and its languages, but returned to Bowdoin to become its first Professor of Modern Languages. In 1834, he moved to Harvard College and married. Longfellow and his new wife left for Europe where he and Greene met in Marseilles.

It was in Marseilles that the two became close friends. Longfellow helped Greene publish the articles he sent from Rome, and Greene kept Longfellow informed of the current publications, books, and literary happenings in Rome and on the continent. This initial connection would become an important path for the development of Crawford's career.

One evening while dining with Commodore Isaac Hull, Commander of the American Naval Squadron in Rome, Greene had an idea. If Crawford were to do a portrait bust of the former Commander of the USS Constitution, it might lead to other important commissions or, at least, Crawford's name might be mentioned back home. He inquired, "Have you taken advantage of the presence of so many fine painters and sculptors in this city?"

"What exactly do you mean?" replied Hull looking up from his meal.

"A portrait. It could be completed and back in America before you finish your command here. You would be able to follow its progress and even be available for more than one sitting. The artists in this city are unique."

"My family has mentioned that idea in the past, but I have never been in one place long enough to look into it. In America there are many portrait painters, but my familiarity with such things is minimal."

"Why a painting?"

"Because that's all I've seen in America."

"I think a sculpture portrait is more appropriate for those in the military. The marble makes a better statement of strength and command."

"I never thought of it that way. I wouldn't know where to begin, but it sounds interesting. What's involved? Sitting in one position for hours while the artist works wouldn't interest me."

"No, no, it's not that difficult. A sculptor makes some quick drawings and then begins a clay model. You go once or twice for the artist to make some corrections. The marble carving is done from the clay or plaster, so you don't have to be present at all."

"Really? You mean I wouldn't have to sit for hours as they do for paintings?"

"Right."

"Well, maybe that's not a bad idea. I'd have to think about it. Do you know of anyone?"

"Well, there are many in Rome. But, there is one American sculptor working here in Rome, Thomas Crawford."

"American! That surprises me. Aren't the Italians supposed to be the best at that sort of thing?"

"They are the best in many ways, but this young man has trained with the best in the world, Thorvaldsen, who speaks highly of Crawford, a recommendation that means a great deal. Why not visit his studio, meet him, look at his work, and get to know him? That might answer most of your questions."

"I just may," answered Hull.

Two weeks later, Commodore Hull visited Crawford's studio. Unimpressed when he first entered the dusty rooms, he felt better after Crawford began to discuss the works scattered about. As he listened to the presentation, Hull, a military commander, leader, and frequent judge of young men's potential, sensed this intense young man had something special. He knew little about art, but what he saw, and the impression Crawford made hinted of eventual success. He decided to have a portrait bust done.

"What is your price for a portrait bust?" asked Hull.

"For a marble bust in the best white marble and with a base of similar material, $250," replied Crawford pointing to one of the completed busts in the studio.

"Would it be that size?"

"Yes, that one is slightly larger than life size."

"How long will it take?"

"About two to three months."

"Does that include packing or crating? I would not want it shipped since I can put it on one of the Squadron's ships or even take it with me aboard my ship when I'm called home."

"Yes, that would include crating."

"Very well then, let's do it. How do you wish to be paid?"

"Half down and the rest on completion. That's the usual manner of payment."

Crawford was pleased with himself and the manner in which he handled this important man. Watching Thorvaldsen deal with significant personalities had taught him well.

More portrait work would come his way, but his real desire was to do a larger piece, something of substance. Crawford completed his first large ideal figure in clay while studying with Thorvaldsen, a supine Bacchante, which never reached the plaster or marble stages. The idea of doing a monument-sized George Washington or Benjamin Franklin was always in the back of his mind. The money from the portrait busts, the small reliefs, and copies of ancient sculptures went to buy marble and pay carvers, leaving some profit, but he lived from bust to bust, not having enough to expand his studio or hire assistants. Without a patron he was stymied.

⁊

Stopping at the studio before one of their evening strolls, Greene found Crawford working on a clay sketch of a full figure and an odd looking dog. The piece was still in the early stage of development, but after viewing the piece from all angles he asked, "If this bizarre dog is Cerberus, I think I know what you have in mind."

"All right, tell me the story which comes to mind," challenged Crawford.

"Well, if it is indeed Cerberus, it could be from any number of stories from Greek mythology. The three-headed dog guarding the entrance to Hades is referred to in several myths."

"But from what you see so far, what is your best guess?"

"Your male figure is holding something in his left arm. My guess is it's Orpheus and he will be holding a lyre. Orpheus was the son of Apollo and the muse Calliope, and when given this instrument learned to play it so well he charmed all around him, including wild beasts. It's said, he could even soften rocks. Am I on the right track?"

"Continue."

"The story is one of my favorites. Orpheus weds the beautiful Eurydice. But of course, being a Greek myth, they would not be allowed to live happily ever after. One day, Eurydice is frolicking about with the nymphs who surround her and is seen by Aristaeus who, smitten by her beauty, makes an advance. In an attempt to flee, she runs through a meadow, is bitten on the foot by a poisonous snake and dies. Orpheus, of course, is heart broken and decides he must find his love even if he has to enter the World of the Dead. To do that, he must get past Cerberus, the watchdog at the gates. Playing his lyre he mesmerizes Cerberus, which allows him to enter Hades and find Eurydice."

"You're right. That makes me feel better. The sketch so far is faithful to the story. I like the final part of the story. It is so poignant, yet, something which could occur when two lovers are desperate to be together. How do you remember the rest?"

"In the darkness he sees Eurydice. Persephone, also charmed by the music allows him to lead her out, but on one condition. He must never look back at her until they are completely outside the World of the Dead. So, she follows him, but he is intent on being certain she is behind, turns around too soon, and she vanishes back into the World of the Dead. A sad tale of sublime love."

"Right. That's how I remember it from my reading."

"But how do you intend to capture the feeling of the deep love and desperation of Orpheus?"

"Well, first, he is the son of the gods, so the figure of Orpheus must be idealized in the sense of the great Greek sculptures, perfectly and classically proportioned. His expression must reflect his torment but also the idea that he is searching in the darkness. This look will take some time, but it will be what either makes or breaks the final piece."

"Right now I am concerned with the overall layout of the figures, the gesture of Orpheus and the drapery. That's how it is with me, I can work fast and as the work progresses, the details evolve. None of my work is an instantaneous or spontaneous idea. First, I have the general conception of the idea, then the initial layout develops in my mind, then as I sketch on paper or in clay and modify the sketches, clarification of the details emerge."

"The more we talk, the more I realize you have read a great deal including Ovid and his Metamorphoses," said Greene.

"I still read whenever I can get hold of a book. I have to thank my sister Jenny for making sure I loved to read. She found the books, I devoured them. My second home after the drawing studio at the New York Academy of Art was their library. I not only read, I looked at all the engravings of sculpture in the collection over and over," said Crawford.

"I would think someone else would have done a piece on these lovers. One can't get much more romantic."

"Canova did individual pieces of Eurydice and Orpheus.[5] I saw the engravings in Thorvaldsen's library. Then I knew I had to attempt to capture the feeling of Orpheus and interpret it in stone myself," answered Crawford.

Crawford spent his mornings on what he considered routine and boring work that allowed him to immerse himself in Orpheus for the rest of the day and often well into the evening. After completing the clay model, he began the full-sized clay. As the enlarged clay began to take shape, he experienced the creative enthusiasm he had felt when he first began to study with Thorvaldsen. The feeling excited him and reignited his drive for success, which had been held in check for the past year as he struggled to make a living as a sculptor in Rome.

Greene followed the progress of Orpheus and thought this might be the piece to launch the career of Crawford in America. He convinced an important Roman art critic, Giuseppe Melchiorri, to visit the studio. Impressed with what he saw, Melchiorri promised to write an article about the piece when the plaster was available and an engraving could be done to accompany the article.[6] In Rome, Crawford was considered a significant young sculptor, quite a compliment to his talent in this city of artists, but in America, he was still unknown.

❦

One morning in the early summer of 1839, George Greene's housekeeper informed him he had an American visitor. Thinking it just another tourist inquiry, he told her to bring him to his office. A tall, slim, well-dressed young man with a firm jaw and flowing dark hair, entered and introduced himself, "I'm Charles Sumner of Boston. A mutual friend, Henry Longfellow, said I should call on you when I reached Rome. He spoke highly of you, your literary interests and knowledge and said if I wanted to learn about Rome, you were the one to see".

"Well, welcome," said Greene as he rose from behind his desk. "I'm certain you exaggerate Henry's recommendation. Is this your first stop on your tour?"

"No, I have been to France and England."

"How are your accommodations? Can I help you with anything?"

"No, I'm getting settled right now, but your office may be of help in the future."

They spent the rest of the morning and then through lunch discussing each other's backgrounds and interests. The instant compatibility between the two, the same age, was similar to the first meeting between Greene and Crawford. Charles Sumner, 29, a lawyer, graduate of Harvard, and fellow faculty member with Longfellow was a prodigious reader, consummate intellectual and protégé of William Storey, Harvard law professor and United States Supreme Court Justice. The practice of law bored Sumner, so he borrowed money from friends for a tour of England and the continent, which would encompass two years of his life.

Throughout his stay in Rome, he read everything Greene could find for him, spending most of the day in his rooms and then joining Greene late in the afternoon to tour Rome and discuss the city, Italy, its history and literature. Sumner was touring, but he had a scholar's hunger for knowledge.

Soon after Sumner's arrival, Greene took him to visit Crawford's studio. Attempting not to prejudice Sumner before visiting the studio, Greene had spoken only of an American sculptor who had apprenticed with Thorvaldsen, giving no hint of his personal strong positive opinion.

After he was introduced to Sumner, Crawford began to show him around his studio, beginning with some of the portrait busts, then the reliefs. When he removed the damp cloths covering the clay of Orpheus, Greene noted Sumner's astonished reaction.

They allowed Sumner to circle the piece uninterrupted. He seemed deep in thought as he pondered the sculpture, viewing it from every angle, up close and then stepping back. Turning back to the two, Sumner said, "It is Orpheus with Cerberus. The tale of Orpheus and Eurydice has been a favorite of mine;

it's such a powerful love story. It never occurred to me a myth with such depth could be expressed in marble. Until now, it was something on a page, a memory in a mind." Turning to Crawford, he said, "I like it. What is the next step in the process? Will you begin carving the work in marble?"

"No, not yet. First I have to finish the clay and then make a plaster, which will require making a mold, then pouring a plaster cast and smoothing or finishing the surface. After that the carving in marble begins," answered Crawford.

"Where will it go?"

"At the moment there is no final destination. It needs a patron."

"What a shame. It needs to be seen. The gesture of Orpheus with his right hand above his eyes lets you know he is looking for Eurydice in the dark depths before him."

"Thank you, for the kind comments."

"This work is already gaining some recognition in Rome within the artistic community," added Greene.

"I love the classic lines of Orpheus, if you will allow me to use the word, 'Phidian' in nature," said Sumner. "It seems to incorporate the classical Greek lines or ideal figure, but at the same time it takes on a new powerful contemporary form. This piece must be seen."

It was early evening when they finished their studio visit and they decided to find a place to dine. Greene suggested Lepre where they could eat and then end the evening across the street at the Caffe Greco where they could introduce Sumner to another side of artistic Rome.

෧෨

After dinner, the three men continued across the street to the crowded, noisy Caffe Greco. Sumner was surprised how many people knew and warmly greeted Crawford and Greene as they looked for a table. Moving toward the back of the Caffe they met Frederick Philip, an American painter who agreed to join them.[7]

Drinks ordered, Sumner, looked around and said, "I visited a few smaller coffee houses in Paris in the area of the Sorbonne. From what you have told me there are some writers and musicians here, but most of the crowd is painters and sculptors, right? In Paris, it was mainly philosophy and revolutionary politics, the artists were in another part of the city."

"Right, but that does not preclude arguments about philosophy," said Crawford. "Politics is not discussed unless it is a group from a country talking about events at home. Rome is a city of perpetual political intrigue and the local government has informants everywhere, except here because the artists are from other countries and absorbed with their art. For that reason, they tend to leave us alone." He paused and asked Philip, "I heard you were thinking of heading home?" said Crawford.

"I plan to go home soon and work, but have serious reservations," said Philip. "I have learned so much about painting here and would like to put it to use at home, but when I left three years ago, I left a developing country still struggling to build cities and expand its commerce. People were interested in family portraits and itinerant portrait painters did well, each producing hundreds of family pictures. In America, that's what people think a painting is and what painters do. I have no interest in doing that, and wonder if anyone will buy, let's say, a landscape painting or be willing to pay more than they are now paying for portraiture," replied Philip.

"You make a good point," said Greene turning to Sumner. "Charles, you have not visited the French Academy of Art in the Villa Medici. I want to take you there next week. The French take their best young artistic talent, in all the arts, not just painting and sculpture, and send them to Rome for two years. They are given studios in the Villa and a stipend. Their selection process must be sophisticated because they are all talented. When one hears the name Napoleon, the first image that comes to mind is war, but, he is the one who purchased the Villa for this purpose. A contradiction, except to the French. Will our politicians at home ever do such a thing? I doubt it."

"You are right," said Sumner, "but the circumstances are so different when you compare the state of the arts in the two countries. Our country has other things on its agenda. Philip raises an interesting point; perhaps it is not only that there are other pressing priorities for the people. Jefferson was interested in all the arts and included niches for sculpture in his plans for Monticello. He had volumes of engravings of art from the continent. Unfortunately, the leaders who followed lacked his interest.

"France has a long history of supporting the arts. In America we do not yet even have a long history. Expecting the government to provide money to support the arts may be putting the cart before the horse. Our people, including the members of Congress, are unfamiliar with the arts. They have little experience beyond what Philip mentioned."

"Congress awards art commissions only to Italians," said Crawford angrily.

"Complaining to Congress is a waste of time," said Greene. "My initial requests to have the consular office changed to diplomatic status have been ignored in Washington. I receive no money from them to keep this consular office open for the benefit of American tourists who in turn complain about my fees. I am not an artist, but I know how difficult it is to get the attention of Congress, unless of course, you have contacts."

"Members of Congress do respond to direct pressure from political connections or supporters," Sumner said. "Ours is not an uneducated population. One has to be connected or at least introduced by an influential person to get their attention. Books are important to our leaders. There are now a number of important colleges other than Harvard. The Boston Athenaeum is building a collection of art, but when most citizens have not seen any art beyond small portraits, how can they become appreciative of other genres of art?

"The Americans studying here and elsewhere in Italy and the continent are the first groups of artists fortunate enough to do so. I suppose it will be their job to convince the people at home creative art is rewarding to see, and that it fulfills some need. The problem interests me," said Sumner.

"In Florence, Greenough and I spent hours discussing this dilemma," continued Sumner. "His sculpture of George Washington is nude from the waist up, his lower body draped in a toga of sorts. The face is excellent and true to the man. He has chosen to depict the great American hero idealistically, ancient and godlike. Americans will probably be shocked by this representation of the father of their country to be placed in the rotunda of the Capitol. When that happens, we will begin to ascertain the status of American artistic culture, or if there is such a culture?"

The following day, Sumner went to see Greene. Carlotta, Greene's spirited Italian wife, greeted him with a warm hug and a kiss. Having noted how her husband's mood improved whenever he spent time with the two Americans, she wanted him to feel welcome in their home.

"How are you today, Charles? I hope you enjoyed yesterday and the evening out," said Greene coming down the hall.

"It was a special day and as you mentioned, evening," replied Sumner. "I've been thinking all morning about Orpheus, and our discussion last night. I have some ideas."

"I could tell that you were impressed. I feel the same way and wanted to see your reaction without prejudicing the visit with my opinion. Thorvaldsen thinks he has the talent and ability to become great. What do you think? Are we dealing with greatness?"

"I'm not an art critic nor even interested in art before this trip," said Sumner, "but I get that feeling. There is no American sculptor of his caliber working at home. Frederick Philip's comments also apply to sculpture in America. However, the problem of the sculptor is compounded by the high cost of marble and the necessity of a patron or commission before even beginning a large work. At least the painter can take the risk of putting together a group of works, other than portraits, at much less expense."

"I agree," said Greene, "Crawford is hesitant to put his toe in the water to test the temperature at this time. He has no money, no reputation in America except for a word-of-mouth praise from the portrait busts done for tourists. I have written Longfellow about his talent, but he, also, is not an art critic."

"Longfellow's poems have been well received and now that he is at Harvard he is becoming influential at the college as well as in Boston. Why not write an article about Crawford, send it to Longfellow, and ask him to get it published? I will also write to Henry."

"Good idea, I can do that."

Greene and Sumner did indeed begin a campaign to get Orpheus shown in Boston. Greene wrote an article about art in Rome with Crawford as the focal point. Longfellow arranged for it to be published. Sumner also wrote Longfellow. praising the work and speaking of Crawford's potential. Sumner even asked his former law associate, George Hillard to promote Crawford's name whenever he had the opportunity. If he had the chance, Sumner hoped Hillard would mention him to Governor Edward Everett and other influential people.

Impressed with Crawford and his work, Sumner decided he would find the money to bring Orpheus to Boston. He asked Crawford his price. He said $2000. Sumner thought the figure low, but it was a sum he could work with. Perhaps he could raise more, but he said nothing.

The three remained close throughout Sumner's three month stay. Before he left, Crawford had Sumner come to the studio to sit for a portrait bust. After Crawford had positioned Sumner and began working his clay, Sumner remarked, "The past three months in Rome have been the best of my trip."

"I will miss your company, as will George," said Crawford

"It has been special. It would be better if you were both in Boston," replied Sumner.

When Sumner returned to Boston, he began planning his campaign to raise money as well as speaking with his friends at the Athenaeum. Shortly after he returned, the Athenaeum received a letter from Catherine Maria Sedgwick, a well-known novelist in the Northeast, as well as an early supporter of women's rights. She had visited Rome after Sumner left and saw Crawford's studio. Impressed, she thought the Athenaeum should show the work of this American sculptor.[8] Now Greene, Sumner, and Sedgwick were promoting Crawford at home. Longfellow could only be impressed by all these reports of the excellent quality of his work.

∾

Stimulated by the possibility of a patron for Orpheus, Crawford worked even longer hours, but could not help thinking about the proverb, 'a bird in the hand is worth two in the bush.' No contract in hand, this piece was still 'in the bush.' He did get four other commissions besides the portrait busts started of Sumner and Greene. These commissions were for smaller ideal figures and reliefs. The advance payments brought temporary improvement to his financial status.

In late October, 1839, Crawford awoke one day feeling odd.[9] He didn't have a cough or diarrhea, which were not uncommon setbacks of life in Rome. He just did not want to get out of bed. His muscles ached and he had a fever, then chills. The chills and fever became worse, so he remained in bed thinking he would feel better the next day. He did not get better, and soon drifted in and out of consciousness. Alone, he remained this way for several days until a neighbor who had not seen him, decided to check the studio and found him delirious. Barely able to write a short note, Crawford told the man to get it to Greene.

There were many theories concerning the cause of malaria - male, bad and aria, vapor or air. It was prevalent between June and October. The popular explanation involved the sun striking the soil resulting in the release of a mysterious vapor which would enter one's body, most often after sundown. For this reason, the Romans lived in the upper floors of their buildings, thinking they would be too high for the vapors to reach them. This also made areas of the city which were higher more attractive, and expensive. The profoundness of the fever varied, and in Crawford's case it would have been called a 'malignant fever.'

When Greene found him, he brought Crawford to a spare room in his apartment. A physician confirmed the diagnosis of malaria, attributing the severity of the 'malignant fever' to fatigue from the stress and intensity of his work. Greene and Carlotta nursed him throughout the winter months, and his condition improved slowly, but his strength did not return until late spring. Hoping to escape the heat and threat of Malaria, Greene took his family and Crawford away from Rome to a summer residence in the hills of Albano, just north of the city.

After a month in the country, knowing he had been a burden to Greene, his wife, and family, Crawford decided he was strong enough to return to Rome and his studio. He had not worked since October, the longest idle period of his life, and he felt guilty and bored.

扙

Crawford could buy his marble in Rome, but with the advance money from several pieces providing extra funds, he decided to visit the marble area in the North and Florence. In Florence, he could visit Hiram Powers and Horatio Greenough.

The selection of blocks at the quarries would give him more choices than he had in Rome. He had heard Thorvaldsen's carvers discuss the subtle distinctions between blocks which would affect their carving. The best carvers could tell the flow of the grain in a block before beginning. The foreman who bought all Thorvaldsen's marble took the carvers selected for a work with him and allowed them to choose their blocks. Crawford needed to know more about the differences in marble. He had heard stories of naive young sculptors buying poor or even cracked blocks from dealers.

Since the quarries were north of Florence, he decided to stop there first. He found a vettura, a coach that could be contracted for a trip. An agreement was made with the vetturino, who drove the coach, and took care of arrangements along the way such as the midday stops, meals, and evening lodging.[10] Typically, they covered thirty-five to forty miles per day with stops for lunch and to rest the horses. He agreed to a contract with the vetturino for $12, including meals and lodging. They could leave in two to three days depending on how long it took for the vetturino to find three additional passengers. To travel from Florence to the quarries he would have to make new arrangements. He felt strong enough for the three-to-four day journey.

Bouncing along in a coach for a day would tire anyone, but if the lodging was halfway decent, one slept well. If the lodging was not so decent, one slept well, anyway. As the coach made its way north, the countryside changed to rolling hills with ancient towns built on and into the highest point. These towns, which looked as though they were growing out of the stone of the hill, fascinated him. Built as fortresses for protection, he wondered what it would be like to look out your window and see the ground three to four hundred feet below. The view across the valley below had to be spectacular.

The land looked more fertile than around Rome. The bread, cheese, and wine differed from region to region, making the best part of the trip tasting these regional specialties. A sheep cheese, found about two days out of Rome, called Pecorino became his favorite. The wine had more body as they neared Florence. After five years in Italy, most of it spent in Rome, he believed he was fluent in Italian, but now he discovered some of the local dialects were difficult to understand.

They arrived in Florence late on the fifth day. He thought the landscape of the Duchy of Tuscany with its rolling hills, olive groves, and vineyards the best he had seen during the trip. His friends at Caffe Greco told him to avoid hotels along the Arno, where the tourists stayed and accommodations were good, but expensive. Someone recommended a small, inexpensive hotel across the Arno, near the Ponte Vecchio, and still close to the center of the city and the Palazzo Vecchio della Signora. The Italian spoken in Florence was classic, so he would have no trouble, and, because he could speak Italian, he would be welcome at the hotel.

The next day, primed by his friends at the Caffe Greco, he knew what he wanted to see and was not disappointed. The narrow streets were cleaner than Rome and lined with buildings with facades of roughhewn stones. Their porticos or entrances were not as impressive as those in Rome and he could only imagine what wonders hid behind the fortified walls and large doors. He spent four days immersed in the art of the Renaissance, the sculpture of Michelangelo and Donatello. After the *David*, his favorite works of Michelangelo were in the Medici Chapel he designed for the Church of San Lorenzo. The figure of *Lorenzo de Medici, Day and Night, Dawn and Dusk*, as well as the *Madonna and Child* consumed his attention for an entire morning. He found it a humbling experience that made him question his own talent.

He visited Hiram Powers first.[11] Powers lived and worked in an old, but elegant, Palazzo, a studio site which Crawford concluded, would make a strong impression on visiting American tourists.

The outer door of the Palazzo opened to a small courtyard surrounded by the studio working areas on the ground level. A servant led him up the inner stairs to a sitting room and asked him to have a seat. As he sat he studied the fine furniture, rugs and paintings on the walls. He could only think of the bed, two chairs, table, bare floor, and bare walls of his living area. After a few minutes, Powers entered, a big man, taller than Crawford with a long, bushy beard, similar to the type worn by many of the artists at the Caffe Greco. Crawford thought the beard made him look older than he probably was. Extending his hand, Powers greeted him, "Welcome to Florence. I understand you are Thomas Crawford, an American sculptor working in Rome. I first heard of you from our Consul who corresponds with yours."

"Yes, George Washington Greene, a good friend," replied Crawford, standing to shake hands.

"What brings you to Florence?"

"I'm on my way to the marble quarries and wanted to see Florence."

"If you need to see so much stone, you must have a large commission?"

"No, but I've been in Rome five years and thought it time to see more of Italy."

"Good idea. I wish I could get away but the work keeps piling up. Where are you from and what have you been doing in Rome?"

Crawford told him of his beginning with Launitz and Frazee, but when he mentioned his apprenticeship with Thorvaldsen, he noticed something off in Powers' reaction. Powers was careful not to dismiss his work offhand, but his comments seemed guarded. Crawford had never met anyone who did not consider the work of Thorvaldsen outstanding. For him, Powers' response was akin to a personal insult, and it would forever affect their relationship.

They then went down to Powers' studio rooms. No workers were present this late in the day, but after looking around Crawford estimated Powers had 15-20 assistants. Everything seemed well organized and the many busts in various stages of development showed excellent technique. He had to admire them; they were good.

The few figurative, larger pieces, left something to be desired. The surfaces of the finished works were excellent, but the figures interspersed with the portraits lacked vitality or any evidence of motion. It was an interesting contradiction.

Powers also showed him pointing machines he had invented as well as smaller tools he had modified to suit his clay modeling and carving. Inventing was his second passion. They spent two hours discussing the art and business of marble carving.

On his way back to the hotel Crawford tried to digest what he had seen, his impression of Powers, his personality, his work. He decided he liked the man but concluded he had not seen anything superior to any of the work by Roman sculptors or for that matter, by his own hand. The busts were well done and seemed to be Powers' specialty. He had to admit any American sculptor he met would be his competitor for the tourist work and commissions at home. This could certainly bias his opinions. He concluded Powers would always be a respectable competitor and should not be underestimated, but he did not have the sensitivity, background, or interest in larger monumental works.

⁓

The next morning, when he visited the studio of Horatio Greenough, he would have a different experience. The studio and home blended in with the surrounding buildings making it difficult to find. An assistant greeted him and led him directly to Greenough who was at work in a large studio. About the same size as Crawford, but a bit older, he had a thin beard extending down from his sideburns that outlined his jaw and chin. Crawford introduced himself.

"What a coincidence, I just received a letter from Charles Sumner telling me all about you. You must be good. Charles does not pass out praise lightly," said Greenough, with a broad smile.

"Charles has been most kind to me," said Crawford.

"And to me. He stayed here before heading to Rome. I hated to see him leave. We spent hours discussing my *George Washington* for the Rotunda of the Capitol. He's quite the scholar. We were friends in Boston and fellow graduates of Harvard, but I was an upperclassman when he entered. Now he's on the Law faculty and here I am in Italy. When I first came to Italy to study, I went to Rome, but after visiting Florence and the marble quarries, I decided to stay here."

"Thorvaldsen mentioned you had been in Rome. Why did you pick Florence instead of Rome for your base?"

"Thorvaldsen, the master, is a wonderful man, unselfish and always willing to help young sculptors," said Greenough. "Rome is impressive, its past can still be experienced in the ruins scattered about the city. That ancient culture has a certain fascination for many. When I came to Florence, I found a culture of a different era, but nonetheless, important to the history of art. It plays a major role in the life of this city, but I had more practical reasons. I visited the marble quarries, which are only a day away, and saw the excellent work done in the ateliers near the quarries, discovered marble would cost half the price closer to the quarries, and assistants, since there are so many in the area, would also cost half. That's why I chose Florence. You should also consider working here. What are your plans?"

"I'm on my way to the quarries now."

"Do you have a large commission?"

"No, but I do need some blocks for several medium-sized commissions," said Crawford.

"Well, good. Do you have any engravings of your work, or did you bring any drawings? I would love to see some."

"No, not with me."

"Can I show you anything in particular?"

"Yes, your *George Washington*."

"It's not here. Because of its size I had to rent a larger space, but it is close and we can walk there in a few minutes," said Greenough, standing and motioning toward the door.

⁊

They walked for about ten minutes, and, after Greenough unlocked a tall pair of double doors on the side of a nondescript building, they entered a large room containing only one object, the sculpture of *George Washington*. Marble dust covered the floor. "It's almost finished. They are just completing some surface details and we should be ready to ship soon," said Greenough walking toward the piece.

Larger than Crawford had expected, it must have been at least ten feet long and twelve feet high. Now he knew what Sumner meant when he wondered how it would be received in America. Even he, an artist, always looking for new ideas, had to think about this a bit. He walked slowly around the piece several times.

This was George Washington, the Greek or Roman statesman, shown as a man of great power and strength, seated on what could only be interpreted as a throne. No question it was Washington, but he had never been seen like this, either in life or in the minds of his people. Nude from the waist up and partially covered in drapery suggesting a toga, Crawford understood the intent, but would average Americans? He could only be impressed by this bold statement.

"Interesting," commented Crawford stepping back to take in the entire work. "It's larger than I expected."

"It is large, but you must remember, it will sit in the Rotunda of the Capitol, a much larger space," replied Greenough. "The face is after the life mask the French sculptor Houdon made when he visited Washington in 1785.[12] Next, we must crate it and somehow get it to Leghorn for shipping to America. Bringing the block from Seravezzo was adventure enough for me. I can only imagine the possible problems ahead on this final trip. My last letter from Congress said Commodore Hull would be in charge of the shipping."

"I did a bust of the Commodore. He is, I hope, a satisfied client," said Crawford. "What do you think your sculpture weighs? My guess would be 15-20 tons."

"You are right, about 20 tons," agreed Greenough.

They spent several more hours talking. When Crawford spoke of Greene's help, Greenough told him he had a similar experience when he started. James Fenimore Cooper visited Greenough's studio and was so excited by what he saw, he became a big promoter of his work in Boston and Washington.[13]

Greenough's asking price for the sculpture of George Washington was $20,000. Congress approved $5000 per year over a four-year period. No other commission for the Capitol had been that large. A pedestal for the piece had to be constructed at a cost of $2000. Greenough also submitted a bill for $8,311.90 covering his expenses for "the lease of the studio, repairs and enlarging of the studio, wages to servants, and foreman, cost of packing, damage to trees on the road from Florence to Leghorn and for a large variety of articles necessary in the construction of a statue of this large size."[14]

Commodore Hull did make the arrangements for shipping from Leghorn. Delays incurred additional fees, and by the time the time the sculpture was in place, the cost above the original fee paid to Greenough came to about $21,000.

Crawford left Greenough's studio knowing he had met a major competitor. All the excellent work he had seen, as well as the man's education, sophistication, and his apparent contacts in Boston and Washington were daunting. Greenough had already received another major commission for the Capitol, The *Rescue Group* was to be a multi-figure piece ten to twelve feet high. At the moment all Crawford had was a potential *Orpheus and Eurydice*, still 'a bird in the bush.'

৩৩

Before returning to Rome Crawford needed to explore the marble quarries and decided to travel by a Posting coach, which delivered the mail. They were faster and he could get there in one day. Greenough had given him the names and locations of his favorite quarries and some contacts.

The trip took him due west for a short distance and then north along the west coast to the area of the two cities, Pietrasanta and Carrara. As they progressed north, he had his first view of the Apennines, the major source of the marble preferred by sculptors for centuries. Above Pietrasanta, the tall peaks were white, not from snow, but quarried marble. Tired from the ride, he decided to leave the coach at Pietrasanta, south of Carrara.

He found a hotel on the central piazza that had an old church at one corner and small shops along the edge. It was already getting dark, so he settled in for the night, saving his first explorations for the next day.

In the morning, he began his tour of Pietrasanta. People in the square were going about their business, and from what he could tell by the marble dust on the shoes of the men, the main business involved working stone. A short distance into the side streets, he found small marble carving shops or *laboratorios*. Madonnas or saints for churches and elaborate headstones for cemeteries were the most frequent products. The carvers (*scarpellini*) worked outside with only a roof for protection from the sun and rain. He liked the idea of working outside, but it would be impossible in a large crowded city like Rome.

Returning to the main piazza, the Piazza del Duomo, he ordered a coffee at the trattoria and asked about the quarries. The owner was more than happy to discuss them and began by informing him that Michelangelo had come to Pietrasanta when he needed the finest marble. "If you step outside and look up at the top of Monte Altissima, you can see where he personally chose his marble," he explained with pride, moving to the door and pointing at the highest mountain.

As he moved through the town he found more studios or *laboratorios* where some were working marble with hand-turned lathes and others were doing ornamental work. The carvers were as good as he had seen in Rome, and the quality of the marble from Seravezzo, between Pietrasanta and Carrara, some of the best.

He found even more *laboratorios* in Carrara. There, he followed a narrow dirt road leading out of town and up a mountain to the quarries. Wide areas of the mountain were stripped of their surfaces, exposing smooth white marble walls. In other areas there were deep pits with marble walls, some filled with clear blue-green water. The brilliance of the sun's reflections off the marble hurt the eyes.

He made sketches of men (the *cavatori*) moving a large marble block on a wooden stone sled down the mountain. It was dangerous work and If a rope broke and they were to lose control, anyone in the way could be maimed or crushed. Large teams of oxen pulled the stone sleds with the large blocks on more level ground. Fascinated, he spent a week watching and learning about marble at its source.

Working here would be cheaper since everything needed was readily available. Greenough had the right idea; maybe he should move closer to the source of the marble, but a studio in Pietrasanta or Carrara lacked an important component: visibility. This was not a stop on the itinerary of Americans on the Grand Tour. George Washington Greene did not serve as Consul here, and his growing reputation identified him as the American sculptor working in Rome.

ᑍᑕ

Returning to Rome, Crawford hoped there would be a letter from Sumner with a contract for Orpheus, but there was none. It was not until March, 1841,[15] that a contract arrived from Sumner. The Boston Athenaeum agreed to show his work, and Sumner said he had the money. Crawford was ecstatic.

Expecting the money to follow soon he ordered a marble block and began working. The carving progressed so well that when Thorvaldsen, back from Denmark, stopped to see it, he gave it more than just his blessing and said it was the best new work in Rome. However, the money Sumner had collected had not arrived.

Three months after Crawford ordered the marble block a representative of the quarry demanded they be paid. Threats were made, and Crawford, an American, with no political connections in Rome, was worried. In retrospect, he knew he should have waited to be paid, at least half, before he began. But the cupidity, typical of a young artist eager to start a work, made him bypass the usual practice of half the fee upfront. He had no cash reserve, his family had no money to forward and he was in trouble.

One afternoon, Greene stopped at the studio. After they chatted awhile, Crawford said, "George, I'm in trouble. I need your advice."

"What kind of trouble? Rome is no place to be in trouble. Please tell me it's not about a young girl, that kind of trouble can only be settled by bloodshed," said Greene with a concerned look.

"No, not that kind of trouble."

"Thank God. Then what kind? You really scared me."

"Money trouble."

"I'm still scared, but this may be solved without bloodshed. How much and who do you owe?"

"I have not paid for the marble block for Orpheus. I owe $400 to the quarry, and they want their money. They are threatening me."

"I assumed when you signed the contract and began the carving, you must have received money. I even talked to Carlotta about it. I noticed how your mood changed once you had the work off the ground and - I assumed - extra money."

"I was so happy to see the contract; my enthusiasm blinded my common sense. I do not know what to do."

"Does anyone owe you money?"

"No, and I should have paid the quarry three months ago."

"You are not the first artist in Rome in this kind of predicament, but most often they are painters with unpaid rent and a few other bills. That is when they disappear, return home and are no longer seen at the Caffe Greco. A sculptor with a studio full of work and a large major piece in progress is difficult to hide. Sumner is part of this dilemma. You told me he said he had the money. If he has the money, where is it?"

"I wish I knew."

"I can write him tomorrow."

"That's not the solution. Another two months will pass, and if we are lucky, we'll get a response. I have let this go too long. They are not willing to wait anymore. They have threatened me."

"What do you mean by threatened?"

"Bring in the police, confiscate my work, damage Orpheus, have me thrown out of my studio. Some or all of that."

"This is serious. There is no one in Rome who can lend you the money?"

"Except for you, all my friends are artists, many in similar circumstances. The Caffe Greco is no place to look for this amount of money."

"Is that why you are telling me all this?"

"No, but you are my best friend. I had to talk to someone about it."

"You cannot give up your work and studio now, not with all the work you have done. I do have confidence in Sumner; he must have the money. Why it has not been sent is a puzzle, but, as you say, even if we contact him and get the answer and the money, it will be too late. Once the police are involved, everything gets out of hand, there is no stopping them. They are not known for their gentle and understanding ways."

"If I use my money to pay them, I will have no money for rent or much of anything else."

"I may be able to get some money from a banker who appreciates the referrals from my office. But we have to get the money from Sumner as soon as possible. Roman bankers can also be impatient. It would be lent to me, not you, so we would now be in this together. Never let my wife know I have done this. And remember, there will be interest on the loan, so by the time the money arrives from Sumner, you will need more than $400 to repay the loan."

"You would really do this? Sumner did say in the letter with the contract he had the money, I can show it to you."

"No, I believe you and Sumner."

"I am amazed you would do this for me, but knowing you as I do, I'm not surprised at your generosity. Beyond the sum of money, I will be indebted to you."

"I can contact the banker tomorrow. If all goes well, I can have the money in three to four days."

Greene did get the loan and the imminent crisis passed. For Greene, however, borrowing money continued. He had a family to support and a Consul's lifestyle to maintain in Rome. His crisis was on the horizon. Sumner did collect $2500, which was $500 more than the original price, but Crawford did not receive the money until five months later, June, 1842,[16] making the interest on the loan higher than anticipated. Crawford, happy and grateful, shipped the bust he had completed of Sumner to Boston.

❧

When Greenough's *George Washington* was placed in the Rotunda of the Capitol, the classical depiction and partial nudity provoked considerable criticism and outrage from the general public. American tourists passing through

Rome, commented on the negative reception of the work. Crawford who wanted no controversy when Orpheus would be shown in Boston, covered Orpheus's genitalia with a leaf.

Close friends of Sumner and Longfellow, Dr Samuel Gridley Howe and his pregnant wife, Julia along with Julia's sister, Annie, were touring the continent and arrived in Rome in December of 1842. They decided to remain in Rome until the birth of their baby and not leave for America until spring, 1844. Greene was a cousin of Julia's father. Their first week in Rome, Greene took them to visit Crawford's studio. Impressed by both him and his work, they included Crawford in many of their Rome adventures and dinner parties.

Orpheus was ready to ship. The winter of 1842-43 was over, with the fresh breezes of spring in the air, Crawford thought he ought to celebrate. He sent a note to Greene asking him to meet him at the Caffe Greco the next evening. Greene accepted.

After ordering wine, Greene began, "You know how to get me to come here. Your note said you would be buying the wine. Why all this sudden exuberance?"

"I'm ready to ship Orpheus. After eight years of hard work I am sending a sculpture to America for my first show. They are coming to crate it next week. It should be leaving Italy in two to three weeks," said a relaxed and happy Crawford.

"About the first of May, right?"

"Right."

"Now it's my turn for exuberance," said Greene.

"Well, what is it, this 'exuberance' of yours?"

"I have not been home for six years, and uncrated, I am leaving for America about the same time."

"Why this sudden decision? The last time we met you said nothing about this."

"Besides seeing my family, there are several reasons. I am beginning the biography of my grandfather, Nathanael Greene, my hero, and as you know the great general of the Revolutionary War and a friend of George Washington. I plan to visit Mount Vernon to see what letters or other correspondence exists between them as well as any letters my family might have. I need to go to Washington and try to change this Consulate to Diplomatic status. I cannot afford to continue spending my limited funds to keep the Consulate open. If it could be changed, there would be a salary for the position and perhaps money for expenses. As it stands, I am almost out of money."

"George, I did not realize things were so difficult. You helped me when I needed money. Can I lend you some now?"

"And you paid me back. This is no time to be shy; yes, I could use $100. The trip will take my savings, and I need to leave some money for Carlotta."

There was a brief pause as Crawford considered this. His finances were still tight, even though they were improved over a year ago, but recalling all Greene had done for him, the answer came quickly, "I can lend you the money, but do me a favor while you are home. Orpheus should arrive about the same time as you. I want you to watch how it is crated. Then, if you could be there when they uncrate it, you could explain to them where to begin and what to avoid to prevent any damage. This showing is so important to me, that's all I think about. I have some drawings diagramming the best way to display the piece, which I was going to send to Sumner, but you could take them. Is that all right?"

"Yes. I plan to be in Rhode Island first to see family, then to Boston to visit Longfellow and Sumner. I will make myself available when they uncrate Orpheus at the Athenaeum. My last stop before returning home will be Washington. I love it here in Rome, but I must change this Consul status. Thanks for your offer, I will feel much better leaving Carlotta with some money. Sam and Julia Howe will be here to keep you company. He's an interesting man."

"He is. He told me about his work with blind children in Boston and the home and school he established for them. One night we had a long discussion about the issue of slavery in America. He was outspoken about the problem. He and Sumner are Abolitionists."

"Indeed they are, as is Julia. Julia thinks I should bring her sister Louisa back with me since she will still be here and Louisa would be a big help when the baby comes."

"Julia mentions her often," said Crawford. "Have you met her?"

"If I have, I do not remember."

"Thank goodness you will be in Boston when Orpheus is uncrated."

"Let's drink to a safe trip for Orpheus," proposed Greene.

"As well as yours," replied Crawford as they raised their glasses.

∽

Greene arrived in America before Orpheus, which was on a ship that docked in New York and transferred to another ship for the trip to Boston. Greene was present, as promised, when it arrived at the Athenaeum. As the first boards were removed, they could see there was extensive damage to Orpheus. One of the heads of Cerebus was broken off and the figure of Orpheus balanced precariously on breaks in the knees and ankles. Everyone thought it would never be shown.

After the initial shock abated, and they stepped back and focused on the areas which were intact, what they saw made them realize they had acquired something unique and finer than promised. Assured it could be repaired, the Athenaeum expanded the project. A special building would be constructed to house the sculpture and include more of Crawford's works. This was what Crawford had hoped for and he had three pieces in the wings for American clients that just happened to be shipped to Boston about the same time as Orpheus.

Greene went on to Washington to plead his case for changing the Consulate in Rome. After two frustrating weeks, he was unable to interest anyone. America did not know where to begin in Italy. The Papal State in Rome represented only one region of the area referred to as Italy, which included other regions such as The Duchy of Tuscany and The Kingdom of Sardinia.

Despondent and running short of money, he returned to New York to stay with John Ward, Julia's uncle. The Ward family were successful bankers and investors on Wall Street. Uncle John was guardian of the trust left by the deceased father of Julia, and her sisters and brothers. Uncle John could best be described as a parsimonious trustee when it came to the distribution of the trust income. An epitome of the conservative Wall Street banker of that time, he required tedious justification for each request, determined to protect the wealth of his nieces and nephews and was convinced he had their best interests in mind.

Part II

Louisa Ward, eager to join her sisters in Rome, persuaded her uncle to let her join them, the decision made easier because she would be accompanied across the Atlantic by her father's cousin, George Greene. Louisa, a beautiful, petite and chestnut-haired, eighteen-year-old had many suitors, but none interested her, and she wanted to see more of the world.

One of her supposed suitors was Charles Sumner. Her sister, Julia, had attempted to encourage a relationship between her husband's best friend and Louisa, but neither showed any interest. Crossing the ocean and visiting London, Paris, and Rome appealed to her more than the predictable routine of high society in New York.

Louisa and Greene arrived in Rome, December, 1843. Depressed, Greene would have to reconsider his stay in Rome as Consul. He loved the city and the access to the social life made possible by his position. His spending was out of control, but surrendering to the glamour of the local aristocrats and wealthy American travelers had taken its toll. How would he tell Carlotta?

On the other hand, the thrill of seeing her sister and staying in this romantic ancient city excited Louisa. Julia welcomed her to their comfortable apartment, which had more than enough room and servants for the additional visitor. Louisa had read as much as she could about Rome before coming, but she found the descriptions did not approach the reality of some of the sites such as St Peters, the Vatican Museum, and the Borghese Gardens and Villa. The pre-Christmas festivities in Rome fascinated her.

༄

A week after her arrival, Greene took Louisa to visit Crawford's studio. Julia and her husband, Sam, had mentioned him several times. She had never met an artist before, let alone, a sculptor, so she did not know what to expect. Her image of an artist was someone who led a Bohemian life, which sounded romantic, but too unpredictable and insecure for someone with her background.

Crawford knew they were coming, but often pretended to be in the midst of modeling in clay or carving marble when visitors arrived. It added to the artist mystique. The inevitable opening questions were always, "How do you know when to stop? What do you do when you make a mistake or take off too much marble?"

The beginning of this particular tour, however, did not follow the usual pattern. As Greene introduced Louisa, Crawford clumsily extended his hand to her, forgetting it still held a chisel. Greene had been through this exercise many times, and this surprised him since Crawford was always in control of himself.

"I think I would make a mess of things if I tried to use that chisel, thank you," a composed Louisa replied.

"Oh, excuse me! I'm so sorry! I was engrossed in my work before you came, and I forgot I had the chisel in my hand," an embarrassed Crawford stammered.

"That would be no surprise to many," said a smiling Greene. "Rumor has it that you work so long you must soak your hands in warm water at the end of the day to get the hammer and chisel free."

"George is a great friend, but he exaggerates. Let me show you around," replied Crawford, having regained his composure. He proceeded to show Louisa his work with a fervor Greene had not seen on any other studio visit with tourists. Louisa responded with dedicated interest. The synchrony of the movement of their eyes between the works and each other could only be interpreted as mutual infatuation. Sensing this, Greene would have left the two alone since his presence no longer mattered, but that would have been improper.

Crawford went into details Greene had never heard before, giving a virtuoso performance which was not for Greene's benefit. After two hours Greene began to make not-so-subtle movements toward the door, which were ignored by the others. After another hour, Crawford finished and asked if he could make some coffee, but Greene insisted he had to get back to attend to Consular business. The reluctance of the two to separate was obvious.

౿

When Louisa returned to the apartment, she found Julia, now in her fourth month of pregnancy, relaxing after an afternoon nap. "Well, did you enjoy your visit with Greene's favorite sculptor?" asked Julia as she folded the blanket which had covered her.

"Yes, such talent and energy, and you can see the results in all the work he has done. I had heard George and Sumner talk about his Orpheus, which they have brought to Boston, so it was fun to see the plaster in the studio. Now I know why they worked so hard to get it to the Athenaeum. I can tell everyone when I get home, I saw the original plaster in Rome before the show in Boston, and with the sculptor. We should invite him to dinner here. Has he been invited to our Christmas dinner?" inquired Louisa, avoiding Julia's eyes.

"He is on the list. Crawford has been a guest here often."

"He is alone as far as I know, isn't he? The Greenes are coming and he mentioned he was looking forward to Christmas, saying it would be the first time he'd enjoy the usual American customs since he left home."

"He is alone. He has no family here; they are in New York," Julia said, sensing a note of urgency in Louisa and her concern about Thomas Crawford.

Julia considered Louisa's comments the rest of the afternoon and during dinner. Perhaps she was over reacting, but being the older sister, she felt responsible for Louisa and Annie. After Louisa had retired, and she was alone with Sam, she said, "Louisa visited Crawford's studio with George today. She was more than impressed."

"What do you mean, 'more than impressed'?" said Sam as he lit a cigar.

"She wanted to be certain Crawford would be here for Christmas."

"He will be here. I don't think I follow you. What are you trying to say?"

"I am concerned she may be smitten with him. It's just a feeling I got after she told me about the visit."

"She only met him today."

"I know, but a woman can tell when another woman is in love."

"In love! All this in one afternoon? Maybe you are being too much of an older sister."

"No, I am serious about this. At home, I often heard her discuss the young men she met. This is different."

"Well, let us say it is an infatuation, she will be going home with us after the baby is born and he will still be here in Rome," said Sam. "That will end it. Crawford has made it clear his path to success requires working in Rome, not in America. I cannot see Louisa making her home in Rome."

"Louisa is intelligent, strong-willed and capable of accomplishing whatever she sets her mind to, which concerns me."

"How could she make a home here? He has no money, and she is accustomed to the best life has to offer, a wide circle of friends, and a close family in New York. Do you think she would give all that up to live here with an artist who can barely keep up with the rent payments?"

"It is possible. You underestimate her."

"I repeat: this fellow has no money and at this time has trouble supporting himself, let alone a wife and family. You have been to the studio; you see how he lives. He is obsessed with his work. She has a steadier income than he."

"I never considered her income a factor, but I suppose that could be in the back of his mind. However, he does not impress me that way," said Julia.

"I hope so, but now you may be underestimating him," concluded Sam.

෴

First thing the next morning Crawford called on Greene, who said, "Yesterday in your studio I witnessed a Thomas Crawford I had never seen before. You were talking about sculpture, but you were not talking about sculpture. Someone has penetrated that hard exterior shell - I suppose you could call it a marble shell - that surrounds you and keeps out all other interests. Am I correct?"

"That's not a bad way to put it. It must have been obvious," replied Crawford with a coy smile.

"Obvious is too weak a word, palpable would be more appropriate."

"I know we are both invited to the Howe's for Christmas dinner, and I am looking forward to it, but I would also like to get to know Louisa outside that setting," said Crawford. "Maybe you could help me do that. Christmas Eve is such a big celebration here, it could be fun to take Louisa to the Vatican and some of the other churches that evening. Would you and Carlotta be willing to be our chaperones for the evening?"

"We usually do go out that evening to visit some of the churches but we have never gone to the Vatican on Christmas Eve. The Pope has a Mass in the Sistine Chapel at 10:00 PM. Is that what you are referring to?"

"Yes, I hear it is quite the spectacle."

"That's also what I've heard, but it's a formal affair. Men must be in formal attire and women must dress in black and wear a veil".

"I didn't know it was formal, but that would be even more impressive. Can you get an invitation?"

"I think so. I have a formal outfit, do you?"

"You know the answer, but if it could be arranged, I would be sure to get one. How is this done, how do I ask her?"

"Carlotta can send an invitation to Louisa to join us for the evening, Julia is halfway through her pregnancy, so I doubt she would go out on a cold December evening among the crowds. It sounds like fun to me and Carlotta would enjoy it. I will talk to my coconspirator, Carlotta, right away," said Greene, now convinced Louisa was more than a passing fancy to Crawford.

As he was leaving, Crawford said, "Thank you, again."

৯৩

The plan played out as intended, Louisa accepted and replied immediately. Julia sent her regrets because of her condition, and Sam would stay home with his wife on Christmas Eve.

৯৩

The necessity of a black dress and veil provided a perfect excuse for Julia and Louisa to visit a dressmaker and the lace shops. Madonnas were displayed on all the street corners for the feast; they were serenaded by shepherds from the south of Italy, playing bagpipes made from goatskins. The shrill sound of the bagpipes pierced the air and ears, but their presence every year heralded the coming of the great feast, surpassed in Rome only by Easter. Louisa found something special for the evening.

The Greenes and Crawford, who had reserved a coach for the evening, arrived at 9:00. The gentlemen looked elegant in their formal attire, as did Carlotta, in her black dress and veiled head. Louisa had not yet made an appearance.

When she did enter the room, all heads turned in unison, the men admired her beauty, the women watched Crawford's reaction. Louisa's bell-shaped black dress accentuated her trim, narrow waist. The sleeves were tight to the arms, and the veil, covering her shoulders and neck, formed a perfect oval highlighting the soft delicate features of her face. A small bit of chestnut colored hair peeked from beneath the veil over her forehead.

"Sorry to keep you waiting," said Louisa. "How elegant everyone looks."

"How lovely you look," replied Carlotta, "I have been looking forward to this evening. We have never been to this Christmas Eve service before."

"I agree. You look lovely," said Crawford who could not take his eyes off Louisa. "This will be a special Christmas Eve for all of us."

"Well, the coach is waiting, and we should get started. The streets will be filled with people and the area around the Vatican will be even more crowded," said Greene moving toward the door. As Crawford helped Louisa with her shawl, their eyes met, and an unspoken message that passed between the two did not go unnoticed by Julia.

While George and Carlotta fretted about the slow progress through the streets of Rome, Louisa kept Crawford spellbound with her impressions of Christmas in Rome and descriptions of all she had seen since coming to the city. As he had hoped, having the chance to be with her like this, gave him the opportunity to talk with her without having to compete with Sam and Julia's friends who were more accustomed to frequent dinner parties and fancy social events.

He was well-liked by his fellow artists and often the leader of both serious discussions and partying at the Caffe Greco, but his isolation in the studio and humble beginnings in New York, made him cautious with what he considered the 'upper class.' It was a world which had not excluded him, but he still considered himself an outsider not yet comfortable with its unspoken rules and boastful ancestries. He did not wish to squander this opportunity to be with Louisa.

෬๑

When they arrived at the Vatican and left the coach, Louisa took Crawford's arm, and the two couples pushed their way through the crowd. Greene had obtained invitations for an area reserved for the staffs of embassies and foreign Consuls. At the sight of the hundreds of candles, which lit the Sistine Chapel and the frescoes of Michelangelo, Louisa gasped and gripped Crawford's arm more tightly. He admired her beauty as she scanned the ceiling and Michelangelo's portrayal of the Last Judgement above the altar.

The ceremony began with the entrance of the College of Cardinals, each accompanied by a valet attending to their flowing scarlet robes with ermine trimmed hoods. There were 71 current members, and they took their seats at the side of the altar.

After all were seated, a hush came over the room in anticipation of the arrival of Pope Gregory XVI. Wearing magnificent white vestments, embroidered with gold, he entered and blessed the crowd as he proceeded to his throne on the altar. Once seated, each Cardinal approached the throne, bowed, knelt, and kissed the Papal Ring. The setting, the pomp of the ceremony, the colors, mesmerized the four American visitors.

As the Pope's a cappela choir sang a Gregorian chant, a High Mass with three celebrants, began. The carefully choreographed movements of the celebrants and servers or assistants in the candlelit chapel with the choir chanting in the background, touched Louisa. Even though it would be midnight before the Mass ended, and the exit procession of the Pope and Cardinals concluded, Louisa could have stayed for more. It was an unforgettable Christmas Eve in an extraordinary setting.

Since it was an unusually warm night for December and their coach was nowhere to be found, they decided to walk. The mood in the Piazza San Pietro and the surrounding streets was cheery so this did not seem an inconvenience.

∾

The Greenes looked in every direction as they walked hoping to find a coach, but Louisa and Crawford, arm in arm trailed some distance behind, enjoying the Christmas spirit of the crowds. They were not so eager to find a coach and end the evening. Louisa delighted in the running commentary of Crawford about the sights of Rome, and as they walked around the Castel Sant'Angelo, Crawford said, "Did you know there is a tunnel leading from the Vatican to this fortified Castel Sant'Angelo? The Popes used it for an escape and barricade from invaders. It was also a prison. I remember the night I arrived in Rome, we crossed this bridge, Ponte Sant'Angelo, and I could see very little. It was a metaphor for the moment, the arrival of a young, naive American with a future enshrouded in fog. The fog cleared slowly, but I think all is clear now, at least to me."

"You love this city, don't you?" replied Louisa.

"Yes, I do. It is a paradise for the artist. Everywhere I look I find some inspiration, and I am sure there is more for me to see. Look, now we are coming to the bridge, and on this clear moonlit night, all Bernini's sculptures along the balustrade stand out against the night sky. I wish I could have seen his studio. He must have employed 200 assistants, because the amount of work he produced has never been duplicated."

"Do you think you will ever return to work in America? How long have you been here?"

"A little over eight years. I would like to work in America, but for now it's impractical. I can get so much more done here. There are no trained assistants there, and I cannot afford to spend all my time training some to create the type of studio I need. My dream is to do monumental works for cities like Boston, New York, and for the new Capitol in Washington. I know I can do that type of work here at less cost and ship it to America. I think Orpheus will help me find patrons."

"You have Sumner to thank for that, and Greene. They know many important people. You have been fortunate. Your choice of friends has been exceptional."

"Including you. I know, and am grateful. Sometimes I feel all this is predetermined, these associations; Launitz and Frazee, Thorvaldsen, Greene, and Sumner. I'm beginning to sound conceited. Forgive me, but I can't help but feel good about my future, and believe me, I am determined to succeed."

"You will, you will. Everyone tells me how hard you work," said Louisa pressing his arm to her side.

Ahead, they could see George and Carlotta waving. They had found a coach.

∽

They were back at Julia and Sam's by about 1:30 in the morning. The combination of the Sistine Chapel, the Pope, the excitement in the streets, and her conversation with Crawford kept Louisa awake for most of the night as she attempted to sort through the different feelings she had about this man. Was it the romantic artist, the attractive man, someone she met on a holiday in this city filled with beauty capable of over stimulating the senses? Should she respond to his unmistakable interest in her? There was no question he would continue to live and work in Rome, a city with no resemblance to New York. Could she live in Rome? At the moment, she had no answers.

Louisa and Crawford, seated apart at the Christmas dinner that evening, were silent as Greene and Carlotta entertained the guests with their account of the events in the Sistine Chapel on Christmas Eve. Watching Louisa, as she watched Crawford, Julia knew what was on her mind.

That winter Crawford saw Louisa often, and she, in turn, was happy to be with him. As he described his work, and all the steps involved from beginning to the completion of a sculpture, she became interested. She realized the result was art, but it was also a business and she felt she could contribute to that aspect of his career. He had been busy enough in 1843 to expand his studio; she counted eleven plasters he had done that year. All this was new to her, and she noted he had tourists visiting every time she was at the studio, something she interpreted as an indication of his future success.

Crawford, who wanted to marry Louisa, was busier and happier than he could remember. The first showing of his work in America, with Orpheus as the centerpiece, was scheduled for May, in Boston. That should result in even more commissions. The only recent disappointment came from Greene who told him the Danish Consul had informed him of Bertel Thorvaldsen's death in March. Reminiscing about his time in Thorvaldsen's studio and all he had learned from him, saddened Crawford who would never forget his mentor.

෴

Under the watchful eye of Sumner in Boston, the small building added to the Athenaeum was being completed. Determined to make Orpheus's unveiling a success, Sumner thought more and more about the other works of Crawford to be included in the show. He decided to add another, his marble bust by Crawford. After all, he had raised the money, persuaded the Athenaeum to add a building to house the show, written articles about the proposed event, and promoted Crawford's work whenever possible among his many acquaintances in Boston. His law practice was stagnant, his life could use some new direction, and perhaps this visibility might lead to another line of work. Few were as articulate, well-educated and traveled as Sumner, but the day-to-day routine of a law office was not a good fit for his diverse intellectual talents.

The exhibition of *Orpheus and Eurydice* opened May 6, 1844, and was a success. Catherine Maria Sedgwick, the popular New England novelist, who had visited Crawford's studio in 1839, wrote part of the catalogue. The reviews in the newspapers were supportive of the work and the potential of Crawford's career.

෴

After the birth of their child in March, 1844, Sam and Julia made plans to return to America. They were to leave in May with plans to stop in Paris and London before crossing the Atlantic. There never had been any doubt in

Crawford's mind about marrying Louisa. Her path to the same conclusion, while not as direct, had nonetheless prompted her to write to her guardian, Uncle John, informing him of her feelings toward Crawford. She knew the pitfalls of marrying someone outside her circle or class would not sit well with her conservative guardian.

Walking in the Pincian Gardens the day before she left, Louisa asked Crawford, "How soon will you come to America?"

"As soon as I can finish some work in the studio. I will not get to New York until sometime in August."

"By then I may have persuaded Uncle John and my brothers you are worthy of becoming a part of the proud Ward family."

"My stomach turns upside down when you say things like that. I work hard. I have a studio full of commissions, and my show at the Athenaeum is a success. What more can I do?"

"They have no idea what a sculptor does. They think of artists as impoverished romantics, an image they have from books and operas. They have never met an artist. Remember, their world is Wall Street and banks."

"A world I know nothing about. By the way, I have not written to my mother or sister about this, but I know they will love you just as I do, and without prejudice. It has been nine years since I have been home. I miss them."

"I'm glad you told me, I was going to stop and see them. That would have been a disaster."

"Perhaps not, they would have been surprised but they would understand and welcome you."

"This view, this city... I would never have dreamed I could live anywhere but New York. You have changed me, but you must promise we will visit America more often than every nine years."

"Agreed," answered Crawford.

∾

When Louisa arrived home in June, Uncle John made it clear he did not approve of Crawford. As she anticipated, the idea that she should marry an artist, a man with no regular income or savings, was a mistake he could not, as trustee of her father's estate, let her make. He did not know this gentleman, nor the family, and he reminded her that her income could be a factor in Crawford's interest in her.

Uncle John was not the only one who felt this way. Julia's husband, Sam, was not as vocal as Uncle John, but he offered no defense of Crawford. Julia, out of respect for her husband, avoided disagreeing with Uncle John.

Invitations to dinner parties arrived as soon as Louisa returned. Her friends were eager to hear about the trip and her extended stay in Rome. Politeness, at these dinners, precluded anyone mentioning Crawford's name, but gossip had already begun, and Uncle John's feelings about this sculptor in Rome were no secret. Once again, Louisa had doubts about leaving New York, her home and friends, to remake her life in Italy.

Arriving in New York late August, Crawford, went directly to see his mother and sister surprising them both. It was a bittersweet reunion, without his father who had died while he was away. His mother and sister, as expected, were thrilled to hear of his plans to marry, particularly his mother, who assumed it also meant he would settle in New York.

After nine years in Rome, Crawford felt out of place. Everything around him was so different from what he was used to. The buildings, the clothing, the food; it was now all strange. When he first arrived in Rome, he stood out because of his American clothes, now he was the oddly dressed European as he walked the streets of New York. Everywhere he looked, he saw new construction. The empty fields he remembered behind his home, were now filled with houses and other buildings. It was exciting, but in a different way than Rome. Here, in New York in 1844, commerce ruled.

Throughout his voyage across the Atlantic, he contemplated what he would say and how he would approach Louisa's Uncle John. Louisa had warned him about her uncle's bias regarding artists, and in particular about the possibility of any artist marrying his niece.

Somehow he had to convince her uncle that he could care for Louisa and a family in the style to which she was accustomed, even though he had no money in the bank and would take her away from her family and New York. His work in the studio was the collateral and for him, wealth, but it was not the wealth Uncle John understood.

He had to sell his reputation as an artist based on the response to his work in Boston, a risky tactic since he was not sure there had been any comment in the New York papers about the Athenaeum show. Julia appeared to like him, Sam maintained his distance, and he had never met her brothers, so he was uncertain how much opposition or support he might receive from them. Carving marble was much easier.

On a warm Sunday afternoon, two days after he arrived, he walked to Bond Street and found the large Georgian brownstone home of Louisa and the Ward family. When she opened the door and saw him, all the mixed feelings she had since her return home and memories of the happy times they shared in Rome blended, leaving her overcome with emotion. She had missed him more than she realized. Yes, she was in love with this man.

∽

Louisa's brother, Sam, was home the afternoon Crawford arrived, anxious to be present at the meeting between him and Uncle John. Annie, Louisa's younger sister already knew him, and Julia and Sam Howe were in Boston. She led Crawford into a large, tastefully furnished room with a piano in one corner. As he looked around at the comfortable, beautifully upholstered chairs, and fine rugs, Crawford felt slightly intimidated by the affluent surroundings.

Uncle John entered the room after Louisa had already introduced Crawford to her brother. Shorter than Crawford, with a thick mustache, balding head, and a slight paunch, Uncle John carried himself with an air of authority and confidence. His well-tailored clothing, starched collar, vest, and well-shined shoes contrasted sharply with Crawford's relaxed casual European dress, giving the opening scene of the drama about to play out, a melodramatic quality.

The conversation turned to polite questions about Crawford's trip and his reactions to New York after having been away for nine years. Coffee was served as Uncle John and the brother took measure of the man. Reserved and letting the conversation continue its natural course, Louisa watched the man she loved present himself for what he was, an artist and sculptor, and no more. This was, she thought, the right approach, giving Uncle John and her brother no chance to question his ability as a business man, an area in which they were astute.

After about an hour, Uncle John asked the men if they would like some whiskey or to have a cigar which was the cue for Louisa and Annie to leave the room. Speaking loud, clear, and with authority, Uncle John asked, "Mr. Crawford, tell us about your business as a sculptor. I see the stonemasons working around the city. It seems like hard, low-paid work. There are others working on gravestones and ornamental decorations for the facades of buildings. Is this the type of work you do?"

"No," replied Crawford. "Everything I do is unique, like a painting, only in stone. I went to Rome to study with the best sculptor in the world, Thorvaldsen, who did many famous monuments in important cities on the Continent. That is what I intend to do in America. Work on the Capitol in Washington requires sculpture and there are no monuments in our cities such as Boston and New York."

"Why do we need monuments? We need better streets, improved waterways, and now railroads for commerce and jobs. That should be our first priority, not art."

"I agree. But we also have to develop a national character as we develop commerce. Where did we come from? Who were our heroes. The ones we should emulate and remember to keep us focused on the freedom for which they fought. You speak of the muscle; I wish to speak of the spirit as it has evolved from our history."

"We can do that with books. They are spending too much money on the Capitol. Monuments do not generate income or wealth."

"But they can generate jobs. Even now, I have one full time assistant and two assistants on a part time basis. Thorvaldsen had up to 40 assistants when I began studying in his studio."

"But, as I understand, you have no, what do they say, what is the word? Ah....commissions to do any monuments, is that correct? And if you did, what kind of money are we talking about?"

"Luigi Persico is currently asking $100,000 for his next commission for the Capitol and may get it," said Crawford.

"$100,000 for what? A statue. I can get a good portrait painting done for $25. That is outrageous and those fools in Washington may give it to him, whoever he is."

"They probably will. He's an Italian sculptor brought to this country because we had no American sculptors 30 years ago. That is why I have trained in Europe to be able to compete with the Italians getting all the work in Washington and why my recent show in Boston has been so important. Now I have more visibility; I am a recognized American sculptor. This gives Congress another choice."

"Louisa mentioned the show," said Uncle John, "but I have not heard anything about it here in New York. The choices Congress makes have little to do with talent, they use political clout as the compass for their decisions. What clout do you have?"

"I plan to visit Washington to promote my ideas for a monument to George Washington, and if not there, perhaps here in New York."

"You have been in Rome for nine years, you are not even a registered voter, have never voted in an election, and you think they will listen to you? Good luck. We haven't even mentioned why we are having this discussion," said Uncle John, vigorously stomping his cigar out in an ashtray. "Louisa has said you have asked for her hand in marriage. As the guardian of the trust her father left her, I have some, shall we say, clout in that decision.

"I love my niece, but have objections to this proposed marriage. You have not demonstrated to me any evidence of consistent income, no collateral as we say in banking, or evidence of financial independence, unless you are holding back information. Louisa's family has a long history in this country. New York is her home, and I do not see her leaving all she has here to follow you to Rome. I am sorry, but I do not approve of this marriage," he concluded pacing back and forth.

Crawford did the right thing, and did not push the man anymore. He politely thanked Uncle John for his time, and rose to leave, but without any indication of defeat. Louisa's brother sat the entire time closed-mouthed, aware their Uncle had been preparing for this encounter since Louisa returned from Rome. He had no immediate opinion of Crawford, but he was impressed he had not given in to Uncle John.

Louisa heard most of the conversation from an adjacent room. When she heard the men move about in the room, she went to the front hallway and waited for Crawford to leave. He forced a smile and took her hand. She signaled to him to not say anything, opened the door and stepped outside with him closing the door behind them.

"I'm afraid I did not impress your uncle," said Crawford.

"Yes, I could hear most of the discussion. At one point I feared it might get out of control," replied Louisa, squeezing his hand.

"I would never let that happen, I love you too much and that was only round one - unless he has changed your mind."

"No, when I saw you today, I knew I would return to Rome as your wife. Let this settle a bit, and give me some time to persuade him. I think I can make it clear to him we will get married even without his blessing, but I would rather not do it that way. As I warned you, he has no idea what you do. He understands the addition, subtraction, and multiplication of money, and does it well. He has me and my sibling's interests in mind. He has been a good guardian. Give me a few days, I will send you a note and we can meet somewhere. I do miss you."

"And I miss you. That's why I got here so soon. After you left, trying to work was useless. I could not concentrate long enough to finish anything. I need you back in Rome."

"It will happen," said Louisa and let her hand slip from his.

∽

Disheartened, Crawford headed for home. The expensive and comfortable furnishings in Louisa's home did not go unnoticed by him. As Uncle John had made clear, Louisa would be giving up a great deal to begin a household in Rome. He had completed eleven sculptures in 1843, enough work for him to expand his studio, but he had no idea how much more he would need to provide for Louisa as well. His best plan was still seeking commissions for works of monumental size.

Louisa sent a note two days later, asking him to meet her the next afternoon for a walk. As they left her house, she took his arm and began, "I thought this would be a good time for you to come to the house. Uncle John is at work and I need to get out for a while. It has been tense at home."

"I feel bad that I have left you alone to fight our battle. Let me come back and speak to him again," said Crawford, pressing her arm to his side.

"No, not yet. The discussions have improved, and he knows I will not change my mind. He just can't bring himself to admit it is my decision. Since you are an artist he continues to warn me that your interest may be based on my inheritance. He feels living with you in Rome can only be a direct road to poverty."

"Did you tell him I had no idea you had an inheritance or income until he brought it up the other night?"

"I told him we had never discussed money but, it did little to change his mind. Let me continue talking to him. I do not plan to elope, but I plan to make my own decision. I'm excited about getting married and beginning a new life together in one of the most romantic cities in the world."

"You're excited? I'm ecstatic that you just said that. This is a love I never dreamed possible. I am humbled by it."

Louisa, stopped and said, "We will make this work. I am already planning the wedding and going through all my things, thinking what I would take with me to Rome. You still have to go to Boston to see Orpheus and Sumner. I wish

I could go, but when you return, Uncle John will welcome you, perhaps with some reluctance, but he will accept our marriage."

"I was so disappointed when I left the other day, but now everything looks different," said Crawford as they returned to her home. He was beginning to understand what a formidable woman she was

༄

The next day Crawford left for Boston. At the Athenaeum he did not identify himself, but bought a ticket and bypassing all the other art on display, made his way to the addition built for his show.

What happened next surprised him. He froze in the doorway, overcome by emotions he had never experienced. After agonizing through the birth of these works for years, they looked different in this setting - and better than he remembered. Now he understood what Thorvaldsen, years ago, meant when he told him, "Only after you have been separated and not seen a work for some time, will you be able to finally judge it and appreciate it." Orpheus was on the platform he designed, the other pieces were on new pedestals. They were in the day's bright, clear light a white he had only seen before in the sunlight on the quarries of Carrara.

Orpheus occupied center stage, the others were placed around the perimeter of the elegant room. Crawford must have stood immobile for at least ten minutes before circling Orpheus several times and moving to the other works. He had underestimated the depth of emotional involvement he had in this, his first public American show. After nine years of nonstop work in Italy, he had come home, accomplishing what he set out to do. Until now, he could only imagine the feelings one would have seeing their monumental work in its final setting.

He did not notice the repairs to Orpheus until he had regained some control over his emotions. They were visible, but well done, and did not detract from the overall appearance of the work. The five other works, *Hyperion, The Bride of Abydos, Anacreon, Christ Blessing the Children* and the *Bust of Sumner,* complemented the presence of Orpheus, providing the viewers additional evidence of the artist's skill. To say he was satisfied would be an understatement.

Next, he thought he should introduce himself to the people in charge of the Athenaeum and thank them. His unannounced visit surprised the director, who thanked him for this addition to the collection of the Athenaeum. The director also brought him up-to-date on the various reviews he had collected from newspapers and periodicals as well as comments of the visitors to the Museum. Orpheus had been and was being well received, and the show was a success for the Museum financially, which had collected enough in admissions to pay for the addition. "The trustees wish to promote American artists and I am certain they would like to have dinner with you, to get to know you and find out what is going on in Italy with the other Americans there," suggested the director.

"It would be my pleasure to join them for dinner, and I hope Charles Sumner would be included," said Crawford, quick to reply.

"He certainly would be, but he has been ill and is recuperating out of town."

"Oh! What a disappointment. I didn't know. My letter from New York may not have even reached him. Do you know what is wrong?"

"No, I know no more, but I'm sure his law partner and friend George Hillard would."

"I'm staying at the Pauline Hotel, and will be there for a week, so let me know when and where you want me to come to dinner with the trustees," said a concerned Crawford.

℘

Grateful for his early support, Crawford contacted Henry Wadsworth Longfellow who invited him to dinner at his home. Greene spoke of Longfellow often and introduced Crawford to Longfellow's novel, *Hyperion* which inspired Crawford to create the bust of the mythological God included in the Athenaeum show. This was an evening he had been awaiting a long time.

Longfellow and his new wife, Fanny, had a home in Cambridge, close to Harvard, where he was a professor, acclaimed teacher, poet, and important faculty leader. On arrival Crawford was greeted by Longfellow, a handsome man with long blond hair, and about Crawford's age. Opening his arms in welcome to Crawford, he said, "We are so delighted to meet you, if only George Greene were also here to enjoy this evening. He has written so much about your talent."

"Yes, he introduced us from across the ocean but I felt like it was across the room," said Crawford as he embraced Longfellow.

"How is George? I miss him and his wit. I hope we get him back to America; he seems too content in Rome."

"He's fine. I know he wishes to return, but he would like to complete his studies of Italian literature first," said Crawford.

"I met George for the first time when he was here in May. After listening to Henry it was obvious why they were so close," said Fanny, smiling as she came forward to greet Crawford. "Birds of a feather, bound by books, would be a good metaphor for the two."

During dinner Longfellow spoke of how much he enjoyed Crawford's show at the Athenaeum and thanked him for including the bust of Hyperion, "You know, there has been criticism of my novel. A critic in Baltimore, Edgar Allen Poe, said it had no direction and worse.[17] According to my publisher, the presence of the bust in the show has sparked interest in the book and increased sales."

"One good favor deserves another. You were one of the first to promote my work four years ago. I shall never forget that kindness," said Crawford, lifting his wine glass to Longfellow.

"But I was a little put out when I wasn't asked to write the catalogue for the show."

"I am so sorry, I didn't even know there would be a catalogue."

"I was just teasing. Catharine Maria Sedgwick did an excellent job with the catalogue. She is one of the most popular novelists in this area and a great fan of yours. When she returned from her trip to Italy, she raved about your talent. She, along with Sumner and Greene, is responsible for persuading the Athenaeum to show Orpheus."

"Yes, I was so pleased to see the catalogue and her description of the myth of Orpheus and Eurydice. She saw my work in 1839, just after Sumner left. I had no idea then how important a writer she was."

"She knew talent when she saw it," said Longfellow.

"Well, thank you. I wish Sumner was here. George is here, in a way, I see the bust of him I sent you," said Crawford pointing to the plaster bust of Greene in a corner of the room.

"Charles should be back soon. In his last letter, he said he was improving, so I think you will see him, if not here in Boston, perhaps in New York. By the way, your bust of Charles, included in the show, has also been a hit."

"I did that bust in appreciation for the encouragement he gave me after seeing my work in Rome. It was a difficult time for me then. I had doubts I would succeed. The three of us had such a good time during his stay in Rome and he has given me an American debut, something I could not have done on my own," said Crawford.

At the end of the night, Longfellow, impressed with the depth of Crawford's knowledge of classical literature as well as his own writing, knew he had helped the career of an artist of substance, and a master of stone. The risk he had taken, based on Greene's recommendation alone, had been worthwhile.

The next night, Crawford dined with a group of trustees from the Athenaeum. The enthusiastic conversation, which revolved around his life and work in Rome exhilarated him as no other dinner conversation before. They found his life exciting and wanted to know more about him. What were his future plans? Where did he get his inspiration? How did he carve such fine detail in marble and make it look so soft? In the Ward home with Uncle John he was seen as a failure with no hope for the future. In Boston he was a celebrity with great promise. Such a dichotomy.

Reinvigorated, Crawford returned to New York after five days, eager to tell Louisa about his warm welcome in Boston, the visit with Longfellow and the potential source of commissions. His return to America at this time could not have been better timed to take advantage of the recognition spawned by his first show.

Before leaving, he visited Louisa's sister, Julia, and her husband Samuel Howe, hoping to gain some support for his marriage to Louisa. Polite, Sam showed mild interest in, as he put it, "getting in the middle of this matter." Julia, who liked Crawford, refrained from commenting out of respect for her husband.

જ્ર

While Crawford was in Boston, Louisa made it clear to Uncle John she would be getting married in spite of his doubts. Rather than lose his relationship with her, Uncle John said he would no longer stand in the way of her marriage, but made her promise any income from the trust would be distributed only to her.

When Crawford returned and went to see Louisa, she opened the door, reached out, and almost leaped out to embrace him saying, "Thomas, I am so glad you're back. I have good news. Uncle John will no longer block our marriage. We can get married!"

Crawford, delighted with the loving reception, at first could only say, "When? When? How did you do it?"

"He only wants me to be happy. He does not want to do anything which will divide us as a family."

"I must thank him. Is he home?"

"No, just Annie and I are here. Tell me about Boston. How was your show? Who did you meet?"

"I need to sit down and take this all in. Since you left Rome, all I have thought about was you, and whether marrying you would really happen. Now it will. What about your brother? How does he feel?"

"He also wants me to be happy. I assure you it will happen. You can relax now. Tell me about Boston."

"So much happened; I don't know where to begin. Orpheus looks better than I remembered in the new addition to the Athenaeum, as do the other pieces. I did not realize how different or how much an elegant setting enhances a work. It was a thrill to see them, but I will admit to my prejudice. I brought a catalogue from the show for you."

"Prejudice, nonsense. Your work is special."

"I had dinner with a group of the trustees who wanted to know everything about my work and Rome. There were many hints of possible commissions, so I want to get back there soon and followup on these leads. If I interpreted the enthusiasm for my work at the dinner correctly, we should be returning to Rome with enough commissions to set up a new studio and household."

"Uncle John will be glad to hear that. How are Julia and Sam? Did you see Sumner?"

"Julia looks good and misses you. Sam is fine, he was reticent to get involved concerning our marriage. A great disappointment for me was not seeing Sumner. He is ill and recuperating in Pittsfield."

"What's wrong? Is it serious?"

"I don't know any more, but Longfellow told me he should be returning to Boston soon and I should see him either there or in New York. That's another thing. My evening with Longfellow and his wife Fanny was special. You must meet them; you would love Fanny. But let's get back to the wedding."

"You must promise to tell me all about your dinners in Boston and everyone you met later. I set a date for the wedding: November 2."

"November 2! You do move fast once you make up your mind. I knew that's one reason why I fell in love with you. My mother and sister will be excited."

"That gives me enough time to have a dress made and work on the other arrangements, I know what I want," said Louisa throwing her arms around him.

"You do, and I know what I want: you," replied Crawford in awe of this determined woman.

ॐ

While Louisa prepared for the wedding, Crawford searched for a patron in New York. He had always dreamt of doing a monumental equestrian sculpture of George Washington in his hometown, New York, but found no interest in the contacts suggested by Uncle John and Louisa's brother. There was little interest in the visual arts, even though this was the largest city in America (312,000 population). This frustrated Crawford who found so much regard for his work and the work of other artists in the much smaller city of Boston (93,000 population).

Discouraged by the lack of potential patrons in New York, Crawford, with basic tools in hand, returned to Boston to pursue the leads from his dinner with the trustees of the Athenaeum. This led to additional dinner invitations and possibilities for work. He decided the best approach would be to make drawings and a clay sketch or model when someone showed interest in a commission, involving them in the development of the work from the onset. He found clay at a local potter. It was not the same quality as he had in Rome, but it was adequate for a quick sketch.

Potential clients were astounded by Crawford's ability to alter either a drawing or clay sketch as he presented his idea of a new work. This modus operandi proved effective for clients who had never purchased an original piece of sculpture, let alone art, and they in turn became champions of this American's work. They would also keep the original drawings, which they could showpiece at their next dinner party. When he had a sale, he made a waste mold of the clay to take back to New York.

Crawford would have stayed longer in Boston but he needed to make his own arrangements for the wedding. Uncle John, in fact, Louisa, had planned a dinner party to introduce him to close friends and relatives. She warned him that there would be more dinners arranged by others. He left Boston with two commissions and $1000 in advance payments, a godsend with the wedding ahead of him.

ॐ

Uncle John's dinner, announcing the engagement of Louisa and Crawford set in motion a series of social engagements that introduced him to her wide circle of friends. Always looking for new patrons, he continued to fill the diary he had begun in Boston with everyone he met, making a special note of those who showed any interest in art. Crawford was the center of attention, not for his artistic talent, but because he had won the heart of Louisa, something many suitors had attempted, but failed. Nonetheless, Crawford delighted being in the spotlight and the realizing how fortunate he was that Louisa favored him.

Accustomed to the peace and quiet of a studio, the fast-paced social life of New York took its toll on Crawford. After nine years abroad, upon returning he had: become engaged, seen his first public show, traveled between New York City and Boston, met Longfellow, and socialized on a scale to which he was unaccustomed. Louisa had changed his life and introduced him to a social world with no resemblance whatsoever to his predictable life in Rome.

The wedding took place November 2, 1844, in the Ward family home with family and a few close friends in attendance. After the ceremony and dinner, the couple left for a honeymoon in a country home north of New York where there were no more commitments to dinner parties or other social engagements. The next three weeks were spent alone together, a time they would remember fondly the rest of their lives.

൦ඏ

After their honeymoon, they left for Boston to visit Julia and Sam who had settled into their new home. Sam, no longer having to deal with the issue of Uncle John's opposition to the wedding, became the perfect brother-in-law, vowing to introduce Crawford to his influential friends. Louisa spent her time with Julia who gave her advice on setting up a household in Rome.

Cured of his illness Sumner had returned to Boston where he and Crawford wasted no time reuniting. They met for the first time in five years at the home of Sam and Julia. As he entered the home, Crawford could not constrain himself and rushed forward to embrace his friend and patron, saying, "Charles, Charles, how long it has been? You look well. I am so glad we get to see each other before Louisa and I return to New York and Rome."

Looking about and chuckling Sumner asked, "Where is your bride? She is the one I came to see, not the American sculptor from Rome. Fame is fleeting, Thomas."

"But it was you who made me famous. Fame is also fleeting for the patrons of artists," returned Crawford, smiling.

"I am afraid you are more famous than your patron for whom fame has not yet materialized."

"Nonsense. Everyone seems to know you; your name has surfaced at all the dinner parties I have attended in this city."

"Without knowing the context, I will take that as a compliment," replied Sumner.

Reminiscences of Italy and Rome dominated the conversation during dinner, each having their particular favorite moment or incident to recall. Most were humorous situations prompting frequent laughter. When it was Louisa's turn, she recounted her first Christmas Eve in Rome and as she told the story it was plain to everyone she was expressing something deep and meaningful, not humorous. With his eyes fixed on his beautiful wife, Crawford could only think of his good fortune.

Dinner over, Crawford had the chance to tell Sumner he planned to go to Washington, where he hoped to find some work to take back to Rome. He knew there was more to be done on the Capitol. "Why this love of Italian sculptors?" said Crawford. "How can the Congress be convinced we have American sculptors who can produce works of the same or better quality?"

Hesitating a moment, Sumner replied, "Don't forget, two major commissions were given to our American friend, Greenough, and the first, *George Washington* has been a clear failure in the eyes of the public. Some of the criticism has been vicious and the members of Congress heard more criticism than they wanted and then they discovered it cost more than planned. Under the guise of poor lighting in the rotunda, Greenough agreed to the removal of the sculpture from the rotunda to the Capitol grounds.[18] His second work, to be called *The Rescue Group*, is yet to be seen."

"But you and I know what a fine work *George Washington* is. I had misgivings when I saw it in Florence, but still knew it was a great work."

"The Italians have been conservative in their approach. They know better than to threaten the viewer and their employers with something avant-garde. The Congress is a political body and naturally equate bad decisions with the loss of votes. Greenough's Washington has sensitized them to the work of unproven artists, and at the moment our list of proven American sculptors can be written on the palm of one hand. Believe me Thomas, I wish it was different."

"American tourists buy my art, and they can be quite sophisticated in their tastes."

"Yes, but in your studio in Rome you are dealing with a well-educated, wealthy clientele coming from the upper one percent of our population. Remember our discussion in Rome about the state of art in America? Greenough proved the point. Americans, the other 99 percent, are not yet prepared for the type of paintings and sculpture seen on the European continent. You covered the genitalia of Orpheus for that very reason."

"You're right, but I still plan to visit Washington even though Uncle John put me in my place when I mentioned it. He may be right, but I'm going to see for myself how the choices are made. Do you have any contacts there?"

"No, however, our former Governor, Edward Everett, a true patron of the arts, understands the important role art plays in the culture of a country and has made it his current mission to promote American artists. I know he's attempting through contacts in Washington, to secure Hiram Powers a commission for the Capitol. Let me see if I can find out more," said Sumner reassuringly.

Crawford left that evening discouraged from the comments about the status of art in America, but he was encouraged Sumner might identify a contact in Washington. With Louisa now at his side, they accepted all dinner invitations. She had a natural business sense and having observed Crawford in his Rome studio wooing patrons she understood the process better than he realized.

◦◦◦

Crawford would leave Boston with three more commissions for ideal figures and a bust of Josiah Quincy, retiring President of Harvard College. The senior class at the college wished to present the school the portrait bust as a gift, and Sumner convinced them Crawford was the best artist to do it. The advance payments for these four pieces plus the previous two from the last visit to Boston, totaled $2000, more money than Crawford had ever seen at one time.

Crawford and Louisa returned to New York to celebrate Christmas with the Ward family and Crawford's mother and sister. Louisa made certain Uncle John understood how many new commissions her husband had as well as the amount of advance money they would be taking with them to Rome. For Louisa and Crawford it was both a wonderful and melancholy Christmas, since they did not know when they would return to New York.

After Christmas, Crawford received a letter from Sumner, confirming Governor Everett's attempt to obtain a commission for Hiram Powers in Washington through Representative John Slidell of Louisiana who would be sponsoring the bill in Congress.[19] Slidell had visited Crawford's studio in Rome, a fortunate coincidence, which Crawford decided to pursue.

Arriving in Washington on a clear, cold January day, he was disappointed at what he saw in this city of about 30,000. Everything in Rome was old; everything in Washington was new with low, uninteresting wooden buildings scattered next to pastures. The street plan of L'Enfant created a sense of organization, but the homes and buildings showed no semblance of order, only hurried construction. His first sense of a center of government came as he approached the hill on which the Capitol stood. From a distance, the exterior of the Capitol, with its copper-covered dome, looked completed. A fence surrounded the partially landscaped grounds, with bare trees lining the street leading to the central steps of the east entrance. Tall columns on the second level extended across the center of the building.

Walking up the steps of the Capitol, he studied the relief by Luigi Persico on the pediment over the central entrance. *The Genius of America*, carved in sandstone, was large, he estimated 70-80 feet with three figures about nine feet tall, which he thought quite rigid and lacking any sense of motion or life. There was a great deal of empty space in the tympanum on either side of the central figures which he felt could have also been used.

When he reached the top of the stairs, above the central doors, there was a relief with a bust of George Washington in the center and on either side, two angelic figures holding laurel wreaths above his head. To him, the drapery covering the angels looked exaggerated and unnatural, detracting the eye of the viewer to the sides and away from the bust of Washington. This also, had been done by an Italian sculptor, Antonio Capellano.

On either side of the central door, were two niches with large figures depicting *War* and *Peace* done by Luigi Persico. Seeing these pieces upset him, and he had a sense of panic, thinking there would be no work left for an American sculptor. As he looked at each piece over and over, he imagined what he would have done instead. He knew he could do at least as well, but deep down he knew he could do better. This reignited his determination to get a commission for this building.

There were more reliefs in the rotunda, which he disliked. They were by other Italian sculptors who attempted to tell the early story of the discovery of America and its first settlers.

He spent two hours exploring the Capitol, then went outside on the grounds to see Greenough's *George Washington*, the only sculpture by an American. The lighting in the small wood building constructed to protect the sculpture during the winter, was poorer than the light in the rotunda. What a pity, thought Crawford. The first sculpture by an American, banished from the Capitol by Americans.

Outside the White House, he found the sculpture of Thomas Jefferson by David d'Angers, a French sculptor.[20] This he liked, it flowed from head to toe, and had a sense of motion or activity expressing the commanding presence of the man. He scanned the bronze surface, comparing the material to the stone surfaces he carved. There was more elegance to the material than he expected. Bronze casting was an area lacking in his repertoire. He needed to learn more about the process.

∾

Crawford had worked for two years developing a sculpture of George Washington in full uniform, mounted on his horse leading his troops. This, he thought, was an image most Americans had of the father of their country. He had made a small plaster of this equestrian group, which he brought with him from Rome, and now to Washington, to convince Congress its appropriate place would be in the Capitol.

Plaster in hand, he found the office of Congressman John Slidell. He welcomed the warmth from the fireplace in the congressman's office. As he stood by the fireplace, the door to Slidell's private office opened, and a short, older man with white hair moved toward him in a brisk manner. Extending his hand and speaking with a firm voice, the man greeted him, "Welcome to Washington. You look familiar; we must have met back home?"

"No, I'm not from Louisiana, but we have met before. Thomas Crawford," he replied, attempting to stay near the fire.

"If not Louisiana, then where?"

"We met in my studio in Rome. I'm a sculptor and you visited with friends touring the continent."

"You know, I do remember. The American Consul took us there. It was filled with statues. Never saw anything like it before, and I'm beginning to understand why you are here. Governor Everett, an old friend, wrote me about your work, but he seems to be very keen on a sculptor named Hiram Powers, and has persuaded me to introduce a bill for him to receive a commission for something or other in the Capitol." Turning to an assistant he said, "Find me that letter; it's recent. What's in the box?"

Crawford placed the box on a nearby table and opened it carefully, hoping it was intact after all the walking he had done. As he removed it from the box, he relaxed; it looked fine. "This is a model of George Washington. A sculpture I think would be fitting for this city, this building." He was thinking he would have liked to have had more time to introduce his idea for the work, but it was too late for that.

Slidell's assistant walked up and handed the letter to the Congressman, which he held as he looked at the plaster. "This is a fine piece of work. What size do you have in mind?"

"It would be larger than life size, about 10%."

The Congressman studied the plaster for a few minutes, then read the letter and returned to the sculpture. "Everett thinks you and Powers have exceptional talent. I know nothing about sculpture, but I know art is an interest of his. He also mentions in the letter that too many Italian artists are being used for the work on the capitol. Is this true? No Americans?"

"Yes, it is true, but now there are American sculptors who can do the same quality of work."

"Wasn't the statue of *George Washington* that was just removed from the Rotunda by an American? Greenough, I think. That was a mess."

"Horatio Greenough."

"The first thing visitors to this office from Louisiana did was complain about 'that thing in the Rotunda.' Every Congressman had to deal with the same problem. After that episode, we are all hesitant to become involved with the art of the Capitol. But I am sympathetic to the fact that we need to give more of the work around the Capitol to Americans. I do see many Italian craftsmen working on the building. At least your Washington has his clothes on. I like it."

"What do I do now?"

"There's nothing you can do now. As I said, I like what I see, and not knowing much about these things, I respect Governor Everett's recommendation of you and Powers. I will submit a bill to the Library Committee of the United States Congress which reviews all proposals for art work on the Capitol. The Committee will discuss the bill and vote whether to submit it to the full Congress. They may or may not wish to meet with you, and it may be some time before they even get to that stage."

"So the Committee does not have the final say?"

"Right. It will be discussed when they meet, but with the current construction there are many other proposals on their agenda, so I cannot tell you when it will be reviewed. Do you know anyone on the Committee?"

"No. All I do is wait?"

"I'm afraid so. The Congress has many demands for money, and you should know art is not high on their list of priorities. Don't give up. As you have seen, they have commissioned art before. You have come a great distance to show me your idea, why don't you join me for dinner tonight? Let me introduce you to some other congressmen."

"Thank you, that is kind of you. I would like that."

That night, Crawford likened the restaurant to a political Caffe Greco. He was introduced to so many congressmen, he could no longer remember names and having nothing to contribute to the conversations, he was glad when the evening was over.

Disconsolate, Crawford returned to New York and Louisa. The other dealings he had with a committee were across the Atlantic, at the Athenaeum, and Sumner had handled that. Every other commission had been on a one-on-one basis with tourists, and in that format he felt comfortable and had been successful. Everyone in Washington had been polite but evasive, which made it clear he would not be hearing from the committee.

∽

Unable to find a home for his sculpture of George Washington in New York or Washington, and with enough other commissions to keep him busy for a year, it was time to return to Rome. Louisa was pregnant and anxious to get to Rome before it would be too difficult to travel. They planned to leave in August, so the months ahead were for packing and visiting friends and family.

Julia and Sam came to visit in late July to see them off and brought news of Sumner's latest exploits. Sumner and Sam had been supporting Horace Mann in his fight to improve the public schools in Boston. He wished to bring all social levels of children together in the classrooms, avoid any sectarian influence in the curriculum, and even wanted to train female teachers. Mann's ideas were too progressive for the Boston establishment.

This was a cause too good for Sam and Sumner to ignore, both for its merits as well as the intensity of the struggle, so they gave him their full support.

Sumner's efforts in the community were noticed by the mayor of Boston, and the city council, who decided to reward Sumner. They invited him to give the 1845 Fourth of July Oration, an honor bestowed each year on one of brightest young men in the city.

Julia and Sam, raving about the eloquence and force of Sumner's delivery, brought a copy of the speech to New York. Entitled *The True Grandeur of Nations*, Sumner spoke about two of his favorite topics, the futility of war and anti-slavery. Both topics related to President James K. Polk's decision to pursue the annexation of Texas.

The southern states supported the annexation of the Texas territory as a new slaveholding state, but this included a large area of land belonging to Mexico. War with Mexico would be inevitable. Sumner berated the Southern states and slave holders, and with the general officers of the Massachusetts militia in the front row, he excoriated the military and their fascination with war, proclaiming all wars dishonorable and unchristian. For Sumner, the grandeur of a nation must be expressed from a high moral ground with a deep intellectual base.

He spoke for two hours, and all were impressed by his ability as an orator, but the large crowd was divided in its opinion of the speech which received no support from the Boston establishment. Others detected the beginning of a new career or direction in Sumner's life: politics.

In September, 1845, Sumner's mentor and dear friend, Joseph Storey, died. He was a former Associate Justice of the United States Supreme Court and, after his retirement, Dean of the Harvard Law School. Sumner had hopes of being appointed as Dean in Storey's place, but he was not selected by the trustees of the College. After this, Sumner, further distancing himself from the practice of law, committed most of his time to work with the Whig Party of Massachusetts.

The Crawford's left for Rome August 8, 1845. It was, of course, a difficult parting for Louisa, leaving a loving family and comfortable lifestyle in New York. Ten years after coming to Rome, Crawford was returning with more confidence in his future, but he still lacked a major commission in America or the Capitol. The next award for a monument in Washington would not go to his American competitors in Italy nor Italian sculptors working in Washington. Instead it would go to an American working at home, and one who was a complete stranger to all the sculptors.

Part III

In 1845, the busy port of Charleston, South Carolina was enjoying a period of growth and prosperity, which provided 35-year-old Clark Mills, with steady work as a plasterer and stucco tradesman. At the time, Charleston was the tenth largest city in the United States with a population of about 30,000. Orphaned in upper New York State, Mills left on his own at age 14, and worked at any job he could find along the eastern and southern coast. In 1831 he became an apprentice to a plasterer in Charleston.

A big, handsome, and outgoing man, accustomed to hard work and good with his hands, he progressed from apprentice to master in half the usual time and became an expert in the decorative plasterwork applied to ceilings and walls. Most of this work was done with molds, but Mills developed new freehand techniques, which became popular with builders and homeowners. Self-taught, he drew unique designs, which, when put into plaster, gave the homeowner something to admire and boast about. He noticed having original plasterwork in a home became, in certain social circles, competitive, with one home owner attempting to outdo the others. Mills' plaster and stucco business became the largest and most popular in Charleston.

One day, because of his reputation, he was asked to make a death mask by the family of a loved one. He agreed and found it easy. It occurred to him that if people wanted plaster facemasks of the dead, wouldn't they also enjoy seeing masks of the living? Mills had an inherently inquisitive nature and experimented with various techniques until he developed a new rapid method of mask-making which caused little discomfort to the sitter.

Seeing an engraving of a bust of President Andrew Jackson in "Harper's Illustrated Weekly" he decided to convert one of his facial masks into a bust, and after several misadventures, began to make progress with another new technique. Word got around and soon he had many requests for portrait busts.

Each bust became easier and more accomplished until, because of the increased demand for these portrait busts, he opened an office and limited his work to plaster portrait busts.

Such was the man. With no formal education, but a risk taker with creative talent, extreme self-confidence and a natural entrepreneurial sense, this business became a success. Mills advertising in a local newspaper, which proclaimed him Charleston's first sculptor, charged between $10-20 per bust.

∾

When Mills worked in the plastering business, he often watched the stone masons and even though he had never seen a marble bust, he recalled that the bust of Jackson in the "Harper's" article was carved in marble. That, he thought, must be the proper way to do portrait busts of prominent people.

Mills asked stone masons many questions and watched the carvers make gravestones. He knew he could carve stone. The next step would be to identify a distinguished political personality and get them to sit for a plaster life mask and portrait bust to be used as a model for a stone carving. A local newspaper editor who admired Mills' work, suggested South Carolina's premier politician, John C. Calhoun, former Vice President, Congressman, and Senator as well as onetime Secretary of War and Secretary of State.

He came up with a novel idea. If he could find 100 subscribers who would pay $5 a person for a stone bust of Calhoun for Charleston, it might impress the Senator enough to convince him to sit for a life mask, as well as pay Mills for his efforts. The newspaper supported his campaign to raise the money, and in April, 1845, after having raised the capital, he wrote Senator Calhoun, saying he wished to come to Washington to make his life mask. Senator Calhoun, flattered by the interest of the 100 subscribers, agreed, and since he would be traveling to Charleston soon, let Mills know he did not have to come to Washington to make the life mask. Mills, never before having worked in stone, completed the bust in October, 1845. The Charleston Evening News reported (October 4, 1845):

> We invite the attention of our readers to the
> bust of J. C. Calhoun, in stone, the production of our
> ingenious townsman, Mr Clark Mills. Mr Mills is a self
> taught artist, and this is his first effort in the noble art

of sculpture. The material is a block obtained from the vicinity of Columbia; and thus on a native mineral of Carolina, our artist, has succeeded in correctly stamping the features of Carolina's favorite son. The studio of Mr Mills is in Broad Street near Church-street.[21]

On presentation of the bust to the Charleston City Council Mills was awarded a medal. His former office was now identified as a studio and his profession as that of sculptor.

∽

In the spring of 1846, three gentlemen from Charleston pledged $1000 to send Mills to Italy to study sculpture.[22] At first, the idea appealed to him, but he had a wife and family, which made it difficult to leave Charleston. Traveling so far from home and living in Italy might be a romantic adventure for some, but his objectives were more realistic. Generating work came naturally to him, and he doubted they could teach that in Italy. The offer was gracious and a pleasant surprise, and If he had to go he would, but he had not heard a convincing argument to persuade him it would be necessary for his career. He was a loner, but a confident one.

South Carolina's former Senator, William C. Preston, now President of South Carolina College, saw the marble bust of Calhoun and was sufficiently impressed to want to meet Mills. Arriving at the studio and looking around, he said, "This is good work. I have seen the marble bust of Calhoun, and it will be here to remind people of his greatness long after you and I are gone."

"It was an honor to work with him and get to know him," replied Mills, sensing he was dealing with an influential man.

"You know there are opportunities for talented artists in Washington. I've been told you have never shown any of your work outside this city."

"Yes, but I'd like to expand my business," said Mills. "I don't know anyone in Washington, or for that matter, in any other city."

"During my tenure in Congress, I Chaired the Library Committee of Congress. It was our job to review and forward for congressional approval all art work proposed for the Capitol and the surrounding government buildings. It turned out to be an education in art as well as the politics of Committee decisions."

"Do you think my work would qualify?"

"Your work is good. Have you any larger works?"

"No, but I'd be willing to try my hand at some."

"Have you seen Houdon's sculpture of George Washington in Richmond?"

"No, but I would like to."

"Well you should, it's good. The Frenchman, Houdon, did it. He's too far away, back in Paris, to submit any proposals for the Capitol. The Italians Jefferson brought to this country are doing well and submitting proposal after proposal to the Committee, but we need American sculptors. I understand they have raised some money to send you to Italy?"

"Yes, Charleston has been good to me."

"I could find some funds from the college to send you to Richmond."[23]

"I would love the chance to go."

"Let me see what I can do. As I said, we need American sculptors and this would be an opportunity for you to see your competition in Washington as well as meet influential people selecting artwork. Besides the Capitol, there are other possibilities for work in Washington."

"Do you have any suggestions on how to get a commission for any work there?"

"While in Congress, I became good friends with one of the congress-man from Tennessee, Cave Johnson, a major supporter and friend of President Polk who appointed him Postmaster General. He told me his friends from Tennessee were raising money to put a statue of their favorite son, Andrew Jackson, in Washington. That might be a possibility. I can give you a letter of introduction."

"I would be grateful. Before you leave, can I make your life mask? It will only take 30 minutes, and then I can make a bust and send it to you in Colum-bia. That's the most I can do for your help," said Mills moving toward a bag of plaster and reaching for a bucket as fast as he could.

"Well, that was not my intent on coming here, but it sounds like fun. You know, you would have an infinite number of self-important politicians wishing to be immortalized in plaster if you worked in Washington. A sculp-tor with your talent could make a lot of money just doing that," said Senator Preston as he was being directed to a chair surrounded by bits of dry plaster on the floor.

∽

The money was raised, and in May, 1847, Mills left for Richmond, the capital of Virginia. With a population of about 20,000 and located along the James River, it had a history dating back to the 1600s. As soon as he arrived, Mills first stop would be the Capitol, which had been designed by Thomas Jefferson in the classical style of a Greek Temple. Set on a hill, it was the largest building he had ever seen.

A long stairway led up to the entrance and as Mills approached, the white stone glowed in the sun. He marveled at the eight Doric columns reaching toward the sky, giving the structure a sense of power. A tall dome covered the center of the building.

On entering the rotunda, Mills had to stop a moment and catch his breath as he saw the sculpture of George Washington above him on its large marble pedestal. He had never seen anything like it. Astonished, he wondered if this might be an actor in a pose before he realized this was a monument in marble. It was the first time he had seen a larger than life-sized full figure carved in marble.

In 1784, the Assembly of the state of Virginia voted to commission a sculpture of George Washington. Since there were no sculptors in America, the Governor wrote Thomas Jefferson, recently appointed Minister to France, for advice. Jefferson recommended Jean-Antoine Houdon, France's best sculptor at the time. Houdon had already done a bust of Benjamin Franklin, so his work was well known by two of America's founding fathers.[24]

Houdon, eager to accept, hoped to convince them to do an equestrian statue of Washington. He agreed to come to America and model a bust of Washington to use when he returned to France. Arriving at Mount Vernon in October, 1785, he took numerous body measurements, and made a life mask and terra cotta bust of the retired Washington in three weeks. From the terra cotta bust, he made a mold and then a plaster to take with him to France. The life mask and the bust, used later, by many sculptors for a likeness of Washington, were left behind at Mount Vernon.

Mills circled the sculpture repeatedly, finding more to see the longer he scanned the surfaces. He thought it amazing, the strength and confidence in the face, the detail of the fringe of the epaulets on the shoulders of Washington's uniform and the spurs on the riding boots. This is how he imagined Washington the General, a powerful leader and Commander-in-chief of the Revolutionary Army.

A member of the Assembly taking a break in the rotunda noticed Mills studying the sculpture and approached him, "A great work isn't it? Everyone admires it, and you seem to be especially interested. You know, the face has been modeled from a life mask taken while Washington was alive. That's how he looked."

"He was a handsome man. Yes, I like it," replied Mills, thinking to himself, "I know all about life masks and how you can make portrait busts from them." The surprise to him was that one of the best sculptors in the world used the same technique. Even though carving a full figure in marble seemed outside his capability, he knew he could model one in plaster. Mills returned the next day to further study the sculpture.

☙

From Richmond, he changed his plans and went to Mount Vernon before heading to Washington. He had to see the life mask Houdon had made. For him, it was also a thrill to see Washington's home. Showing the letter from Senator Preston as an introduction, he was allowed to see the life mask and the terra cotta bust of Washington made from it. Mills made a copy of the bust, which he would treasure the rest of his life, but he also realized the potential future value of his plaster copy.[25]

When he reached Washington and the Capitol, his first impression from a distance, was the large size of the building with its columns larger than those in Richmond. Stopping to take it all in, he studied the relief carving above the columns (Persico's *Genius of America*) which reminded him of the type of decorative work he had done in plaster, except there were three figures and not just a design.

When he saw the sculpture to the left of the steps (Persico's *Discovery of America*) he could not believe there would be another marble carving larger than the *George Washington* in Richmond, but this was larger and more complex. Everywhere he looked he saw stone and had doubts, unusual for him, that he could carve stone figures.

Senator Preston had told him about the sculpture of *George Washington* done by Greenough and the hassle it had caused while in the rotunda. When Mills found it outside the building, he was angry. Washington, naked and draped in a long cloth, was disgraceful to the memory of the man. He agreed it should not be in the rotunda. If this is what they learned in Italy, he had another reason not to go.

He was surprised by the sculpture of Thomas Jefferson he found outside the White House. He wondered what the metal was? He asked a passerby, and they told him it was bronze, the same metal used to make bells and cannons. This intrigued him because if they could cast a bell, why couldn't he learn to cast a sculpture from a plaster model, using a similar technique?

∿

Next, he went to the office of Postmaster-General Cave Johnson. As he entered the large, ornate, and well-furnished suite of rooms, Mills knew he must be an important man. As far as he was concerned, the more important, the better, because those were the people who made the decisions. Greeted by an assistant, he introduced himself and gave him the letter from Senator Preston.

After a short wait, the door to an inner office opened, and Postmaster-General Johnson came toward him. With the letter in his hand, he greeted Mills with a big smile and said, "Welcome to Washington. A sculptor and American at that, we need people like you in this city. My old friend, Senator Preston says you are an excellent sculptor. You should be working here."

"I wouldn't mind that," replied Mills, trying to look humble.

"You're an artist, let me show you something," Johnson said leading Mills into his office. There, drawings of George Washington and Benjamin Franklin with the number five on each side below the images and U.S. Post Office above, lay on a table next to the desk. "This is something new for mail. What do you think? It's called a postage stamp."

"What do you mean postage stamp?"

"Instead of receivers paying when the mail is delivered, senders will be able to buy these ahead of time and stick them to their letters. They are printed in sheets, and when people buy them at the post office, the clerk will cut off one or more."

"How big will these stamps be?"

"About an inch tall and three-quarters of an inch wide. They're already using a similar system in England."

Mills liked the enthusiasm of this man, and the conversation moved on to some of Johnson's other ideas for the Post Office such as boxes for collecting mail, which he was going to place around Washington. Johnson asked him how he did the portrait busts Senator Preston mentioned in his letter. Their mutually inquisitive and inventive personalities made them instant friends, and Cave Johnson suggested they continue their conversation at a local tavern.

They walked to a nearby tavern exchanging more ideas along the way. After drinking several whiskies, Johnson mentioned the subject Mills came to hear. "You know, my fellow Tennesseans and I think there should be a statue of Andrew Jackson in Washington. We even purchased a plot of land across from the White House. We have been looking for an artist, and we wanted it to be an American, but we only knew of Greenough, and the donors were leery of asking him because of all the trouble we had with his statue of George Washington. Would you be interested?"

"I might be. What do you have in mind?" replied Mills, doing his best to keep his enthusiasm under control.

"Jackson was a great leader. Everyone thinks he should be on his horse, rallying his men at the Battle of New Orleans."

"What size did you have in mind?"

"Big. Big as his reputation, larger than life-size. Do you think you could do something like that?"

"I think I could, but I would not do it in stone. I would do it in bronze, just like the sculpture of Jefferson in front of the White House."

"Everybody likes that statue. Do you think bronze would be all right? They seem to be making everything around here out of stone."

"It should be fine. The sculpture of Jefferson has weathered well," answered Mills, thinking to himself, cannons and bells are always outside, and they do fine.

"While I was in Congress, these Italian artists were always bringing models of work they proposed for the Capitol. They had a name for them, which I can't remember. Anyway, it was a good way to get somebody's attention. Can you make a smaller version of what you would propose for the statue? Then I can show it to the others who have given or raised money for the project."

"That I can do."

"How long would it take?"

"Three to six months."

"Well, if you can bring back a model that will impress the group, I can get the job for you," said Johnson touching Mills' arm with one hand, and signaling for another round of drinks with the other. "We have raised $12,000 for the statue. It will have to be done for that amount."

"That would be agreeable to me," said Mills, dumbfounded by the amount, but keeping his composure. With that amount of money, he could do just about anything, even though he had no idea what it would cost or how to cast something in bronze.

∽

The idea of the $12,000 fee for doing work he enjoyed preoccupied Mills on the return to Charleston. There was money to be made in this business of art. Now he had to decide how to sculpt a man on a horse rather than another portrait bust.

Supporting the plaster as he modeled the piece would be a problem. A plaster portrait bust could be developed over a central metal rod or piece of wood. A man on a horse with four thin legs was a much more complex undertaking. Casting the bronze, would be the other hurdle. He knew of shops which cast small iron objects, but had never seen it done and had no idea whatsoever what bronze cost.

When he returned to Charleston, he began working most of the day on the Jackson project, saving time later in the day to review the work done on the portrait busts, which paid the rent and fed the family. His successful plaster and portrait bust business had provided enough money for him to purchase a slave, Philip Reid, at an auction in Charleston, for $1200. Intelligent and strong, Reid had a natural talent for working with plaster and enjoyed converting the life masks to busts which allowed Mills to concentrate on the Jackson project. Mills would make the life mask of new clients, and Reid began the final busts. The master would then do the final touches. They made a good team.

The first month was one disaster after another. The wet plaster dripped from the armatures he designed. Having no training in the construction of armatures, Mills employed his usual method, trial and error, to find the eventual appropriate support structure.

As the horse took shape in the studio, people began to stop and watch Mills work. The newspaper, always a fan of the work of Mills, reported on the progress and this, in turn, resulted in more portrait bust clients. It took Mills six months, longer than he anticipated, to get the model completed. He had Jackson, saluting the troops, hat in his right hand, sword at his side, and his horse up on its hind legs.

Mills liked the manner in which Houdon depicted Washington, in full dress uniform, and he convinced one of the officers stationed at Fort Sumter in Charleston Bay to pose for him. He made the model three feet by four feet for several reasons. It had to be large enough to impress Johnson and his friends, but not too cumbersome to take to Washington. The enlargement of the model by a factor of three would give him a final sculpture one-third larger than life-size.

∽

By the end of February, 1848, Mills was ready to return to Washington. He and his slave, Reid, made two crates, one to hold the model and the other filled with all his equipment for working with plaster. If the Committee liked the model, and he was confident they would, he would stay in Washington and find a studio where he could enlarge the model to full size. For added income, he planned to promote his portrait bust business among the Washington politicians. If he got the job, he planned to leave his family in Charleston.

On March 5, he and Reid loaded the crates onto a hired wagon and hauled them to the dock in Charleston. As they bounced down the streets, Mills wondered whether the plaster model would survive the trip intact. He had written Cave Johnson when to expect him. Knowing the Tennesseans would be eager to see the model, he would not have much time for repairs once he arrived in Washington.

As they sailed up the coast to Washington, he could not get the other unsolved problem out of his mind - the casting of the piece in bronze. He had visited every foundry around Charleston, but found no one with experience casting sculptures. The varied and conflicting advice they offered only confused him.

When they docked in Washington, he left the crates with Reid, and went to the Post Office Building. Cave Johnson saw him walk into the office and said, "Well, I've been expecting you. Where's the sculpture, do you have it downstairs?"

"No, no, it's too large to bring up to your office," replied Mills extending his arms to give some indication of the size. "I need to find a large space to uncrate it for viewing."

"In your letter you mentioned I should keep an eye out for a vacant building. I made some inquiries and found one on the corner of 15th Street and Pennsylvania Avenue, near the Treasury Building. It looked large enough and the rent was reasonable. Let's walk over and see what you think of the building."

∽

The wooden building must have been a storage area for materials used in the construction of the Capitol. Large enough, it had a high ceiling and a set of doors opening to the back. There would also be room for Reid to sleep. Mills returned to the dock and brought the crates to the space for unpacking. He promised Johnson the Committee could see the model in two days.

When Mills and Reid opened the crate they were surprised and relieved there was only minimal damage to the plaster model. They used a few boards from the crates to build a platform on which to place the model, so it could be viewed above eye level as it would be when set in place on the final pedestal. The bare room had enough windows for adequate light. As promised, Mills was ready in two days.

꩜

An excited Johnson convened the Committee and invited the Senators and Representatives from Tennessee to the unveiling. On a pleasant spring day in March, with everyone in a good mood because of the weather and anticipation of this unusual event, they met at the Post Office Building and together walked to Mills' new studio.

When the introductions were concluded, but before uncovering the model Mills talked about his ideas of the hero Andrew Jackson and the difficulty (he embellished a bit) of transforming them into plaster. Mills, the salesman, now prevailed with his usual entrepreneurial confidence. At the moment he felt he had generated the appropriate amount of enthusiasm, he walked over to the model and removed the cloth cover.

There were a number of gasps from the group. Mills said nothing, letting them take their time looking at the model as he watched their faces. When he thought he detected a few tears in the eyes of some of the group he felt it was time to set the hook, "Well gentleman, what do you think, is this what you had in mind?"

"By God, it certainly is," responded Johnson with obvious emotion in his voice. "That's our man, our Tennessee general and President. That's the best damn thing I've ever seen, that's Old Hickory, even the horse is perfect."

Similar accolades came from the rest of the group, in spite of the fact none had ever seen an equestrian sculpture before. Then Mills, walked over to Johnson and said, "When do you think the group will reach a decision?"

Johnson looked at his fellow Tennesseans and answered, "I think we might be able to come to a decision right now. Do any of you have any questions of Mr. Mills?"

"Yes," replied one of the committee members, "when do you think it could be finished?"

"If all goes well, I should be ready for casting next summer," replied Mills. "I have to find a supply of bronze to cast it and construct the furnace to melt it."

"All the cannons Jackson captured from the British in New Orleans were brought to Washington and are just sitting at the arsenal," interjected Johnson. "I wonder if we can't get Congress to release them. That would give you a supply of bronze, and it would be unique. The statue of Andrew Jackson made from the spoils of his great victory in New Orleans."

The members of Congress who were present, were excited by the idea, and said they would sponsor a bill to release the cannons to Mills and make certain it passed. On March 23, 1848, a contract was signed between Mills and the committee to commission a bronze statue of Andrew Jackson for a fee of $12,000.[26]

◌◌

Contract and money in hand, Mills began building the armature or infrastructure for enlarging his model. The studio, close to other government buildings, brought many visitors as well as members of Congress to view the model and meet the American sculptor. The Italian sculptors they had watched and admired before, produced idealistic figures, beautiful in their own right, but not always understood by the people of Washington. Mills was creating a monument to an American hero and President (1829-1837) and many had seen or knew Jackson. This was exciting to the people of Washington.

Mills felt confident he could make the larger-than-life plaster sculpture, but still had to reckon with the process of casting the sculpture in bronze. There was a Foundry in the navy yard producing cannons, but they were accustomed to casting solid cylinders, or wheels and symmetric parts for the cannons. He could not interest them in attempting to cast a sculpture. Remembering his idea about the casting of bells from bronze, he heard of a bell founder in Baltimore and decided to visit him.

Once assured Mills was not a competitor, the founder explained how he cast his bells. It was a technique, which, because of the symmetrical shape of a bell, Mills could not follow step-by-step because of the complex asymmetrical structure of his sculpture. However, he did learn about building a furnace to melt the bronze, the composition of the materials used for making molds, and the use of wax which created the space into which the bronze was poured. He even watched them pour the bronze for a small bell. The trip gave him enough information and confidence to feel he could, with a little experimentation and reading, or trial and error, cast a bronze. After all, he had never sculpted a man on a horse before, but now he had, and everyone loved it.

Mills with his slave, Reid, decided not to return to Charleston and his family or bring them to Washington. He loved the attention and excitement generated by working in the center of the nation's government. Through his friendship with Cave Johnson, he met important people of the city, and his personality was such that he was at ease with them as well as the visitors to his studio. Family and Charleston began to fade from his world.

He bought a horse to study its anatomy and dissected a dead one. He borrowed Jackson's uniform, sword and saddle from the Smithsonian Institute. It was no longer just trial and error. He was beginning to understand the craft of sculpture. Mills worked with solid blocks of plaster, carving different sections one at a time which could be assembled later.[27] The technique was unique to Mills and baffled the Italian sculptors in Washington. The large plaster sculpture of Jackson on his horse was the talk of the town, but winter had arrived, and he had not yet built his foundry and furnace. It took until November, 1849 for him and Reid to complete the plaster enlargement of Jackson and the horse. The final completion date of July, 1850 was now unrealistic.

Part IV

ART AND POLITICS
A MONUMENT AND A MONUMENTAL DEBATE

As Clark Mills struggled with his first equestrian sculpture, Thomas Crawford and Louisa were settling in Rome. They had arrived in the fall of 1845 and were welcomed into the home of George and Carlotta Greene until they could find their own apartment. The first order of business for Crawford was to check his studio to see if everything was still there. Things were just as he had left them, even his tools, which he was afraid would be stolen after such a long absence. As he walked around the room, the smell of clay and marble dust welcomed him back to the world he understood best.

One evening after the spouses had gone to bed, Greene, who Crawford thought looked worried and distracted, said, "Remember all our talks about money problems in the past? They never seem to go away."

"And probably never will," replied Crawford.

"Mine are now worse. I love this city. My wife has taught me how to live as an Italian, but I cannot afford this lifestyle on the small fees I make as Consul. I've been depressed ever since I left Washington with no hope of establishing an embassy here. I'm afraid to tell Carlotta. You are my closest friend in Rome, the first I'm able to talk to."

"How about fees from your writing?"

"The periodicals are happy to take an occasional article I send to Longfellow, but it pays little." "And your book about your grandfather?"

"Nowhere near completion. I'm too depressed to work on it. My debt is strangling any attempt at creativity."

"How much debt?"

"More than you care to know."

"I have some money. Let me pay you for your help."

"Thank you, but it would not be enough."

"Maybe if I knew I could help you work through it. How much?"

"Thousands."

"Thousands!" said an astonished Crawford. "When we arrived I knew there was something going on in your head, but I had no idea it was this serious. Does anyone else know?"

"I have written to Longfellow and asked him if he could find me work in America. He should be getting the letter about now."

"So you plan to return to America?"

"I have not had the courage to tell Carlotta, so please don't tell Louisa," said Greene with a sheepish look.

Crawford decided it best not to ask any more. His good friend appeared embarrassed enough. That night he slept little, pondering the disintegration of the dreams of his best friend in Rome and wondering how it would be to live in this city without him. He would give Greene as much money as he could spare, but not as much as he wished, now that he had a wife and imminent family to consider.

With the help of Greene, the Crawfords were able to rent an apartment on Via San Niccolo da Tolentino, very close to the Piazza Barbarini where Crawford had spent the first nine years of his life in Rome. He found a larger studio space with more rooms close by and began to move everything from his former studio, so he could begin work on the commissions from Boston. Louisa, in the final months of her pregnancy, busied herself with furnishing the apartment and preparing for their second Christmas together in Rome.

Longfellow and Sumner responded quickly, and together raised enough money to get Greene back to America. Things only became worse for Greene after he let Carlotta know of his dire situation. She had family in Rome, a typical close Italian family, and the couple did not want to let them know how serious the problem was. Telling them would cause an emotional explosion which would only complicate the situation.

Under the guise of an outing to the Campagna, George Greene and his heartbroken wife, Carlotta, left Rome and their possessions. It was a sad end to his tenure as American Consul in Rome from 1837 to 1845.

Longfellow was able to get a position for Greene at Brown College as an instructor of modern languages. Crawford no longer had his close friend who had encouraged his development as an artist, referred clients, and found him patrons in America. George Greene had been, without a doubt, the trigger for Crawford's career.

࿇

After living alone for nine years in Rome as the proverbial 'starving artist,' Crawford delighted in the new luxury of a family life. Their first child, a girl, was born in January 1846. The commissions from Boston allowed him to hire two assistants who had worked at Thorvaldsen's studio and some part time help. Now, instead of working on into the night alone, he left the studio at the end of the day to be with his family.

To celebrate the birth of his first child he began a bust of Louisa which became an immediate success. No other bust he made would come close to the virtuosity of the portrait of Louisa, and he eventually sent it to Uncle John in New York. Perhaps, he felt, in some way this might compensate for the absence of Louisa from the Ward family.

Business, if not brisk, was consistent, and he always had work although nothing monumental. Crawford might not have admitted it, but Louisa never hesitated to make Uncle John forward money from her inheritance to supplement their life in Rome.[28] With Greene gone, Crawford opened his home to the many American painters and sculptors now in Rome. Caffe Greco, was still popular with the artist colony in Rome, but it no longer escaped the scrutiny of the papacy because of the long reign of the ultraconservative Pope Gregory XVI who was suspicious of anything new or innovative. The American artists preferred the privacy of Crawford's home.

Throughout Europe, political change was moving to the left, and Pope Gregory XVI wanted no part of it for his papal state. Papal spies were everywhere, and with the press under the control of the papacy, people avoided open political discussion. Italians also wished to end the Austrian control in the Northern part of Italy and hoped the ideas of the revolutionaries, Vincenzo Gioberti (*On the Civil and Moral Primacy of Italians*) and, Giuseppe Mazzini, would somehow take hold and lead to the formation of a unified Italy. The American artists, children of a recent revolution, with nothing to gain in such a struggle, nevertheless were naturally attracted to Mazzini's cause.

Pope Gregory XVI died in June, 1846, after a reign of 15 years. The newly elected Pope Pius IX, began his reign granting amnesties to many of his predecessor's opponents and decreasing the censorship of the press. Mazzini saw this as an opportunity to revitalize his revolutionary agenda, and over the next 18 months the movement gained momentum. The potential of a unified Republic of Italy became more of a possibility than ever before. By the end of 1847, even Crawford and some of his fellow American artists became directly involved, and volunteered for the citizen's militia of Rome, or their local version of a National Guard. Given uniforms and swords, the militia trained for the defense of Rome from attack by the Austrians.

Crawford and Louisa had their second child, another girl, in November, 1847. Louisa wanted more room for her growing family as well as a place for the children to run and play, other than the streets or parks. In the summer of 1848, they heard the Villa Negroni, on the eastern edge of Rome near the Baths of Diocletion, was available to lease. It was surrounded by gardens filled with wild flowers, cypress, and scattered orange and lemon trees, between once elegant but forgotten fountains. To the southwest, across an empty field was the church Santa Maria Maggiore, and the Pincian Hills were above to the north. It had once been a famous grand estate, but now, only the original main building remained. It was the size of a small palazzo.

Larger than they needed, the beautiful setting convinced them they should make an offer to Prince Massimo, the current owner. They were able to negotiate a long term lease for $250 per year, which for the size of the building, was quite reasonable and within their budget.

The Prince agreed they could build a separate building on the grounds for Crawford's studio. In the summer of 1848, they moved to the Villa Negroni, their home for the rest of their married life. It was less than a mile form their original apartment, and Crawford's studio, so he could still work there until they had enough money to build the studio at Villa Negroni.

It was a happy and anxious time for the Crawfords. The Austrians began to battle the revolutionaries in the north. In November, 1848, after the assassination of the Minister of Justice of the Papal States, riots followed in Rome, and Pope Pius IX fled Rome to Gaeta, south of Rome, in the Kingdom of the Two Sicilies. Governance in Rome became unpredictable and chaotic. Louisa, fearful they would be trapped in Rome as the different factions fought for control of the city, wanted to leave before the battle began. Crawford had mixed emotions about leaving. He was still enamored with the dream of a Republic of Rome and a unified Italy, but he also was concerned for the safety of the family, the villa, and the work in his studio.

When it became clear that Catholic France was sending troops to reclaim Rome for the Pope, Crawford realized it was time to leave Rome and return to America. They were able to depart in March, 1849, before the French army arrived. They reached America in May. By July 1,1849, the Roman army had surrendered to a French army which had surrounded the city, and the Pope returned to Rome

∾

Back in America, they decided to stay with Louisa's sister, Julia, and her husband, Samuel Howe, in Boston. From this great distance, they could only hope Villa Negroni would not be damaged during the French siege and occupation of Rome. They could also be with Charles Sumner who had, since they left, become a major political force in the Whig Party of Massachusetts. His strong antislavery feelings were unchanged, in fact, they had intensified.

In 1848, Sumner had run for the House of Representatives but was defeated. Now, he followed every move of Senator Daniel Webster, who, along with Senator Stephen Douglas of Illinois, hinted at compromise with the Southern States to avoid their possible secession from the Union over the slavery issue. Sumner and the abolitionists could never agree to such a compromise.

One morning in November, 1849, as Crawford read the *Boston Post* he saw a notice which read as follows:

VIRGINIA WASHINGTON MONUMENT
By virtue of an Act of the Assembly, passed on the 22nd of February, 1849, providing for the erection of a Monument to GEORGE WASHINGTON, the Commissioners appointed by the Governor of Virginia hereby offer a premium of Five Hundred Dollars for a plan for the Monument, to be approved by them, accompanied with the necessary estimates for its erection.

The Monument will be located on the Capitol square, in the City of Richmond, be constructed of Virginia granite or marble, or a combination of both, and cost one hundred thousand dollars.

Plans and estimates required by the first day of
December next, enclosed to the Governor of Virginia.[29]

It was signed by six commissioners with William F. Ritchie, Chairman

This was the commission Crawford craved. After all his unsuccessful efforts to convince people in New York, Boston, and Washington they needed a monument, he had found the first real opportunity to design one while reading a newspaper. He could not believe it. Away from his studio the past five months he had become bored, but now his heart pounded as he rushed to find Louisa and show her the notice.

But could he prepare a model on such short notice? As far as he was concerned, he must. The next day on the advice of his brother-in-law, he rented a space in Amory Hall on the corner of Washington and West Streets in the center of Boston. Amory Hall hosted many different events including lectures, performances, and art shows, so there was a constant flow of visitors to the building.

He had brought from Rome a standing figure of Washington in uniform, but he preferred his previous model of the equestrian sculpture of Washington, which he failed to sell to anyone the last time he was in America. That could be the focal point of the monument. As he made drawings the project expanded, and he thought there should be other prominent Virginians represented who were important in the early development, of not only Virginia, but America. He could work fast, but completion by the December I date seemed improbable.

Sumner visited often, and one day Crawford asked, "Charles, do you know any of these commissioners or anyone who knows the Governor of Virginia?"

Sumner thought awhile before he answered. "You know, this monument will be in the heart of slave territory. These are people diametrically opposed to my views on that issue. Any relationship you have with me may make you suspect. They have no idea what your position is on the subject, but you are submitting your proposal from Boston, the capitol of the abolitionists."

"You mean they will be considering the viewpoint of the artist on slavery as one of the criteria?"

"Not formally, but it is always in the back of their minds. You are an unknown. This is an issue which occupies their every waking moment. You live in Rome. I don't know how that may effect their thinking. It would be marvelous if these decisions were based on talent alone, but the human factor is impossible to gauge when a committee meets."

"What do you suggest?" asked a concerned Crawford.

"Well, don't let me discourage you. I just want you to be aware of the obstacles you may encounter. I like what I see, and rare as it may be, this could be an instance in which talent will prevail. Let me write to a lawyer friend in Richmond and see what he can do. It would be a mistake for me to contact any politicians on your behalf. They know my views down there and I could poison the well."

∾

To meet the deadline, Crawford needed to work rapidly to complete all the drawings and the model with the equestrian Washington at the top. He returned to his old habit of working well into the night, and many nights he slept in the temporary studio. Soon people stopped to watch this impassioned sculptor and how he intended to design a monument. Only those who had visited Europe had ever seen one, so Crawford and his work became a popular curiosity. Other hopefuls had the same problem with the December 1 deadline, there were many complaints, and the committee extended the deadline to January 1.

Crawford decided the equestrian Washington would be fifteen feet tall and the complete monument 65 feet high. It was an ambitious plan with many figures as well as the fifteen-foot equestrian Washington.

Crawford finished the model two days before Christmas, leaving him just enough time after the holiday to pack and travel to Richmond. Once he had read the notice of the competition in November, he had thought of little else. Christmas would be his first full day home for over a month. As he prepared to leave for Richmond, Louisa said, "Write every day and let me know what's happening. The suspense will drive me crazy."

"I will. You know this could mean so much for my career. If I get this commission, we will not have to worry about money. The prestige of being chosen should lead to other jobs, and those will be icing on the cake. I must get this commission and will," answered Crawford.

"Don't forget what Sumner said about Virginians, said Louisa. "You are dealing with the Commissioners, but they are dealing with the Governor, the Legislators, and the newspapers. Control your temper, and don't tell them they know nothing about sculpture. Avoid any discussions about slavery because you will only lose."

"I know, I know. I will be on my best behavior and hold my tongue. It won't be easy."

"That's right, I know you better than anyone. Try to remember when you were telling Uncle John that we wanted to get married. You knew when to stop pressing then and it worked. You can be quite impatient and blunt when you disagree with someone, so avoid arguments. Promise me," said Louisa who knew her husband did not suffer fools lightly.

"I promise," said Crawford, knowing his wife was right.

&

Arriving in Richmond on January 5, 1850, Crawford found the office of Conway Robinson, Sumner's friend, on the second floor of a building overlooking a circular empty area in front of the Capitol. As Crawford was waiting to meet Robinson he gazed out the window and began to visualize how his proposal could be placed in the setting before him. His thoughts were interrupted when he heard, "Sorry to disturb your concentration, I'm Conway Robinson, and you must be Sumner's sculptor friend, Thomas Crawford?"

"Yes, excuse me, I was wondering if that's where they will be placing the monument," said a startled Crawford pointing to the open circular space outside.

"That is the approximate area. Welcome to Richmond. Come into my office and have a seat. I hope your trip was pleasant," said Robinson, who looked about the same age as Sumner but was shorter and thinner.

"It was. Thank you for taking the time to see me."

"Sumner is an old friend, and his excellent recommendation persuaded me to become involved in this project. Your many years of study in Rome and success in Boston are impressive. Richmond does have Houdon's *George Washington* in the rotunda of the Capitol, so we have prior experience with sculpture, but that was many years ago."

"I haven't seen it yet, but plan to. Houdon was a master, and I'm certain it's good."

"We're proud of it. My concern is our lack of experience in judging the entries. Notices of the competition were placed in newspapers all over the country, and I anticipate most will be from dreamers who have no idea of how to design and construct a monument. There are few Americans with such experience, and it would be good to have an American win the competition."

"I brought drawings and a model which might help the commissioners get a better perspective of my design."

"Good idea. It will also help me. I have no idea of how one designs a public monument of this scale. Let's start by going to the Governor's office and locating where your model will be displayed. I checked the other day, and a few entries were only written descriptions, but many included drawings. One other model has been received."

"How many entries were received?"

"Yesterday, at the end of the day, they had received 63. You would be number 64 and the competition has been extended to January 8."

∾

On the way to the Governor's office, Robinson greeted everyone with a cheerful comment and often a handshake, addressing many by name. The same was true in the Governor's office, where the staff welcomed him as an old friend. With gentle persuasion from Robinson, the staff found a place in the entry area of the office for Crawford's model. Satisfied Crawford had received an appropriate reception and sufficient help, Robinson bade him goodbye, promising to return later in the day to see the model. Crawford knew he had an important friend, again, thanks once again, to Sumner.

Tired from the trip but excited, Crawford unpacked the model. Visitors to the office stopped to watch and ask questions, which distracted him, but he remembered Louisa's admonition and answered them with all the patience he could muster. He asked the office staff if he could see the other model submitted, and they directed him to a room across the hall. On entering the room, he immediately guessed the probable designer.

As he stood there, all he could think was "another column." This looked like the work of Robert Mills (no relation to Clark Mills), an important architect, at one time Architect of the Buildings in Washington. He had designed the first two Washington monuments - the Baltimore Washington Monument and the Washington Monument in the nation's capitol now under construction.

Crawford had seen Mills' drawings for that giant obelisk on his last visit to Washington. He considered them imaginative and bold, but Crawford lived with numerous obelisks in Rome and those were enough for him. The monument in Baltimore was 178 feet high with interior steps leading to the top where the visitors could view the city. Mills had one of the Italian sculptors, Enrico

Causico, carve a 16-foot sculpture of Washington, which he placed on the top of the column. Crawford had not seen it, but a friend with a stereopticon had shown him pictures.

The model of the column Mills submitted for the competition had a few minor differences from his Baltimore monument.[30] Balconies were present at several levels but, again, there was a sculpture of Washington at the top. He could not guess the height and wondered if Mills had already asked Enrico Causico to carve another Washington.

∽

Robinson returned about four that afternoon and found Crawford explaining his model to two legislators who were from rural areas in the northwest part of the state. He stood back and listened, attempting to get a feeling for their reaction to the model. They seemed confused by the complexity of the work, and when they were told it would be sixty-five feet high they were politely skeptical. Robinson could detect no other strong negative reactions, but it was clear they were overwhelmed by this piece of art and hesitated to ask questions to avoid looking ignorant. He wondered how they would describe it to their fellow legislators over drinks in the local tavern that evening.

When they left, Robinson asked Crawford to give a detailed description and explanation of his model. Aware this was an important beginning of his quest for the prize, Crawford began, "The focal point, of course, will be the equestrian sculpture of Washington, in uniform, mounted and directing his men. For the face I plan to work from the facial mask Houdon prepared when he visited Washington in Mount Vernon."

"How tall is your sculpture of Washington and the horse?"

"Fifteen feet." Pointing to the bottom of the model, Crawford explained, "This is the lowest part, also referred to as the plinth, a circle with eight steps around the entire circumference. There are four levels to the monument. Starting with the lowest level there are eight eagles seated on low pedestals. At the top of the steps are six pedestals on which are seated allegorical figures six feet high."

"Have you decided who or what these allegorical figures represent?"

"I have. Colonial Times, Revolution, Independence, Bill of Rights, Justice and Finance. The next level is the base, which will be a six-pointed star, and on five points of the star there will be a figure of a prominent Virginian. On the sixth point, will be another allegorical figure, Virginia. These will all be nine feet high."

"Who will these prominent Virginians be?"

"I thought I would let the Commissioners make those choices, but I hoped it would include Thomas Jefferson and Patrick Henry."

"That's a clever idea."

"The next level, the highest segment, is the octagonal pedestal for the equestrian Washington. On two sides of the pedestal will be a relief of the Seal of Virginia."

"Thirteen figures, eight eagles and two reliefs, how long will it take you to carve them?"

"The figures and relief will not be marble, they will be bronze."

"Bronze. I'm not sure I have ever seen a bronze sculpture."

"If you have been to Washington, there is a sculpture of Jefferson outside the White House. Have you seen it?"

"Yes, I have, and I liked it. Everyone likes it. I forgot it was bronze. Why did you choose bronze?"

"The figures will weather better. The monuments in Europe use bronze for the figures and stone for the support structure. As indicated in the competition notice, Virginia granite or marble will be available for the artist. The plinth, base, and pedestal will be Virginia marble, and the sculptures bronze."

"You know," said an awed Robinson, "the model alone is worth seeing. At sixty-five feet high, the completed monument will dominate the center of the city. I can't say enough about it. By the way, did you see the other model submitted?"

"Yes, it's in a room across the hall. Let's take a look at it," answered Crawford.

Moving across the hall, Crawford let Robinson examine the column before he said, "My guess would be this is the work of Robert Mills who has done two Washington monuments."

"If you are correct, you have a formidable competitor. Robert Mills, from Charleston, South Carolina, has important political connections in the South. This is a man who Thomas Jefferson mentored, and has designed buildings in Washington, South Carolina, Philadelphia, and here in Richmond."

"I had no idea he had done so much. How old is he?"

"Quite old, but tough. You will have a struggle, perhaps a better word would be battle, competing with him. I don't mean to scare you, but you should realize who you are up against. That being said, I prefer your model," said Robinson. "It is something new and different from anything I've seen. It would be good for Richmond. No other city has anything like it."

"Thank you for the background on Mills. As an outsider I hope he can count on your advice and support. You're the only one I know in this city," said Crawford.

"I forgot to mention, we have an invitation to dinner tomorrow at the Governor's residence, 8:30 sharp. I hope you can make it. This would give you a chance to meet some other people from Richmond."

"I will be there," answered an elated Crawford.

~

Leaving Robinson, Crawford found a hotel, unpacked and checked the box which contained another equestrian Washington. He had no idea how long it would take six judges to make a final decision from 64 entries. While they were deciding, there might be enough time to take this second model to Washington.

Settled in his room, he opened the box and found the thin legs of the horse broken. He could fix that, but he decided to wait until he reached Washington since the next trip might have the same consequences. What Robinson told him about Robert Mills concerned him more. Jefferson's protégé, It was hard to top that. On the other hand, Robinson's reassuring comments about his model being a new approach (for America) gave him hope. In the daily letter he promised Louisa, he told her of Sumner's superb choice of Conway Robinson as a contact in Richmond.

It was cloudy and cold the next morning as he walked to the Virginia Capitol. The wind cut through his coat, and he yearned for the milder January weather of Rome. The wooden buildings intermixed with the larger state buildings had little character, but he tried to remind himself he lived in Rome, the ancient capitol of the world, with palazzos and stone buildings hundreds of years in the making. As the Capitol came into sight, his mood improved. The stone temple designed by Jefferson was as classical in style as any in Rome, or Greece, for that matter.

On entering, the large size, soaring height of the rotunda before him presented the perfect space for Houdon's sculpture of *George Washington*. This was a masterpiece. White marble, carved with great skill, it could just as well have come from the atelier of Canova or Thorvaldsen. Few sculptors could match the work of Houdon. Crawford spent most of his time studying the face of Washington and made sketches for future reference. Everyone in Richmond would be searching for those features in a new sculpture of the General and President. If he did not win the competition, seeing Houdon's work would partially compensate for the long trip to Richmond.

After his lengthy study of Houdon's work, he returned to the Governor's office hoping to find someone who could tell him when the winner of the competition would be announced. No answers were forthcoming. He decided his best choice for the rest of the day would be to return to his hotel, write to Louisa and then rest, something he had not done since November.

That evening, it was a short walk to the Governor's residence located on the Capitol Square. As he came to the large Federal style building, he remembered Louisa's two cautions: do not tell them they know nothing about sculpture, and do not get into a discussion of the slavery issue. He was further reminded of this when he was greeted at the door by a slave servant who took his coat. From the entry area he could see a group of about ten men in animated conversation across the room. His eyes moved quickly among them in search of Robinson, who noticed him, came over, and greeted him, "Welcome. Before I introduce you, let me give you some background on the group. Three are competition Commissioners, one is in charge of the buildings of the Capitol, four are legislators, and one is the State Treasurer."

"Where's the Governor?" asked a nervous Crawford.

"He comes just before dinner is served. There must be interest in your proposal because the guests invited tonight have all been involved in this project. Relax. I'll jump in whenever I think the conversation is getting close to dangerous territory, such as your friends in Boston."

"I'll try my best," replied Crawford, grateful for Robinson's presence.

Just as Robinson finished introducing Crawford to everyone, Governor John B. Floyd joined the group. He came up to Crawford, shook his hand, and giving no hint if he knew why Crawford was there, welcomed him to Virginia. The guests were then seated around a long oval table which conformed to the curved shape of the elegant room.

Bills currently before the legislature dominated the initial conversation, and Crawford began to relax and enjoy the meal. Then, to his surprise, the Governor addressed him asking him to give his impression of the state of affairs in Rome, specifically the French occupation of the city, and whether he thought Pius IX would regain control of the Papal State.

Crawford began cautiously, not sure how much they knew, and as he described his experiences in the city from 1848 until he left in 1849, all appeared interested. The many questions asked by the Governor indicated he was well-informed about the aborted revolution. Avoiding any suggestion of his involvement with Civil Guard of Rome (afraid they might think he preferred being an Italian), Crawford kept their attention for the remainder of the evening. The competition or any discussion of art and artists never surfaced.

The dinner over, Crawford left with Robinson, and as they walked, Crawford asked, "Were they aware I had submitted a proposal for the monument? I was puzzled. There was not one question about that."

"Of course they were. The three commissioners present do not wish to show any evidence of favoritism. Your model must have caught their attention; leave it at that for now," said Robinson.

"I don't know whether to stay or go on to Washington. Can you ask when they will have a decision?"

"I may be able to. I'll let you know when I do. Good night," said Robinson as they parted ways.

As he walked on to the hotel, every detail of the evening's conversations came back to him. He could think of no blunders, but he knew if the situation were reversed and he was a sculptor from the South having dinner in Boston with a similar group, the issue of slavery would not have been avoided. He had heard of southern hospitality, but now he understood what it meant.

❧

Unable to get a definite date for the Committee's final decision, Robinson suggested Crawford go to Washington, but let the Committee know where he could be reached. Crawford had busied himself sketching the Houdon Washington and the Capitol Square. On one of his walks, he noticed a sign for a photographer's studio. Photographs, or daguerreotypes, were becoming popular, so he hired the photographer to take pictures of the Capitol Square, which he could show Louisa and take to Rome. He thought this new invention could also become a method of recording his work and be used to give clients in America the opportunity to see a clay or plaster model before the carving began.

He left Richmond for Washington on January 13, hoping to find support for his other equestrian Washington. Reluctant because of his well-known association with the new abolitionist Free Soil Party, Sumner sent Crawford a letter of introduction to Senator Salmon Chase of Ohio. Crawford was received graciously by the Senator, but found him preoccupied with the issue of slavery, as were all in Congress. Crawford sensed little attention would be paid to his proposal, even though the Senator promised to sponsor a bill to commission his sculpture.

Wherever he mentioned he was a sculptor, people told him he must visit the studio of Clark Mills and see his wonderful sculpture of Andrew Jackson. More than one person characterized him as "a self-taught genius." The first thing Senator Chase had asked when they met, was did Crawford know Clark Mills? Mills was obviously a popular and well-known figure in Washington. Crawford had never heard of this sculptor, so he decided the only way to clear up this mystery would be to visit his studio.

He had no trouble finding the studio near the Treasury Building because of the sign over the door: CLARK MILLS SCULPTOR. That in itself was different. No sculptor or painter in Rome had a sign outside their studio. He could not decide if this was good or bad. When he entered the large room and saw the plaster of Andrew Jackson on his horse, he experienced a range of emotions which perplexed him. Surprise, envy, anger; he was not certain which was strongest and had to take a moment to control himself. Who was this Mills, and how did he get this commission in Washington when Crawford had no success?

Telling himself he should be calm and objective, difficult as it might be, he began to look at the piece from the perspective of a sculptor. The plaster work was well done, but Jackson in the saddle, had a rigid back, and was anatomically incorrect. The arms and legs were out of proportion when compared to the body length. The sleeves of the coat and the pants seemed empty. The horse, reared back on its hind legs with the front legs high in the air, astounded him. He had seen that pose only in paintings. He could see no suggestion of pins in the hind legs, anchoring the piece and preventing it from falling forward. Could it be balancing in that position by its weight alone? If so, that would be impressive. He had assumed (if he won the competition) his equestrian sculpture would be the first in America. What a shock. There was not only one in America already, but in Washington.

He walked to the other end of the studio where a man worked on a plaster bust with an assistant, a black man whom Crawford assumed was the sculptor's slave. Setting a tool down, and with a big smile, a tall man about the same age as Crawford said, "Welcome to the studio, I'm Clark Mills. Can I answer any questions?"

"Yes, where did you study to do this work?" asked a still unsettled Crawford.

"I learned everything on my own. I guess you would say I am self-taught. It just comes natural."

"Did Congress commission this piece?"

"Oh no, a group from Tennessee did. Congress has nothing to do with it."

"Are you going to carve it yourself?"

"No, it won't be done in marble, it will be cast in bronze."

"I didn't know there was a foundry in America casting sculpture," said a confused Crawford.

"There will be, I plan to cast it right here," said Mills with a chuckle.

"So you have been in the foundry business before?"

"No, but I have been studying the process and I am ready to begin after I build a furnace. It's too cold now. In a few weeks it should be warm enough to lay the bricks," answered a confident Mills.

Perplexed by what he had just heard, Crawford decided it was a good time to leave before he became, as Louisa warned him, blunt. Discovering an untrained sculptor with a studio in Washington, as close as one could get to the Capitol itself, depressed Crawford. He was getting nowhere in this city, but this popular 'self-taught genius' had a commission for a monument, and apparently did it by declaring himself a sculptor and caster of bronze. After fifteen years of struggle in Rome, this was a bitter pill for Crawford to swallow.

⁊

Over the next two weeks Crawford waited in Washington, dubious he would have success with Congress. He was about to pack and leave for Boston when, on January 28, an article in the paper said the Commissioners in the Richmond Competition had narrowed the finalists to six, none of which were identified. On January 30, the boredom of the past two weeks came to an abrupt end when he received a telegram asking him to return to Richmond to meet with the Commissioners. He left immediately, and when he reached the Governor's office in Richmond, was told the competition committee was eager to meet with him the next day.

Crawford took this all to mean he was a serious candidate for the monument and his mood now changed to cautious jubilation. That evening he wrote Louisa telling her of the good news and promising to not be 'blunt.' That night, unable to sleep for any length of time, possible questions from the committee passed through his mind over and over. In the morning, on his way to the meeting, he felt nervous, but at the same time confident in his proposal. A lack of confidence was never a weakness of Thomas Crawford.

When he entered the meeting room he found the Commissioners seated around a table with his model in the center. After introducing Crawford to the Commissioners (he remembered those who had attended the dinner at The Governor's Residence), the Chairman, William F. Ritchie began, "Yours is the last of the finalists to be reviewed. We would like you to explain your model and the drawings you submitted. When you have finished, we have some questions."

For the next hour, Crawford moved step-by -step from the bottom of the monument to the equestrian sculpture of Washington, explaining his rationale for the various components. Given this opportunity, he knew he could make a convincing case for his work and his nervousness vanished. His presentation completed, Chairman Ritchie asked, "Why have you chosen bronze instead of marble for the figures?"

"Long term, bronze will weather better than marble, particularly the finer details of the figures," answered Crawford.

"Have you done other works in bronze?" continued Chairman Ritchie.

"No, but I plan to use one of the finest foundries on the Continent. They have done many monuments and their work is excellent. An excellent example of a bronze sculpture is the statue of Thomas Jefferson in front of the White House. It was cast in Paris, and I'm sure you have seen it."

"I have and it is good. Aren't there any foundries in America that can do this? I understand the fellow in Washington doing the Andrew Jackson sculpture will be casting it himself. Can you use him?" asked one of the commissioners.

"No, there are no foundries in America capable of doing these complex figures. As for the sculptor in Washington, I did visit his studio last week. In my opinion, since this will be the his first attempt at casting a bronze sculpture, he will have a difficult, if not impossible time."

"I have listed some changes we discussed when we reviewed your proposal. First, the final height. We feel it should be 60 feet. Do you have a problem with that?" asked Chairman Ritchie.

"No."

"The Committee wished to have the monument include the remains of George Washington, but that looks unlikely. Instead, we discussed enlarging the pedestal to contain Virginia and Washington archives as well as an interior staircase. How do you feel about that?"

"That sounds like a good idea, and Virginia granite is the perfect material for the plinth, base and pedestal," answered Crawford relieved they had no major revisions of his figures on the monument. This was going well.

"Your detailed explanation of the model clarified the other questions I had. We plan to make a formal announcement of our selection in the next few days. In case any further questions arise, perhaps you could remain in Richmond, if that is not too great an inconvenience," said Chairman Ritchie.

"No, I will stay. The Governor's office knows where to reach me. Thank you for your consideration and time," answered Crawford, as he shook the hands of all the commissioners.

Returning to his hotel Crawford did not think he was too optimistic, nevertheless sensed his design would be chosen. Tired from the quick trip back to Richmond, the sleepless night, and the stress of the committee presentation, he fell on the bed and slept until the next morning.

⚬⚬⚬

Crawford did not have to wait "a few days" to hear from the Competition Committee. The next day, Chairman William Ritchie came to the hotel and told him he had won the competition. He immediately sent a telegram to Louisa and then rushed to see Conway Robinson. Entering the office, Crawford's smile and unmistakable excitement told the story. "I did it, I won. You are the only person I know in this city and you have been such an important part of this quest, I had to tell someone," blurted out a euphoric Crawford.

"Well, the best man won. Congratulations," said Robinson. "I've been keeping my ear to the ground the past three weeks, and there were rumors the committee favored your proposal. Your model helped sway their decision because it was different from all the other proposals and included great Virginians."

"I had that feeling when I made my presentation to the committee. Drawings are a poor way to present a three-dimensional idea such as sculpture. Now I can return to Rome and my studio where my days are less stressful."

"Although there has been no formal public announcement," said Robinson, "word of this is spreading all over town. You are a stranger to Richmond, and there will be people who question whether you are American since you have lived in Rome and plan to return. Others who submitted proposals may think they can use that to change the committee's mind."

"Could the committee really change their decision at this point?"

"I doubt it, but be prepared, and ask me when to respond or better yet, not respond, especially if criticism of the Committee's choice becomes unpleasant. This is a major project and expenditure for the city for the next five years," warned Robinson.

"I can't return to Boston," said Crawford. "They plan to lay the cornerstone for the monument on Washington's birthday, February 22nd, and they want me to be present. I'm not one to shy away from a fight, but until then I'll try to avoid any critics that surface."

Robinson's prediction materialized with lightening speed. The following day, a legislator introduced a bill to nullify the decision of the committee. The rapid organization of the legislators suggested to Robinson someone familiar with Richmond and its politics was in the background orchestrating the protest. He wondered if Robert Mills could be involved, but there never would be any proof he was.

Within two days, the Virginia House of delegates, voted 85 to 40 to indefinitely postpone the bill to nullify the committee's choice, but the criticism continued, and the heated debate moved to the newspapers which Crawford could not avoid reading.[31] On February 6th, the official announcement of the selection of Thomas Crawford as the winner of the competition was published in the *Richmond Enquirer* and preparations for the laying of the cornerstone began. Crawford had two influential supporters who assured him there would be no change in the final choice for the monument - William Ritchie, Chairman of the Competition and Editor of the *Richmond Enquirer*, and Conway Robinson.

❦

The night before the laying of the cornerstone, Crawford was again at the Governor's residence for a dinner, which included President Zachary Taylor, who along with Vice President Millard Fillmore and former President John Tyler would participate in the parade and ceremonies. The elaborate celebration included a long parade ending at the site of the monument followed by the usual political oratory and Crawford setting the cornerstone.

As thousands surrounded the monument, Crawford set the cornerstone, using the silver trowel made for George Washington when he laid the cornerstone for the United States Capitol in 1793. The box enclosed in the cornerstone included a piece of wood from Washington's coffin, copies of the Declaration of Independence, his Farewell Address, the United States Constitution, a Bible and two coins from the short-lived Roman Republic contributed by Crawford.[32] The celebration concluded that evening with a Ball in the Masonic Hall.

This hectic and stressful period from November, 1849 to February, 1850, gave Crawford the national notoriety he had sought. There was no question in his mind he deserved to be a candidate, (he felt so confident at the moment, *the* candidate), for any new sculptural work contemplated for the United States Capitol. To further pursue this consuming ambition, he stopped in Washington before returning to Boston and Louisa, but found his proposal for an equestrian Washington in the Capitol would likely die a slow death in the Library Committee of Congress.

He arrived home to Louisa and children the first week in March, 1850, with $500 for winning the competition and hours of stories. The next task would be to make architectural drawings for the granite structure which would incorporate the changes suggested by the committee as well as watercolors of the monument from several perspectives. When these were completed, he could then return to Richmond to sign the contract and receive his first payment of $10,000.

◌◠◦

Well behind schedule in May, 1850, Clark Mills found someone with experience in bronze casting to help him. Charles Ludwig Richter, an immigrant from Germany, who had worked in Germany casting sculpture, visited Mills at his studio. Both were risk takers and innovators, and Richter found the challenge of building a foundry and casting this large sculpture fascinating and agreed to work with Mills.

Mills built a small building behind his studio where he and Richter designed a furnace that did not have the tall chimney seen in the Naval Yard Foundry furnaces or any other foundry. In fact, it had no chimney, only scattered holes for the escape of air. They thought this would cut down the heat loss up the chimney allowing a more intense and efficient transfer of heat to the bronze. Whether the idea was Richter's or Mills', no one ever knew, but over the years both would claim it as theirs.[33]

Philip Reid, Mills' slave, paid careful attention to their discussions knowing he, along with the masons, would be constructing the furnace. Richter had the experience, Mills the temerity, and Reid the common sense necessary to implement their plans. Even with the addition of Richter to the team, it would still be an exercise in trial and error.

The plan was to first cast a bell, giving the team a chance to practice making a mold and pouring the bronze. Proud of their new furnace, they started the fire which burned for three days before they considered it hot enough to melt the bronze. Reid and a hired slave, who were to handle the melted bronze and the pour, never had the opportunity. The bronze overflowed and spread freely within the furnace destroying the mortar between the bricks and parts of the furnace collapsed. Fortunately, no one was burned.

It would take six weeks to clean up the mess resulting from their first attempt at casting and build a new furnace. However, Reid had learned enough from this disaster to supervise hired slaves in the cleanup, leaving Mills time to pursue his other business, making face masks and busts of politicians and other dignitaries in Washington. Mills' had celebrity status in the city, and in turn, he made it a point to meet as many members of Congress and important people in the city as possible. This brought him customers.

The next attempt would be to cast a bell. Richter and Reid, who now understood the process, supervised the slaves hired by Mills for this first successful casting. It was a start, but by July, 1850, the original date given by Mills for the completion of the sculpture, no part of the sculpture was cast. Reid's team then cast three more bells and a bust of Apollo, sculpted by Mills.

Fifty-thousand pounds of bronze, which included the canons captured by Andrew Jackson in New Orleans, were appropriated by Congress for the casting of the sculpture. Mills' lack of progress concerned the original committee members who persuaded Congress to assume control of the project. It would have been an embarrassment not to continue the Jackson monument, and besides, Mills was well-liked and well-connected in Washington.

They decided to begin by casting Jackson first. Mills and Richter spent two weeks determining where to place the shims or thin metal strips which outline and divide the surface of a model before applying the mold material. Careful study is necessary to be certain each segment of the mold on the surface can be removed freely and in one piece. The mold material is applied between the shims, which are removed when the segments of the mold are pulled from the surface of the sculpture. This gives sharp and accurate delineation of the different segments, which assures they can be joined accurately after casting. They finally decided they could cast Jackson in six segments.

Making the molds went smoothly, but the first attempt at casting failed. The edges of the casting were uneven which meant they would not join side to side with the adjacent casting without leaving a gap. There were many similar failures, and it would take until the fall of 1851, before Reid and his team could produce the six usable castings for the figure of Jackson. Mills, now twelve months behind schedule, had wasted most of the original fifty-thousand pounds of bronze and had not begun the casting of the horse.

∽

While Mills struggled with bronze casting, Crawford was completing his drawings and collecting engravings and portraits of Virginians likely to be selected for the monument. He and Louisa continued to stay with Julia and Samuel Howe in Boston where Sumner was a frequent visitor. At dinner one Sunday, Samuel said, "Webster continues to appease the slave states."

"Yes," replied Sumner, "he has lost his moral compass. These compromises which the Senate are discussing will never abolish slavery. Webster's current obsession is preserving the Union at any cost, but he forgets the blight slavery has placed on our nation."

"He thinks allowing California to enter the Union a free state is a victory, but what about the territories of New Mexico, Arizona, Nevada, and Utah which will be next in line? To further placate the slave states, he agrees these territories should make their own choice when they become states. How can he justify a compromise that could increase the number of slave states?" said Howe.

"He no longer represents the views of the people of Massachusetts. He's in bed with Henry Clay of Kentucky and John Calhoun of South Carolina, the other members of this Senate triumvirate. He believes they are helping him preserve the Union, forgetting they represent slave states."

"And this latest compromise issue, abolishing the trading of slaves in Washington, but allowing all those who now own slaves to keep them. How ridiculous is that?" said Howe.

"It's becoming worse. Only President Taylor's opposition prevents passage of these compromises. A bill which permits former slave owners to pursue runaway slaves in free states is now being debated. If found, and captured they can be returned to the owners without a trial. This might even apply to slaves who have been freed."

"How can we stop Webster?" asked Howe.

"He must be defeated at the next election, but even that will be too late. The debate has gone on for months and this fugitive slave issue is the last part of the package. Unfortunately, it looks as though it will pass," said Sumner.

Similar discussions between these two dedicated abolitionists were frequent while Crawford stayed at the Howe home. He listened respectfully, but felt ill-prepared and unmotivated to participate in their conversations.

∽

It would be three months before Crawford returned to Richmond to sign the contract. His last visit to Richmond had been in January and February when it was cold, the trees bare, the streets dirty, and the cloudy days of winter cast a somber shade of gray over the city. The trees, now covered with leaves and the warm, bright June sunshine changed Crawford's impression of the city. It had a charm he had not noticed before, but on his last visit, absorbed in the competition, he probably had not made an effort to look.

His first stop would again be the law office of Conway Robinson. He trusted Robinson and he needed someone to represent him while he was away in Rome. Robinson, welcomed him back and said, "I hear you are here to sign the contract. That means you will be heading back to Rome soon."

"Yes, and your friend Sumner said it would be a good idea to get a lawyer. Would you be willing to represent me during the construction while I'm in Rome?" asked Crawford.

"I have no experience with sculpture, but yes, it could be interesting. What's the agenda? When do you sign the contract? We should review it before you sign."

"I can go to Chairman Ritchie's office now and get a copy. Have you heard anything about the project since I left?"

"The barrage of complaints gradually diminished. Time heals. You still have a few harsh critics in the Legislature, but it's in summer recess and they are all home working their farms. Your timing is perfect. The sooner the contract is signed, the better," said Robinson.

The contract was ready, and they sat down to review the long document. Robinson guided him through the opening legal language, but when they reached the financial details, Crawford could only smile. For the equestrian sculpture, $30,000, the two prominent Virginia figures, $9,000 each and the shields, $2,000. These were to be completed before February 22, 1856. He was to receive an advance of $10,000.[34] Thomas Jefferson and Patrick Henry were to be the first prominent Virginians completed.

One paragraph bothered Crawford. Because he would be in Rome, the committee designated Robert Mills as the supervising architect for the construction of the granite portion of the monument. He asked Robinson if they could add a paragraph to the contract which made it clear Robert Mills could not revise the design or change any of the measurements in Crawford's drawings without his approval. Robinson thought that reasonable and Chairman Ritchie agreed. Crawford signed the contract June 27, 1850.

Ten months later, the costs for the construction of the monument in Richmond were up to $42,000. This included the purchase of five slaves and their upkeep (they were sold about a year later to raise money for the escalating costs). Robert Mills was retained at a salary of $88.33 per month.[35]

◦◦

Crawford returned to Boston in time to celebrate the Fourth of July with his family and two daughters. He hoped to leave for Rome in three weeks, stopping in Paris to research the bronze foundries, but his plans were interrupted by the sudden death of President Zachary Taylor on July 9, 1850.

The President, who had appeared healthy and in good spirits at the Fourth of July celebration in Washington, became ill the next day and died four days later. Vice President Millard Fillmore was sworn into office as the thirteenth President of the United States and asked Daniel Webster to be his Secretary of State. On July 17, 1850, Webster resigned his seat as Senator to accept the offer.

Sumner and Howe were elated. Howe quickly campaigned to have Sumner appointed to the seat, but the small Free Soil Party had little influence. Webster, still in control of the Whig party in Massachusetts, made certain Sumner would have no chance of being selected to fill his vacated seat or the seat of Representative Robert C. Winthrop, appointed to the Senate by the governor.

Webster considered Sumner an extremist, who, with his incisive and often inflammatory oratory, could only play havoc with all the work done to achieve a compromise with the slave states. However, in 1850, as the Constitution specified, Senators were not elected by popular vote but by a majority vote in both the House and Senate of the State Legislature. The Massachusetts Legislature was scheduled to meet after the first of the year, 1851, to either elect Winthrop, the governor's temporary appointee, or choose someone else. Sumner denied he had any interest in becoming a Senator, but some others in Boston felt otherwise, and began to build a case for his candidacy.

President Taylor had opposed the compromises with the slave states, but President Fillmore would offer no opposition. Led By Senator Stephen Douglas of Illinois who had joined the Triumvirate, the compromises after passage, included the admission of California as a free state, the abolishing of slave trade in the District of Columbia (but allowing those who had slaves to keep them), compensating Texas for money owed Mexico after their war, and granting territorial status to New Mexico. The Fugitive Slave Act, which passed September 18, 1850, made Federal Marshals available to assist slave owners in finding their escaped slaves.

~

Amidst all this excitement, Crawford and Louisa left for Rome July 20, 1850. As they crossed the Atlantic, returning to what he considered home, Crawford was already planning the expansion of his studio to house the sculptures for Richmond.

In Paris, Crawford visited bronze foundries to learn more about the technique and evaluate their previous work. Sending a plaster of each sculpture would be all they needed, and this would allow him to move on to the next figure while the previous was being cast.

Once he had completed a clay model, he could turn it over to the assistants to make the molds and pour the plasters. When the plaster had been poured, he would make any final revisions necessary, and the plaster figure could then be shipped to the foundry. He would need to hire additional assistants, but now he could afford the new expense.

From Paris he went to Munich, and after visiting the Royal Bavarian Foundry, concluded it the best he had seen. Work on the Richmond monument could begin and when he returned to Rome, decided to start with the figure of Patrick Henry. Louisa, happy to be in her own home, set about decorating and furnishing additional rooms in the villa for the children and guests.

Louisa's two sisters, vacationing in Europe, joined them later making their Christmas celebration in Rome special. It had been 15 years since Crawford arrived in Rome, the only American sculptor in the city. Now Louisa could plan a party, inviting the many American sculptors and painters who worked in Rome.

The extensive coverage of the Richmond competition in American news-papers made Crawford well known. For American tourists visiting Rome, a stop at Crawford's studio became a necessity, leading to new commissions. Crawford decided to enlarge the equestrian Washington from twenty to twenty-three feet and the figures of Patrick Henry and Jefferson from nine to twelve feet. This he did at no extra cost to Richmond. The new studio he constructed to accom-modate the large figures and massive horse became the talk of the artistic com-munity of Rome and a fascination for American tourists.

By the spring of 1851, he employed 25 assistants and the figure of Patrick Henry was ready for shipping to Munich. Crawford could not help recalling the days spent in Thorvaldsen's studio when he marveled how the maestro kept so many projects moving at the same time. Now, in a similar situation, he realized that the excitement of watching the figures evolve was the fuel, which kept the creative drive of the sculptor vibrant. He had never been happier and did not hesitate to accept even more work.

෫෨

One evening when Crawford returned to the Villa, Louisa handed him a package from Richmond. When he opened the package, it contained some sketches and a letter. He scanned the sketches and then read the letter. "This man is mad," shouted Crawford. "Who does he think he is?"

Louisa who had never heard him react so vehemently before, rushed to his side and asked, "Who are you talking about?"

"Robert Mills. He even has the impudence to add the title Architect of the Richmond Washington Monument after his signature."

"What has he done?"

"What hasn't he done would be more appropriate. He has presented the governor with these sketches, claiming they would, "improve the overall appear-ance of the monument."

"I thought you had them include a clause in the contract preventing him from making any changes?"

"I did, but guess what he wishes to add?"

"I can't believe it," said Louisa as she looked at one of the sketches.

"Neither can I. He has added his favorite structure, a tall column, elimi-nated the pedestal for the equestrian sculpture, and placed Washington on the ground. He thinks I will approve of this? As I said, the man is mad. He also wants the figures to be stone not bronze. This is beyond impudence."

Everything had been going well, and now he had to deal with Mills' attempt to undermine his dream. Did Mills have enough power to make these changes? Contacting his lawyer, Conway Robinson, in Richmond would be the only way to deal with Mills.

He wrote two letters, one to Robinson and another one he should present to Mills. He asked Robinson to remind Mills of the wording in the contract, tell Mills to never make another attempt at changing Crawford's drawings, and confine his involvement to supervising the construction of the pedestal and the surrounding base. His emphatic letter to Mills made it clear he had no interest whatsoever in his column or any other changes and included the following comment:

> ...you propose to place the main feature of my design (I allude to the Grand Pedestal and the Equestrian Group) upon the ground and offer to me as substitute the most hackneyed of all architectural forms, a kind of bastard column that you would dignify if possible by the sounding appellation of 'the column of the revolution.'[36]

Robinson again proved to be an excellent lawyer for the absentee Crawford. Robert Mills apologized and promised he would make no changes to Crawford's drawings. However, living in Rome, so distant from Richmond, the incident gave Crawford several months of angst as he awaited the responses from Robinson and Mills.

Crawford could now turn to the figure of Jefferson and the two reliefs of the seal of Virginia. Visitors to his studio from America saw the figures and reliefs, on returning home, gave enthusiastic reports to their local newspapers.

⁊

When the State Legislature of Massachusetts met in early 1851, the Whig party had lost much of its power in the recent November elections. The original term of Daniel Webster filled by the Governor's appointee, Winthrop, ended in November, 1850, requiring the State Legislature to elect either Winthrop or another candidate to the United States Senate. A coalition of Democrats and Free Soiler Parties nominated Charles Sumner as their candidate to oppose the Whig, Winthrop.

Sumner's candidacy passed the State Senate quickly, but took three months and 26 votes in the House of Representatives before he was elected to the Senate, April 24.[37] It was a great victory for the abolitionists who were upset by Webster's support of the Compromises of 1850 and the Fugitive Slave Act, which particularly perturbed Sumner. Sumner would take office in November, 1851. He was assigned the desk in the Senate chamber formerly occupied by Jefferson Davis who had resigned to run for Governor of Mississippi.[38]

Sumner's reputation clearly preceded him. The small Free Soil Party had little power in Congress, and his history as an outspoken abolitionist and zealous moralist was well known. When the new Senators were to be introduced in the Senate chamber, the other Senator from Massachusetts, John Davis, "overslept," and Sumner had to be introduced by the Senator from Michigan. It was a clear affront to Sumner.

His first months in office passed without Sumner taking the floor to debate an issue, which did not go unnoticed at home. The newspapers were beginning to question his ability to represent the people of Massachusetts as well as the cause of the abolitionists.

On May 26, 1852, he rose to speak and read "a memorial from the Society of Friends in New England" which proposed an amendment to repeal the Fugitive Slave Act. Senator Douglas of Illinois and the southern Senators considered Sumner the loose cannon of the abolitionists and were prepared to block any attempt by Sumner to discuss what they considered his extreme abolitionist views. Douglas feared he would resurrect the acrimony which existed between the North and South before the Compromises of 1850. They moved to table the amendment, which passed, preventing any further discussion.

Embarrassed by this defeat Sumner bided his time until July 27, 1852, and again asked permission to speak regarding his amendment to repeal the Fugitive Slave Act, which had been tabled. After a brief debate, Sumner's amendment was defeated 32 to 10.[39]

However, on August 26, 1852, when an appropriation's bill for 'extraordinary expenses' came to the floor of the Senate for discussion Sumner knew the government needed this extra money to enforce the Fugitive Slave Act. He had been working for months on a speech titled *Freedom National; Slavery Sectional* and determined this was the time to take on the slave states. He caught his opposition off guard, gained control of the floor and moved to repeal the Fugitive Slave Act.

Sumner then began his speech before the Senate:

> Painfully convinced of the utterable wrongs and woes of slavery; profoundly believing that, according to the true spirit of the Constitution and sentiments of the fathers, it can find no place under our *National* Government - that it is in every respect *sectional*, and in no respect *national* - that it is always and that it is everywhere the creature and dependent of the *States*, and never anywhere the creature or dependent of the *Nation*, and that the Nation can never, by legislation or other act, impart to it any support, under the Constitution of the United States; with these convictions, I could not allow this session to reach its close, without making or seizing an opportunity to declare myself openly against usurpation, injustice, and cruelty, of the late enactment by Congress for the recovery of fugitive slaves.[40]

And, after the three hours, he concluded:

> Finally, sir, for the sake of peace and tranquility, cease to shock the Public Conscience; for the sake of the Constitution, cease to exercise a power which is nowhere granted, and which violates inviolable rights expressly secured. Leave this question where it was left by our fathers, at the formation of the National Government, in the absolute control of the States, the appointed guardians of Personal Liberty. Repeal this enactment. Let its terrors no longer rage through the land. Mindful of the lowly whom it pursues; mindful of the good men perplexed by its requirements; in the name of charity, in the name of the Constitution, repeal this enactment, totally and without delay. Be inspired by the example of Washington. Be

admonished by those words of Oriental piety - 'Beware
of the groans of the wounded souls. Oppress not to
the utmost a single heart; for a solitary sigh has power
to overset a whole world.'[41]

When he finished, Senator Jeremiah Clemens of Alabama took the floor
and responding said, "The ravings of a maniac may sometimes be dangerous,
but the barking of a puppy never did any harm."[42] Sumner's oratorical skills
impressed the chamber, but no one rose to support his motion to repeal the
Fugitive Slave Act and it was defeated 38-4.

∽

In the same year, 1852, casting failures continued for the team of Mills,
Richter, and Reid. It took six attempts and twelve months before they finally
cast the horse in four sections. The repeated castings had made Mills' slave,
Philip Reid, an expert in foundry work. In November, 1852, the casting completed, Mills was two years behind schedule, in debt and had not been back to
visit his wife and children since leaving Charleston four years earlier.

Despite the chaotic progress of the casting Mills continued to be
popular with the politicians and people in Washington. In contrast to
Crawford's formal approach in Washington, Mills needed no letters of
introduction to develop personal relationships with the Washington decision makers. When not struggling with the bronze casting, he spent his
time eating, drinking, and socializing with members of Congress and promoting himself for the next commission being discussed by Congress, an
equestrian sculpture of George Washington for the nation's Capitol. An
important supporter, John Walker Maury, lawyer, banker, and local politician, who would later become Mayor of Washington, lent him the money
necessary to complete the casting.[43]

The dedication ceremony of Mills' Andrew Jackson was January 8, 1853,
the anniversary of the Battle of New Orleans. The ten cast bronze sections
comprising the sculpture weighed fifteen tons and Mills, concerned he would be
unable to move the complete sculpture from the foundry, chose to assemble its
ten sections on site in Lafayette Square. A major factor in the excessive weight
of the work was the extra bronze Mills used in the hindquarters of the horse,
which allowed the sculpture to sit balanced on its rear legs without any attach-

ment to the base or pedestal. Mills had created a fifteen-ton freestanding bronze horse and rider, probably unique in the world at the time.

A parade down Pennsylvania Avenue preceded the formal dedication, which was attended by thousands as well as President Polk and his Cabinet. During his oration, Senator Stephen Douglas of Illinois, the main speaker at the dedication, described Mills as follows:

> It is the work of a young untaught American. I cannot call him an artist. He never studied or copied. He never saw an equestrian statue nor even a model. It is the work of inborn genius, aroused to energy by the triumphant spirit of liberty.[44]

When Mills unveiled the sculpture, the monument to their hero, former friend, and President was an immediate success. Few in the audience had seen an equestrian sculpture before, but now they had one in Washington of a man they remembered and could immediately recognize - *and* it stood on its hind legs without any support. It was an exciting day in the Capitol followed by a Grand Ball in the evening.

Well-known in Washington before, Mills was now more popular than the President and did not have to pay for drinks or dinners for months, thanks to his many admirers. Congress showed its appreciation by appropriating $8000 for a pedestal, the construction to be supervised by Mills, and $20,000 for the work of the sculptor. Up to that point, Mills had done all the work with the $12,000 received from the Monument Committee four years earlier, which was now spent, leaving him in debt. The total government allocations came to $28,000 (plus the copper), and with the original $12,000, the cost of the Jackson Monument had reached $30,000.[45]

The final $20,000 appropriated had a caveat which made it unique in the history of Congress. The fact he had been separated from his family for four years, not returning to Charleston to visit them or bringing them to Washington, was an obvious issue not only for Mills, but others. The appropriation specified that $10,000 was to be invested for the family, and how he intended to accomplish this had to be documented. With the remaining $10,000, Mills paid off his $5,000 debt to John Walker Maury. Mills used the $10,000 for the family to buy (invest in) a farm three miles from Washington where he planned to build a foundry and establish an American art school.[46]

꩜

Three weeks after the dedication, Congress passed a resolution to commission an equestrian sculpture of George Washington, something that had been discussed on and off since a Continental Congress resolution in 1783. The timing couldn't have been better for Mills. He was the foremost sculptor on American soil, and awarding the commission to him was popular and a surprise to no one. The appropriation was for $50,000, the same amount Crawford was to receive for his Richmond equestrian Washington. Crawford's fee, however, included the figures of Patrick Henry and Thomas Jefferson, as well as the two reliefs of the Seal of Virginia and the cost of shipping to America.

Still smarting from the defeat of his amendment in August, Charles Sumner quietly watched the rapid passage of the George Washington commission to Mills, knowing he was in no position to mention Crawford as a possible candidate. It was apparent any opposition to the popular Mills would only further annoy his Senate colleagues as well as everyone in Washington.

Mills, who declined the opportunity to study in Europe, decided two of his sons should, and sent them to Munich to study sculpture and bronze casting. The success of his Jackson also brought him a commission to cast another, this one for the City of New Orleans, the site of Jackson's famous battle. They agreed on a price of $35,000, and Mills would use the original molds for this casting. Richter had left, Philip Reid could act as a supervisor for the casting and he hired a Frenchman, Francois Antoine Picart, trained in Paris, to chase or finish the surfaces of the castings. Mills was now, not only popular, but wealthy and could concentrate on sculpting the model of Washington and building the first fine art bronze foundry in America.

Part V

A New Patron

In May 1852, Crawford left Rome for Munich to visit the Royal Bavarian Foundry and discuss the casting of Patrick Henry, his first attempt at a bronze sculpture. The director of the foundry, Ferdinand von Miller, immediately recognized the genius of Crawford. They became close friends, they understood each others craft, and, from that point forward, their work together continued smoothly.

When he returned to Rome in June, Louisa handed him another letter from Conway in Richmond. From her expression he could tell it was not good news. Indeed, Robert Mills continued to lobby the legislature regarding his plan to add a column to Crawford's monument. Furious, Crawford wrote a strong denunciation of Mills. The committee, the governor, and legislators must have agreed and they discharged Mills from the project in October, 1852.[47]

While Crawford was in Munich, one of the Richmond commissioners visited Rome and saw the busy studio, the clay sculpture of Jefferson and the Virginia State seals. Louisa made certain the time he spent in Rome would be memorable, and when the commissioner returned to Richmond, he assured the committee they had chosen the right sculptor for their monument.

By August, Thomas Jefferson and the Virginia State seals were completed and shipped to Munich. Crawford could now begin the clay equestrian George Washington, a major undertaking, considering the size of twenty-three feet. The horse would be attached by only two hooves, one front, one back, a new variation for an equestrian sculpture. Placing the armature on a stand with rollers, allowed him to complete one side, and turn the horse to complete the other. Rome had not seen a sculpture of that size before, and as the word spread throughout the city there was a constant flow of visitors to watch him.

Things were certainly going Crawford's way and they were about to get better. Congress had approved an extension of the Capitol in 1850. A competition for the design of the extension was announced, but with no conclusive winner, the Architect of the Capitol, Thomas Walter, was asked to do the design.

Franklin Pierce of New Hampshire, the Democratic nominee for President, won the November, 1852, election. After taking office, President Pierce, changed the supervision of the construction of the expansion from the Department of the Interior to the War Department and its Secretary, Jefferson Davis.

Jefferson Davis, in turn, chose Captain Montgomery C. Meigs of the Army Corps of Engineers to supervise the construction. Secretary Davis and Meigs considered the appropriation passed by Congress for the expansion also included selection of the artists for the paintings and statuary.

A graduate of West Point, and an engineer by training and military service, Meigs, originally had been brought to Washington to work on the city's aqueduct system. A large man, confident, capable, and efficient, he wasted little time taking charge. He had a remarkable eye for talent and excellence when it came to the arts.

Wisely, he did not hesitate to ask for advice before considering the selection of sculptors for the new wings. The members of Congress continued to question the use of Italian artists and he agreed. He asked Edward Everett of Massachusetts, someone known for his knowledge of both art and American artists, to give him names of sculptors.

Everett had always championed the work of Hiram Powers, but he had also visited the studio of Crawford in Rome in 1841 and seen his *Orpheus and Eurydice* and other works in Boston. Everett suggested these two Americans.

∾

On August 23, 1853, Meigs sent drawings of one pediment from each new wing to Crawford and Powers, as well as requests for a door to each new chamber with a sculpture above. In his introduction of the requests he wrote the following:

> The pediments and doorways should be a part
> of the original construction of the building, and I do
> not see why a republic so much richer than the Athe-
> nian should not rival the Parthenon in the front of the
> first public edifice. Permit me to say that the sculp-
> ture here by our artists is not altogether adapted to the

taste of our people. We are not able to appreciate too
refined and intricate allegorical representations, and
while the naked Washington of Greenough [who died
in December, 1852] is the theme of admiration to the
few scholars, it is unsparingly denounced by the less
refined multitude.

...In our history of the struggle between civilized
man and the savage, between the cultivated and the
wild nature are certainly to be found themes worthy
of the artist and capable of appealing to the feeling
of all classes.[48]

In the letter, Meigs asked Crawford not to discuss this request with other
artists. If others, particularly members of Congress, knew money was available
for art, they surely could find an artist in their district or state willing to submit
a proposal.

The transfer of the construction to the War Department was not popular
with many members of Congress, and Meigs, aware of this, made decisions
quickly and quietly. Secretary Davis was always available and willing to intervene
if trouble developed. On the other hand, Meigs' relationship with Thomas Wal-
ters, Architect of the Capitol, who was unhappy with this arrangement, would
begin to deteriorate.

᭤

Crawford, who had almost given up on receiving a commission in Washington, was overjoyed when he read the letter from Meigs. It implied the job
was his if he proposed a suitable design. He would not have to agonize through
another competition as he had in Richmond.

The base of the triangle forming the pediment was eighty feet long and
it was twelve feet high at the peak. He remembered Persico's relief, *The Genius of
America*, in the pediment over the central entrance of the Capitol. It was approximately the same size. Persico had placed only three allegorical figures and an
eagle in the center, leaving the remainder of the space on either side bare. Meigs
made it clear he wanted a story, not just an allegorical symbol.

Crawford replied quickly to Meigs:

> I fully agree with you regarding the necessity of producing a work intelligible to our entire population. The darkness of allegory must give place to common sense. I have faith enough to believe that poetry and grandeur are inseparably connected with the history of our country's past and future and that the dignity of sculpture may well be devoted to the perpetuation of what the people love and understand. As yet, I have not had the honor of being employed by our national Government, but the Washington monument I am now engaged upon for the state of Virginia will serve as a practical exponent of my desire to illustrate American history without having recourse to sculpture as practiced in the age of Pericles.[49]

Excited over this request from Meigs, Crawford could think of nothing else and immediately began sketching his ideas for the pediment. The figure of George Washington for the Richmond monument and one side of the horse were almost completed. He could let his assistants finish the other side and devote his time to the pediment.

Meanwhile, Meigs received a surprising reply from Powers who wrote:

> I fully coincide with your views which seem both natural and just and I thank you for the kind spirit in which you have written to me. But I have not the time to prepare designs for the decoration of our Capitol Buildings even if it were a desirable object with me to propose for a commission from the Government of my country.[50]

Crawford concluded the distance of the pediment from the ground was too high for a low or bas relief. The depth of the pediment, thirty inches, was enough for three-dimensional figures making them easier to be seen from below. For him, a drawing would not adequately demonstrate this perspective, so he sculpted, to scale, a complete clay pediment twelve feet in length with all the three-dimensional figures in place. He completed this model in two months, a remarkable feat.

Taking the clue from Meigs' letter, he called his work, *The Progress of Civilization*. A figure representing America stood in the center, and to her right was a woodsman, a hunter, an Indian chief, an Indian mother with her child, and an Indian grave. These represented the beginning of America. To her left were a soldier, a merchant, two youths, a schoolmaster, and a mechanic, representing human endeavor. Photographs of the model, with his explanation and costs were sent to Meigs on October 31,1853.

Meigs received Crawford's photographs and proposal on November 30, 1853. In his personal journal Meigs wrote:

> It illustrates the progress of civilization and the
> decay of the Indian race, and it is a very fine composi-
> tion I think.[51]

The next day, he took it to Secretary Jefferson Davis who liked it except for the Liberty cap on the figure of America in the center of the pediment. He mentioned this to Meigs who, puzzled, asked, "I do not understand. Why?"

Davis replied, "We are not a country of previously enslaved people. We are a free people. The cap is a symbol and usually worn by people emancipated from slavery."

"Should I tell him to change the cap?"

"No, I do not like it, but no one else will probably notice," said Davis. "You can tell the President I approve of the design of the pediment."

The Liberty cap, or Phrygian cap as it was known in ancient culture, had slightly different meanings throughout history. Roman slaves freed by their masters wore them. Secretary Jefferson Davis of Mississippi was particularly sensitive to the slavery issue and rights of the southern states to maintain the status quo.

The following day, Meigs brought it to the President who likewise approved the design. This rapid approval of a major sculpture commission is a record which stands to this day. Meigs wrote Secretary Davis:

> The time which he estimates necessary for the
> completion of the life-size models in plaster ready for
> marble is thirty months. The price $20,000.[52]

This, also was approved.

The price did not include the costs for carving the marble pieces. Crawford told Meigs he thought it would be less expensive to have this done in Italian statuary marble, either in Rome or Carrara, where he could follow the progress himself. Meigs, by now an expert in stone and stone quarries because of the extensive use of marble in the construction of the Capitol, thought otherwise.

Quarries from every state, looking for work, were constantly sending his office samples of their marble. Every time he passed Persico's sculptures of *Peace* and *War* on either side of the central entrance to the Capitol, he noticed the deterioration occurring on the surfaces of the Italian marble. Alerted by his engineering background, he was unwilling to have the figures carved in Italian stone until he studied the American marbles.

◦◦◦

Crawford now, often had fifty assistants in his studio, the largest in Rome. The Perkins family of Boston added another commission, a seven-foot bronze sculpture of Beethoven for the Boston Music Academy.

Next, Crawford had to consider a design for the door Meigs had requested. Ghiberti's door for the Baptistry in Florence was considered the best in the world, and approximately the same size. Before beginning sketches for his doors, he wanted to again study this famous door and, while there, visit Hiram Powers to look at his design for the other pediment.

He left for Florence after Christmas. The rains and hints of snow made the trip difficult, but studying Ghiberti's door gave Crawford the final inspiration he needed. He measured the panels and admired Ghiberti's ability to tell his story in low relief with the background of each panel looking like a drawing rather than sculpture. Crawford decided he would tell the story of the American Revolution on his door. He also noted Ghiberti had placed a bust of himself next to one of the panels.

Powers greeted him warmly and showed him his latest portraits which Crawford considered excellent. After the tour, they sat down to coffee and Crawford asked, "Have you prepared your design for the pediment of the Capitol extension requested by Captain Meigs?"

"I certainly have not," answered Powers angrily, "and will not."

Crawford, stunned by the response said, "You mean you are not interested? That surprises me."

"I am not in the habit of replying to requests from a Captain in the Army who wishes to judge whether my work is up to his standards. I decide what is appropriate for any commission I accept. Others may have to compete for work, I do not."

"So you are not interested in any work for the Capitol?"

"I have something else in mind and when it is finished, I will send it to Washington at my price. I will not bargain with a construction boss. I have no respect for any artist who does."

"Your refusal to send a design for the pediment is final?"

"Yes," said Powers.

When Crawford left he could not believe what he had just heard. Any sculpture included in the Capitol would become part of America's heritage, and yet Powers dismissed the commission so casually. Crawford immediately sent a letter to Meigs describing his visit to Powers and asked if he could do both pediments.

When Meigs read the letter, he knew that letting Crawford do both pediments would be a mistake. This would give members of Congress and other artists additional ammunition for their battle to curtail his power. He tactfully told Crawford it would be better for them both if he considered someone else. Crawford already had the pediment, a door, and the sculpture above the Senate door.

Crawford decided the sculpture above the door should be two allegorical figures representing *History and Justice*, together eleven feet wide and four feet high, which he planned to complete in Italian marble in his studio

❦

1854 began with an amazing amount of work for Crawford. He had to complete the equestrian group for Richmond, start the first of the fourteen figures for the pediment, design a door with its overhead sculpture, and continue all the incidental commissions from tourists.

By May, the first four figures for the pediment were completed in clay. After the plaster castings were finished, pictures were taken and sent to Meigs. Hoping for other commissions, Crawford wanted to deliver results to Meigs in the same rapid manner with which Meigs had approved his proposal for the pediment. He had not met the man, but through their correspondence it was apparent they understood each other quite well.

Under Meigs, the construction of the Capitol extension proceeded at a pace not seen before in Washington. His excellent managerial skills, quick decisions and, as many thought, autocratic style did not sit well with members of Congress and other American artists. On June 14, 1854, Congressman Stanton of Kentucky, addressing the House of Representatives complained:

> He makes contracts with whom he pleases: he purchases materials when and where he chooses: he employs mechanics and laborers, and pays for all them by his own check or order. I cannot see the authority for all this. I look in vain for the law of Congress which authorizes it: and if I say that Captain Meigs occupied his position against the express enactment of this body I Give utterance only to what any candid man will believe who examines the subject.[53]

Meigs, however, would not be intimidated by Congressional pressure.

Louisa, pregnant, did not wish to spend the summer in Rome and left with her daughters for Bagni di Lucca, west of Florence. This allowed Crawford to devote all his time to this extraordinary amount of work.

૭૦

In July, the plaster casting of the Richmond equestrian group was ready to ship to Munich and had to be cut into multiple sections for the long trip. Crawford planned to be in Lucca in time for the birth of his fourth child and then follow the Richmond equestrian group to the Munich foundry. He arrived in time for the delivery of their first son, Francis Marion, on August 4, 1854. Crawford, anxious to get to Munich, spent only three weeks with Louisa and the four children, before he left for Munich.

At the foundry, Crawford discovered his sculptures of Patrick Henry and Thomas Jefferson were on display at the Munich Exhibition of September, 1854. Thousands of visitors to the Exhibition enjoyed these large bronze figures cast locally before they left for America. He visited the Exhibition often to watch the German viewers admire his work. It was the first time Crawford experienced the thrill of such broad public acceptance of his sculpture, and hoped the same enthusiasm would occur when they were shown in Richmond. The anguish of the selection process and trauma of the post competition criticisms in Richmond had not been forgotten.

When the Munich foundry finished casting the Beethoven sculpture, they displayed it outside their music hall and planned a week long Beethoven Music Festival in March, 1855, to celebrate. Crawford received an invitation and took Louisa. They were invited to meet the King, Maximilian II, who had been following, and admired, Crawford's work.[54] His German fans would always be his favorites.

After reassembling the equestrian group in Munich, Crawford returned to Rome to work on the pediment figures and design the door. A letter from Meigs came with more good news. After Powers's refusal to submit a proposal for a pediment design, Meigs could not remember whether he had asked Crawford to design one or two doors. When he reviewed his records, he discovered he meant to ask for two. Crawford, delighted, happily accommodated Meigs.

The additional door meant more space to tell his story of the American Revolution. When finished, they were to become the entrances to the Senate and the House of Representatives. Remembering how Ghiberti included a bust of himself in his door for the Baptistry, Crawford included his image in a panel in the first door which depicts Washington entering Trenton on his way to the Capitol. He placed himself, as well as Louisa and the children, in the crowd watching the passing parade

◦◦◦

After studying the many marble samples sent to his office, Meigs decided to have the figures for the pediment carved in Washington, using stone from a quarry in Lee, Massachusetts, which he felt would better withstand the climate changes of Washington. When Meigs informed Crawford of his decision, he also asked him to send a plan for a studio for the carvers and recommend one of Crawford's assistants who could train American carvers. Crawford initially thought he would rather have the pediment sculptures carved in Rome where he could oversee the work, but the more he thought about it, he realized delivering plasters saved him the trouble of dealing with carvers and their idiosyncrasies.

Meigs also wanted him to explain his method of copying the plaster casts in stone. Crawford sent a description and drawings of the apparatus used in his studio and included drawings and measurements of each marble block needed to carve the figures of the pediment.[55]

Meigs had already employed sculptors Francis Vincenti, and later Guido Butti. Crawford sent Tomasso Gagliardi from his studio. These three Italian sculptors would eventually carve all the figures of the pediment, but their infighting, jealousies, and tantrums (at one point Gagliardi threatened to kill Butti) did make Meigs have second thoughts about his decision.

In another letter, Meigs described architect Thomas Walter's final design and dimensions for a new-enlarged Capitol dome. He commented, that he and Thomas Walter agreed the dome should be crowned with an appropriate work of art. Crawford, of course, took this as a request for another sculpture proposal. Wasting no time, he made a clay model for the top of the dome.

෴

Included with photographs of Crawford's first door sent to Meigs were photographs of this clay model called *Freedom Triumphant in War and Peace*. On July 12, 1855, Meigs wrote in his journal:

> I received today from Mr. Crawford a very grace-ful and beautiful design for the statue and crown on the top of the dome of the Capitol. It is a figure of Freedom, triumphant in peace and war, a draped figure of a female. The height being 15 feet, it will be a large statue, to be executed in bronze. He says nothing of the price, except that if his design is approved, we can then enter into particulars. I think I must be able to get the Secretary to approve and adopt this design. Mr Walter is making a copy of the upper part of the lantern of the dome to the same scale as the photograph in order to see how they fit.[56]

Meigs took the photographs to Secretary Davis who after looking at them, said, "I like the door. You said there would be two?"

"Yes, he has agreed to do two, and the panels on the second will continue the story of the American Revolution. I recently saw a plaster reproduction of the famous Ghiberti door in Philadelphia and think ours will be better," said Meigs.

"That's quite a statement. Do you really believe that?"

"I do. Crawford is a genius. People wonder why no one else is getting sculpture commissions. The reason is simple. I've only seen work of his quality by one other American sculptor who I am considering for another door."

"Who is that?"

"Randolph Rogers. I am waiting for his design. This should be an interior door; the other two are for the exterior entrances to the Senate and House."

"Good, an American sculptor. I am getting all sorts of pressure from members of congress to give a commission to their favorite sculptor. The supporters of Hiram Powers continue their crusade to include his work. How much does Crawford want for each door?"

"Six thousand dollars for each," said Meigs.

"Where will they be cast?"

"He wants them cast in Munich, but I think only one should be done there and the other here in America."

"I agree, and if you think it can be done, have them both cast here. The more work we have done here, the quieter our lives will be. Members of Congress are constantly promoting companies from their states or districts. Sometimes I think it would have been better to have all the construction workshops set up away from the Capitol. That way they would not always see and hear all the Italian workers we are employing. Do you think the price is fair?"

"I do. There is one other set of photographs Crawford sent. In a letter I described Thomas Walter's new dome for the Capitol, and he made a model of a figure to crown it," said Meigs.

Secretary Davis, looking at Crawford's model, said, "I did not know there was to be a sculpture on the dome."

"I think it would be a striking addition, particularly at that height. It could be seen from anywhere in the city," answered Meigs. "Walter has seen it and made a sketch to scale with the figure on the dome. I sent the sketch to Crawford."

"It's an interesting figure, but it seems a little weak to me. The shield is too small to protect anything," said Davis. "I do not like the olive branch in the other arm."

"I will let him know. The design may change when he sees the actual dimensions of the dome and Walter's sketch," answered Meigs

When Crawford received the sketch made by Thomas Walter, he showed it to Louisa and said, "I want this commission. What a great place for one of my works. When Meigs told me about the new dome, I took a chance and sent a photograph of this model. I think they like the idea. Now it looks too small for the size of the dome. What do you think?"

"It does look small. I think she could be bolder and stronger. As she is now, she looks defenseless."

"I think you're right. I'm going to make another model and get it back to him quickly. If others hear of another Capitol commission, they will flood Meigs office with their offers."

Within a month, Crawford completed another model with a sword in the right hand and a larger shield in the left. Crawford studied the dome of Saint Peter's in Rome to get a better perspective of how his figure might look on the smaller Capitol dome and enlarged his figure to eighteen-feet-five-inches. When Meigs saw the new photographs he entered the following comment in his journal dated November 16, 1855:

> I also received today a design from Mr. Crawford. He has revised his first design since I sent him a tracing of the dome and has made a light and beautiful figure of Liberty upon a pedestal, separated by fasces and [laurel?] wreaths. The figure is lightly draped. It has upon it the inevitable liberty cap, to which Mr Davis will, I do not doubt, object.[57]

He sent the photographs to Secretary Davis January 11, 1856, and told him Crawford asked $3000 for the plaster figure and globe. Secretary Davis replied to Meigs on January 15,1856:

> Sir: The second photograph of the statue with which it is proposed to crown the Dome of the Capitol impresses me most favorably. Its general grace and power, striking at first view, has grown on me as I studied the details.
>
> As to the Cap, I can only say, without intending to press the objection previously made, that it seems its

history renders it inappropriate to a people who were born free and would not be enslaved.

The language of art, like all living tongues, is subject to change; thus the bundle of rods if no longer employed to suggest the function of Roman Lictor, may lose the symbolic character derived therefrom, and be confined to the single signification drawn its other source, the fable teaching the instructive lesson that in Union there is strength. But the Liberty Cap has an established origin in its use, as the badge of the freed slave; and though it should have another emblematic meaning today, a recurrence to that origin may give to it in the future the same popular acceptance which it had in the past.

Why should not armed Liberty wear a helmet? Her conflict being over, her cause triumphant, as shown by the other emblems of the statue, the visor would be so as to permit, in the photograph, the display of a circle of stars, expressive of endless existence, and of a heavenly birth.

With these remarks I leave the matter to the judgement of Mr. Crawford, and I need hardly say to you, who knowing my high appreciation of him, that I certainly would not venture, on a question of art, to array my opinion against his.[58]

Meigs wrote Crawford of the Secretary's approval as well as his concerns. When Crawford received the letter from Meigs telling him Secretary Davis approved Armed Liberty with reservations regarding the liberty cap, he immediately changed the liberty cap. He even followed Davis' preference for a helmet with stars and decorated it with an eagle's head and feathers. Their support and patronage could not be risked.

On May 1, 1856, Meigs entered the following in his Journal:

I wrote today to Crawford to tell him that the Secretary was pleased with his design for the dome

figure as revised and to ask him to send me a sketch for
the other pediment.[59]

∽

The slavery issue still dominated the agenda of Congress. In March, 1856,
Senator Stephan Douglas, a major power in the chamber, took the floor to
discuss the status of the territory of Kansas. Settlers from both the north and
south, hoping to begin a new life on their own land in the territory, found
themselves in the middle of an ideologic battle between slave owners and abolitionists.

Those favoring the entry of Kansas to the Union as a slave state, sent
activists from Missouri to promote their cause. The New England abolitionists formed the New England Emigrant Aid Company and sent settlers
to reinforce their cause. Violent confrontations broke out between the two
groups.

Senator Douglas continued his support of the southern slave states, but
Senator Seward of New York surprised Douglas by moving to have the Kansas
territory admitted as a 'free' state. The lengthy discussion of the motion led to
increasingly bitter feelings between the two sides.

Senator Butler of South Carolina, an outspoken enemy of Sumner, did
all he could to denounce and embarrass him after his first major speech against
slavery in 1852 (*Freedom National; Slavery Sectional*). This only reinforced Sumner's
determination to oppose slavery in any existing state, new state, or territory. The
debate lasted for months.

During the early debate Sumner never rose to speak but drafted a rebuttal
to the slave state's opposition to Seward's motion. On May 19, 1856, Sumner,
feeling the time right, demanded the floor and began the speech he called *The
Crime Against Kansas*. There had been rumors Sumner was preparing to speak,
and when he rose, word spread throughout the Capitol, and the gallery quickly
filled to overflowing. With the confidence, passion, and the self-importance of
an erudite scholar he began:

> Mr President,
>   You are now called to redress a transgression. Sel-
> dom in the history of nations has such a question been
> presented.....

It is the rape of a virgin Territory, compelling it to the hateful embrace of Slavery; it may be clearly traced to a depraved longing for a new slave state, the hideous offspring of such a crime, in the hope of adding to the power of Slavery in the National Government........[60]

Sumner then proceeded to attack Douglas and Senator Butler of South Carolina:

But before entering the argument, I must say something of a general character, particularly in response to what has fallen from senators who have raised themselves to eminence on this floor in championship of human wrongs; I mean the senator from South Carolina [Mr. Butler], and the senator from Illinois [Mr. Douglas], who, though unlike Don Quixote and Sancho Panza, yet, like this couple, sally forth together in the same adventure..... the senator from South Carolina has read many books of chivalry, and believes himself a chivalrous knight, with sentiments of honor and courage. Of course he has chosen a mistress to whom he has made his vows, and who, though ugly to others, is always lovely to him; though polluted in sight of the world, is chaste in his sight; - I mean the harlot Slavery....... If the slave States cannot enjoy what, in the mockery of the great fathers of the Republic, he misnames equality under the constitution, - in other words the full power in the National Territories to compel fellow men to unpaid toil, to separate husband and wife, and to sell little children at the auction-block, - then, sir, the chivalric senator will conduct the State of South Carolina out of the Union! Heroic Knight! Exalted senator! A second Moses come for a second exodus! [61]

Sumner continued for the remainder of the afternoon until the Senate adjourned for the day. No one talked to Sumner as he gathered his papers, and

all avoided him in the halls of the Capitol as he left. The next morning, when he
concluded his three-hour scathing attack on slavery and the slave states, instead
of shouts of support or anger from the gallery an ominous silence fell over the
chamber. The senators, eyes downcast, sat at their desks dumbfounded by what
they had just heard.

Senator James M. Mason of Virginia asked to speak in reply and said:

> I am constrained to hear depravity, vice in its
> most odious form uncoiled in this presence, exhibit-
> ing its loathsome deformities in accusation and vilifi-
> cation against the quarter of the country from which
> I come.....because it is necessary in my position, under
> a common Government, to recognize as an equal,
> politically, one whom to see elsewhere is to shun and
> despise.[62]

A furious Senator Douglas, shouting, called Sumner's speech, "the most
un-American and unpatriotic that ever grated on the ears of the members of
this high body."[63] Senator Butler had not been present either day. When the
Senate adjourned, two of Sumner's colleagues, afraid he might be attacked, suggested they escort him home. Sumner refused their help.

Two days later, as Sumner worked at his senate desk, Representatives Preston Brooks and Laurence M. Keitt of South Carolina entered the chamber and
approached Sumner. Brooks carried a cane with a large metal top. When Brooks
reached Sumner he announced, "Mr. Sumner, I have read your speech twice over
carefully. It is a libel on South Carolina, and Mr. Butler, who is a relative of
mine."[64] With that, in a ferocious rage, he began beating Sumner with his cane.
His rapid, well-placed blows gave Sumner little chance to defend himself as he
was beaten to the floor.

The few senators present rushed to help Sumner, but they were threatened by Keitt who also had a cane and some claimed a pistol. As blood gushed
from Sumner's head, covered the floor, and spattered empty desks, he lapsed
into unconsciousness. Brooks delivered more blows to the fallen Sumner and
stopped only when the shaft of his cane shattered. Brooks and Keitt turned,
gave no indication of regret for what happened to those who watched in horror,
and walked away.

As the news of the beating reached the cities in the south and north, interpretations of the event were partisan. An editorial in the Richmond Enquirer read, "Our approbation is entire and unreserved. We consider the act good in conception, better in execution, and best of all in consequences."[65] For blacks and abolitionists, the beating symbolized and dramatized the evil of slavery on democracy's foremost stage.

The physical and emotional effects on Sumner lasted years. He did not return to the senate chamber for three years, but, even though absent for so long, was returned to the senate by Massachusetts. The abolitionists were not about to let the slave owners think they had been intimidated by the act.

A committee of the House of Representatives, voted to expel Brooks and censure Keitt. Brooks, who became a hero in his district and the south, was later reelected. A Federal court in Baltimore fined Brooks $300 for assault.

∽

In January, 1856, while working on a plaster figure for the Capitol pediment, Crawford struggled to focus on the surface. Thinking it just a mild case of whiteout, something which can occur when focusing for a long time on a brightly lit white surface, such as plaster or block of white marble, he thought little of it. When it bothered him again as he modeled in clay, he attributed it to long hours in the studio, eye strain or fatigue.

His work had gone well. The pediment figures were completed, their plaster casts would be shipped by the end of summer. The foundry in Munich had notified him the equestrian sculpture for Richmond was ready and wished to know when he planned to approve it.

It had been six years since Crawford and Louisa had been to America. She missed her family, and the children needed to spend some time in America. They spoke English with their parents, but their native language was definitely Italian. Crawford and Louisa decided she would leave three months before Crawford, giving him time to complete his work in Rome, stop in Munich to check the equestrian sculpture, and then follow them to America.

Crawford was also eager to find out more about Sumner. The news of his beating on the Senate floor had made the newspapers in Rome after Louisa left. Visitors to his studio brought more details, but Crawford wanted to see his friend and patron personally.

The week before Crawford left, he received the letter from Meigs with the final approval of *Armed Liberty* or *Freedom* and the pleasant surprise regarding the second pediment. He wondered what caused Meigs to change his mind. Previously, Meigs told him it would be a mistake to have the same sculptor do both pediments. Whatever the reason, he could make sketches while traveling and a clay model when he returned. While he was away, he would have his assistants begin the clay enlargement of *Freedom* to full size.

He looked forward to his visit to the foundry in Munich. Things always seemed to go well for him in that city. Miller and his workers cheered when he saw the equestrian sculpture for the first time. The surprise was a bit overwhelming, but he was pleased with the result of the casting. The surfaces had been worked beautifully. When they wrote him the horse would be cast in one piece, he feared the worst. Nothing that large had ever been cast in one piece. He spent the next fifteen minutes circling the piece.

"Well, are you satisfied?" asked the foundry director.

"Of course, you always do such good work. I am amazed the horse could be cast in one piece," said Crawford.

"We thought a long time about that, but there is so much symmetry in a horse it seemed possible to do one casting."

"How are we going to ship this?" asked Crawford.

"That may be difficult. Our measurements indicate the horse will require a shipping crate 22 x 16 x 8 feet. It may not be possible to get that large a crate below the deck of most ships. The crate for the figure of Washington is no problem."

"I know they shipped Greenough's *George Washington* from Italy on a U.S. Navy ship. Perhaps the Governor of Virginia can persuade the Navy to do it again. I will write the chairman of the committee and explain the problem to him."

∾

Crawford left for America July 2,1856. To escape the heat of Boston and, more likely, to be a part of the New England summer social scene, Louisa had taken the children to Newport, Rhode Island, where Crawford met them at the end of July.

Their reunion was a mixture of happiness and tears, most of which were Crawford's. Louisa said, "The children missed you, I missed you."

"I missed all of you, too," said Crawford.

"The children have been looking forward to this and have all sorts of things to show you. We can spend the rest of the summer here together."

"I would like that, but first, I must leave next week for Richmond to finalize the contract for the next four figures on the monument. On my way back, I plan to stop and see Meigs in Washington."

"None of this can wait until you are rested and spend more time with us?" asked Louisa.

"These two jobs are our livelihood for years to come."

"You will not see Sumner in Washington. Have you heard?"

"Yes, but tell me what you know," said Crawford.

"A Congressman from South Carolina beat him severely after he insulted its Senator and the state in a speech. He's recuperating in Boston, and they say he may not recover fully for a long time. Everyone here is talking about the attack and the increasing tension between the abolitionists and slave-holders."

"Well, that has always been Sumner's mission, to end slavery."

"Yes, but must violence be part of the solution?" said Louisa. "You will hear a different viewpoint in Richmond. They must not know how close you are to Sumner."

"I think they know, but we have an agreement and they are satisfied with my work. Don't worry, I do not plan to discuss the event there. Anyway, I think they consider me a Roman," said Crawford.

"Is there something wrong with your left eye? It looks different."

"I'm not sure, but I have been working hard and it could just be eye strain."

"Does it hurt?"

"No, but when I close the right eye and use just the left, I see less."

"What do you mean, less?" asked Louisa.

"My field of vision is smaller than the right."

"Have you seen a doctor?"

"No, I think it's something temporary. As I said, I have worked harder this past year than any other time in my life," said Crawford.

∽

When he reached Richmond, he found the sculptures of Jefferson and Patrick Henry on display on the steps of the Capitol. Satisfied they had survived the ocean crossing in good shape, he walked to the office of Conway Robinson.

When Robinson saw him, he reached out to embrace Crawford, "Welcome back to America. It has been six years since your last visit to our city."

"Too long a time," said Crawford. "Richmond looks bigger than I remember."

"It is growing fast; the entire country is growing fast. Immigrants are arriving every day from Europe. The word is out. America is the country of the future; the place with free land and where you can make your fortune. Unfortunately, that is not always true, but at least they have a chance."

"I saw the two sculptures. Anymore critics in the legislature?"

"No, that's over. Everyone likes them. The committee is ready to offer you a contract for the next four pieces. Are you ready to sign?"

"Of course. Thank you for all your assistance."

"Have you seen Sumner?" asked Robinson.

"Not yet, but hope to see him before I leave. Louisa told me how serious a beating he suffered."

"Yes, indeed, from all accounts it was brutal. His speech resurrected every animosity imbedded in the souls of both sides on the slavery issue. When or if this will end, I have no idea. Avoid any discussion of the incident here."

The four additional Virginians selected for the monument by the committee had changed. Chief Justice John Marshall, Thomas Nelson, George Mason (ancestor of Senator James M. Mason one of the Senators insulted by Sumner during his Crimes against Kansas speech) and General Andrew Lewis were the final choices of the committee. The contract Crawford signed stipulated $9,000 for each twelve-foot bronze figure.

When Crawford brought up the problem of shipping the equestrian group, the committee reminded him the contract specified it was his responsibility to deliver the piece to Richmond. They told him Governor Wise received the letter Crawford wrote from Munich and had written to the Secretary of the Navy who had not yet replied. They were planning a celebration of the dedication of the equestrian George Washington piece in 1858 on Washington's birthdate, February 22, and expected the sculpture to be in place then.

Crawford wondered if Meigs could use his influence to get a U.S. Navy ship to bring the crates to America. Washington would be his next stop.

&

Washington, like Richmond, looked bigger to Crawford as he passed through the city. It was August 5, and the heat and humidity made Crawford uncomfortable. The rapid growth and expansion had, however, left a chaotic mixture of buildings.

Approaching the Capitol, he saw stacks of building materials outside work sheds which surrounded the building. Workmen were everywhere. Scaffolding circled the empty space, previously occupied by the original dome, and the beginning of an ironwork superstructure circled the base of the new dome. The external walls of the two new extensions of the Capitol appeared complete. Everything Crawford saw confirmed his impression of Meigs who he knew only through correspondence. This was a man of action.

Ascending the steps of the east entry to the Capitol, Crawford stopped to look at Luigi Persico's *Discovery of America* and Horatio Greenough's *Rescue Group*, placed to the left and right respectively, on either side of the staircase. He preferred Geenough's work. Looking up, at the pediment above the massive columns at the top of the steps, he could only think his pediment over the new east Senate wing would look better and tell much more about the history and people of the country than Persico's *Genius of America*.

Crawford paused at the top of the steps and looked back. The construction activity all around him generated a sense of excitement. The pleasure he experienced creating his sculpture in the studio was one thing, but seeing this impressive structure, where it would be placed and viewed forever, that, he could only describe as exhilarating.

When he finally found Meigs' office he was not there. As he looked around, everything in it reflected the large scale project he witnessed outside. Stacks of architectural drawings covered a large table at one end of the room. Neatly piled correspondence filled another. The front of his standup desk contained multiple compartments stuffed with more papers.

⁊⁊

After about fifteen minutes, a large man with a narrow beard outlining his jaw from ear to chin, entered the room and said, "Good morning, were you waiting for me?"

Crawford, with a big smile, stepped forward, extended his hand and said, "Thomas Crawford. What a pleasure it is to finally meet you."

"Crawford, the pleasure is also mine. I was expecting you this week. Welcome to Washington. I think you said you were coming from Richmond?"

"Yes, I just arrived today."

"I hope everything went well there. All Virginia is waiting for your General Washington. Will it be coming soon?"

"There is no definite date. It is finished and on display in Munich, but shipping the oversized sculpture is a problem," said Crawford

"Please sit down, we have a lot to talk about. Is your wife with you? I hear so much about her. She has many friends."

"I know, more than I. No, she's in Newport with the children."

"Too bad. My wife wanted to meet her. How long are you staying?" asked Meigs.

"As long as it takes to finish our business. Before we go any further, I want to tell you it has been my distinct pleasure to work with you. I am grateful for your support and encouragement."

"Well, thank you. It has been a pleasure to work with you also. By the way, did you get my May letter about *Freedom*? Secretary Davis liked the changes you had made to the head dress."

"Yes, I did, just before I left. Thank you for the opportunity to design the other pediment. I have some ideas, and when I return to Rome it will be my first project. I consider it my highest priority," said Crawford.

"Remember, you have no guarantee of getting the project. You know I hesitated to give both pediments to you, but all the other designs submitted so far have not come close to equaling your first pediment design. It is still risky to award both pediments to one artist. My political critics are always watching and quick to criticize everything I do," said Meigs.

"I understand. It's better to be in Rome away from all of that. I had my fill of legislators in Richmond when they awarded me the commission. How are the carvers doing?"

"We can walk down there and you can see for yourself. They are a difficult bunch to handle. I call them my Italian prima donnas. Do you have the same trouble in your studio?"

"Yes, but multiple it by 40 or 50. At times, I employ eighty or ninety assistants. It is a price you pay for the best. They are always, as you say, prima donnas. I try to keep my foreman between me and the craftsmen," said Crawford.

"Unfortunately, I have no foreman to deal with this small group, and if I put one of them in charge all hell would break out," said Meigs. "I have learned to ignore their disagreements and slow work because in the end, the carving gets done and it is good. Let me show you some of the drawings of the new dome."

"Like it or not, I think they have made you a little bit Italian," said Crawford, laughing.

∽

For the next hour, Meigs showed Crawford Thomas Walter's drawings of the new dome. As he moved from drawings of underlying iron infrastructure to the finished surface, Crawford kept visualizing his sculpture on top of the dome. Nothing, he thought, would surpass seeing his work on this magnificent dome where it would be seen from every part of the city.

"How is the work coming on *Freedom*," asked Meigs.

"They are working on the clay enlargement in my studio now, and it should be finished when I return to Rome," said Crawford. "Then, after about six months molds will have been made and the plaster cast."

"The dome will not be finished for another four to five years, so there will be plenty of time to cast the bronze," replied Meigs. "I know you prefer the foundry in Munich, but we need to develop art foundries in America. I am trying to convince the owner of the Ames foundry in Chicopee, Massachusetts, to do one of your doors and *Freedom*. We have time to decide on a foundry, and I want to keep that decision open."

"Last time I was here, I visited the studio of a sculptor who said he would be casting his sculpture of Andrew Jackson. What happened to him and his foundry?" asked Crawford.

"You mean Clark Mills. He built a foundry on his farm about three miles away. They tell me he finished another bronze Jackson for New Orleans and is now casting an equestrian George Washington for this city."

"Has he asked to cast anything for the Capitol?"

"Clark Mills has many friends in this city who have approached me to give him work. Have you seen the Jackson across from the White House?"

"No, but I am going to walk over there when I leave here. I did not like the plaster when I saw it. The figure was awkward."

"You are not the only one who disliked the sculpture. The people like it; the art critics do not. After the initial emotional acceptance by the public passed, critics began to write negative reviews. Then, when he finished installing the Jackson, he worked hard convincing his friends in Congress and the city to give him the commission for a bronze Washington. I understand he is casting it now and is almost finished," said Meigs.

"So, you think he is too busy?" said Crawford

"I just do not think his work is as good as yours and the work of other sculptors. Everett, who recommended you, feels the same way. I have made it a point to avoid any connection with him or his friends. Some of them, I know, are my enemies. I have a small furnace for casting bronze on the grounds. The staff from the Naval Yard foundry helped me construct it. We use it for the small ornamental pieces designed by the architect, Thomas Walter."

"When I heard Congress awarded the George Washington commission to him, it came as a surprise and disappointment. I tried twice to interest some members of Congress in doing a Washington sculpture but hit a stone wall," said Crawford

"Everett told me it happened quickly. No one else was considered or even asked. Mills' timing and connections were excellent. Come, we can tour the Capitol and workshops," said Meigs.

❧

The perimeter of the Capitol included workshops for carpenters, stone masons, iron workers, bricklayers, blacksmiths, and, of course, marble carvers as well as others. When they reached the workshop of the carvers, Crawford saw all his plasters for the pediment had arrived.

The Rome assistant he had sent to Meigs, Tomasso Gagliardi, greeted him and introduced him to the other carvers, Vincenti and Butti. What Crawford saw pleased him. The marble Meigs found interested him. He took a chisel and, for a few minutes, worked on a block. It certainly was not as soft as the Italian marble he used, but it cut almost as easily. When he put the chisel down, he said, "It works fine. The slightly darker shade of white may bleach in the sun. It reminds me of a Greek marble I have seen. Where did you say it comes from?" asked Crawford.

"Lee, Massachusetts. I have heard no complaints from the carvers," answered Meigs.

"Si," said Gagliardi. "We are used to it now and like it."

"That makes me feel better," said Crawford. "I did not know what to think when you told me about this marble. Captain Meigs, your sculpture studio has passed my test."

"That's good to hear. After all, we organized it according to your directions," said Meigs.

When they finished the tour, Crawford asked Meigs if he knew anyone in the office of the Secretary of the Navy. Meigs asked why and Crawford told him of the difficulty in finding a ship to bring the enormous crate with the Richmond horse to America. Meigs agreed to take him to the Navy Secretary's office on the following day, but he could not guarantee success.

That afternoon, when they parted, Crawford felt even better about his patron, Captain Meigs. Just as in their correspondence, they understood each other perfectly, and he knew his work was in competent hands. When Meigs returned to his office, he made the following entry in his journal:

> ....Mr. Crawford seems to me a man of somewhat rough manners. He has a pleasantness which is honest, no doubt, but which looks like the effect of a rather rough early education. I have had it upon my tongue today to ask him several times from what state he came, but I was prevented by some turn in the conversation. He will be at the office again tomorrow, when I expect to go with him to see the Secretary of the Navy.[66]

ॐ

The next day, the Secretary of the Navy would not make a firm commitment to allow a government ship to transport Crawford's equestrian sculpture. Modifying the deck of a U.S. Navy ship to transport oversized crates containing a sculpture, would probably not escape the notice of Congressmen, who were always quick to complain of an unauthorized expense. He promised to continue considering the possibility, but his lack of enthusiasm for the project was apparent.

Meigs then took Crawford to the White House to meet the President. As they walked, Meigs said, "After his election, President Pierce decided to make completing the Capitol expansion a priority of his administration. When he changed the oversight to the War Department, the President and Secretary Davis agreed they wanted a Capitol which would compare to any Capitol in the world."

"The President, like Jefferson, must have an interest in art?" asked Crawford.

"No, not like Jefferson who collected books of engravings of art for his library. President Pierce gives final approval to the works we recommend and has seen all your proposals, but he depends on me and the Secretary to find the best artists. The architect, Thomas Walter, concentrates on the structural details. By default, the Secretary and I have assumed the responsibility for decorating the building."

The conversation puzzled Crawford. He had not met Walter, and such a meeting did not seem to be on Meigs' schedule. He knew there was a message Meigs was trying to convey, but since his dealings with Meigs had been successful, he decided not to probe the relationship between the two.

This would be the second meeting Crawford had with a President. His first, in Richmond, the pleasant dinner with President Zachery Taylor and the monument committee, went well. This meeting with President Pierce, lasted less than thirty minutes. The President, familiar with Crawford's work, praised his proposals and acknowledged having seen the completed carvings for the pediment.

The President spent most of the time discussing a proposal of Hiram Powers for his sculpture *America*. He questioned Meigs about the status of the negotiations with Powers, and told him to complete them. He was bored listening to the frequent inquiries from members of Congress about the proposal.

When they left the White House, Meigs said, "I must excuse myself now; I have to get back to my office. I suppose you are wondering what the problem is with the Powers' sculpture?"

"It sounds as though there are many supporters of his work in the Congress," said Crawford.

"Yes, there are. No one wants to believe he refused the offer to design a pediment. They think I am prejudiced in your favor when it comes to commissions. I am prepared to give him $20,000 for his sculpture, *America*, but you have met him and understand his personality. I'm waiting for his reply. If he turns down our offer, I do not know what to do next."

"He is strong willed. Good luck. We are meeting for dinner tonight at eight, right?" asked Crawford.

"Yes, I will see you then," said Meigs.

〜

That evening, Crawford asked Meigs, "Did you receive my proposal for the possible frieze around the Capitol rotunda?"

"Yes, and I still like the idea, but I have not decided whether to do it," answered Meigs.

'You estimated the dimensions as 300 feet by 6 feet. Since it would be indoors, I thought plaster would be the best medium."

"Yes, plaster would work. What price did you quote?"

"$50,000," said Crawford.

"Don't make a design or model yet; we may not make a decision for at least a year. That would be an ambitious project. I would think you have enough work for now."

"Thanks to you, Captain Meigs, my studio is now capable of producing just about anything. The assistants I have are the best in Rome, and I would like to keep them busy and not lose them to another studio. I wrote you about this before. I could do all the sculptural work for the Capitol faster and cheaper than anyone," said Crawford.

"At the moment, that's impossible. I surprised myself when I convinced Secretary Davis you should do another door and pediment. You know other American sculptors, some in Rome, are also asking me for a commission and each has a Congressional patron," said Meigs. With that, they parted.

Walking home, Meigs, looked back on the past two days with Crawford. He found him even more ambitious than the impression he conveyed in his letters, yet Meigs' opinion about Crawford's talent, remained unchanged.

Meigs' detractors in Congress had previously begun a campaign to end his control of the construction of the Capitol extension. On May 26, 1856, Congressman Ball of Ohio took the floor of the House of Representatives and made the following comments:

> Another item of these Capitol expenditures demands our particular attention. Are you gentlemen aware that this Government has become an extensive manufacturer of statuary? It is even so. Just around the corner may be found two shops filled with Italian and German sculptors busily engaged in manufacturing

statuary to be placed in the east pediment of the two
wings. This too is with no authority of law that I can
find unless under the general authority to construct
the two wings.

The statuary in question does not seem designed
to commemorate any historical events or person-
ages connected with this country. It seems to be a
mere amateur collection and deserves no place in the
national Capitol. The graven images have the likeness
to nothing in the Heaven above or earth beneath - I
beg pardon, however - one was pointed out to me as
the wife of one of the foreign workmen. Yes, Sir, we
are to have this copy of a living original to adorn our
Capitol.[67]

In July, Mr. Ball continued his attack on Meigs, and the House passed a
resolution requiring Meigs to submit detailed information on all the marble
work and sculpture for the Capitol and the Post Office Building, also under
Meigs' authority. Meigs supplied all the information requested by the House
committee.

August 7, two days after his meeting with Crawford, Congressman Ball
resumed his criticism of Meigs and attempted to remove him from his position by sponsoring a bill which would eliminate any military supervision over
Capitol projects. The assault continued over the next week and finally ended, for
the time being, when Meigs' allies in the Senate gave him three separate votes
of confidence.[68]

Part VI

Unforeseen Circumstances

The excitement of meeting Meigs, and all the construction activity at the Capitol, temporarily distracted Crawford from the trouble with his left eye. Staring out the window at the passing landscape as he traveled on the train to New York, he again noticed subtle changes in his vision. When he closed the right eye, what he saw in the left had an irregular outline along one edge, and the same margin appeared blurred.

The only other time his health prevented him from working was his bout with malaria in Rome years ago. That was now a distant memory, and it had left as quickly as it came. Surely, this too would pass.

In New York, he visited his mother and sister Jenny. She never had been to Rome or even out of New York. He missed her. She had recognized his talent before anyone, and he remained grateful for her encouragement when his parents were unable to understand his interest in art. Now she wished to visit Rome and see all the sights described in his letters. It did not take much to convince her brother to take her back to Rome with him.

When he returned to Louisa in Newport, she wanted to know everything about Washington and Meigs. "What kind of man is he?" she asked.

"He's just as I thought, strong, intelligent, and organized. The construction at the Capitol and the new Post Office Building are completely under his control. No detail seems to escape him. Not many men could accomplish what he has in such a short time."

"Did you find out where Sumner is?"

"Yes, they told me he is recuperating at a clinic in the mountains of Pennsylvania. No one knew how long he will be there. Apparently, the injuries were quite serious. They say he is not the same man."

"The children miss you. They liked it when you were with them every evening at the Villa Negroni. Now they never know where you are and don't understand why you have to be away all the time," said Louisa.

"I miss them just as much."

"I do have some good news," said Louisa

"Tell me, what?"

"George Greene will be here this weekend."

"Wonderful. I stopped in Boston for two days and saw Longfellow. George will be interested in our conversation."

"Are you certain nothing is wrong with your eye," asked Louisa as she looked closely at the left eye. "Does it hurt?"

"You are the only one who mentions it. No, it does not hurt. Quit worrying, it will be all right," said Crawford.

⁏

It had been six years since Crawford had seen George Greene. When Greene arrived, their conversation immediately turned to the plight of their mutual friend, Sumner. Crawford said, "It is still not clear to me exactly what happened to Charles. Why did this man beat him, and why, in the Senate chamber. Did no one come to his defense?"

"Two days before the beating, Sumner delivered a scathing attack on the slave states, and singled out South Carolina and its Senator, Andrew Butler. His cousin, Preston Brooks, a Congressman from South Carolina, decided to defend the honor of the Senator, his state, and all the slave states. Why no one came to Sumner's defense is not clear. Eyewitness accounts of the incident vary. We shall probably never know the answer."

"I'm an artist, and politics is a puzzle to me. Have there been other violent incidents like this?"

"I can understand your confusion. Politics generally implies compromise. You and I know Sumner. When it comes to slavery there is no place for compromise. For him, it is immoral, period. This was well-known in the Senate where they prevented him from taking the floor to discuss slavery several times."

"He must have made some really offensive comments to cause such a response."

"I have read the speech and he did, but I'm certain he would never take them back. Should he have personally insulted Senator Butler? Perhaps not, but with the expansion of our country, the slavery issue must be faced. Should we have a country with both free states and slave states? That's where we are in our history, but that does not justify the beating."

"Will Sumner return to the Senate?"

"My guess would be yes. Since the attack, Sumner has become somewhat of a folk hero. When he will return is another question. You and I know him well enough to remember how he handles illness. He does have a tendency to be a bit of a hypochondriac, but I do not wish to diminish the seriousness of the attack. He was beaten senseless," said Greene.

"I wish I could see him before I return to Rome, but from your description of the beating, I doubt I will," said Crawford.

"You just got here and already you are on your way back?"

"I have to leave in two days. There is too much work waiting for my review and completion as well as new work to begin."

❦

As planned, Louisa and the children were not to return to Rome until the spring of 1857. The day Crawford left in September, 1856, Louisa pleaded, "Please stop in Boston and have a physician look at that eye. There are excellent physicians in Boston."

"If it continues to bother me, I will have it checked when I get to Rome. Stop worrying," said Crawford.

"But that may be another month."

"I think it will clear on its own. Nature has a way of healing most ills. I have been sick before and survived. This should be no different."

"You are stubborn. Write me every day. Spring seems a long way off. We will miss you," said Louisa.

"You and the children need this time with your American family and friends. It may be another five or six years before we return again. Jenny will take good care of me until you return," said Crawford.

Before leaving New York, Crawford gathered images of the four distinguished Virginians to be added to the Richmond monument and even met with Senator James M. Mason, one of the Senators Sumner had personally attacked in his recent, fateful speech. Senator Mason's ancestor, George Mason, was one of the distinguished Virginians to be sculpted.

Crawford sailed from New York, September, 1856. The long, boring days at sea left him with time to think. Denial was no longer an option; he could not see well with his left eye. This prevented him from working on the sketches he planned to make during the trip. The ideas for his many commissions, exciting and clear in his mind, would have to wait. When they reached London, he would ask friends to recommend a physician.

∾

The oculist in London, after examining the eye, suspected the most likely diagnosis was a growth or tumor in the back of the eye. Since Crawford said he would be stopping in Paris, rather than expressing his serious concern outright, the physician suggested he see a famous oculist there, Dr. Louis-August Desmarres.

The London physician did not give him a final diagnosis, but his carefully chosen words, as well as what he did not say after the examination, alarmed Crawford. Fortunately Jenny was traveling with him. The uncomfortable feeling caused by vision changes in the eye, and the uncertainty about the future of his work left him depressed and moody. With Louisa back in America, Jenny's support would be essential.

Dr. Desmarres was, indeed, a famous oculist. He had written the foremost book on diseases and surgery of the eye, invented specialized surgical instruments, and trained many oculists throughout Europe. Crawford, tormented by the uncertainty of his future vision, needed an answer. His first stop in Paris would be the famous oculist.

Dr. Desmarres' office looked more like an artist's studio than a physician's examining room with north light from a large skylight illuminating the room. Instead of paints and canvases scattered about the room, there were piles of books, papers, and cabinets filled with oddly shaped surgical tools. Dr. Desmarres, a serious and softspoken man about the same age as Crawford, asked many questions before he began examining the right eye first. After spending more time than Crawford thought necessary for the unaffected eye, Dr. Desmarres stood back to look at the left eye. "When did you first realize this eye was being pushed forward?" asked the doctor.

"I noticed a difference between the two eyes about two months ago," answered Crawford.

"Now you must be very still and focus on one spot over my shoulder. I am going to use some magnifying lenses to look closer at the eye and into it if I can," said Dr. Desmarres and placed a tall stool in front of Crawford.

Dr. Desmarres, examined the eye from every possible angle for at least twenty minutes. Then he asked, "What type of work do you do?"

"I'm an artist. A sculptor," replied Crawford.

Dr. Desmarres, still seated, remained silent for at least a minute. Crawford felt the long pause which followed, could only mean bad news.

Finally, Dr. Desmarres said, "Have you ever had a piece of stone injure your eye as you carved?"

"No, never."

"Mr Crawford, there is something in the back of your eye. I am not 100 percent certain, but almost certain it is a growth, or what is also called a tumor. Some use the term melanosis of the eye."[69]

"Can it be removed," asked Crawford.

"It can, but only by removing the eye."

So many things suddenly went though Crawford's mind; he could not speak or fully comprehend what he had just heard. What about his work, family - what, what, what? Composing himself after a few minutes, he asked, "Can't you just remove this, whatever you call it, tumor? Is this the only alternative, assuming your diagnosis is correct?"

The experienced Dr. Desmarres waited before he replied, "I'm afraid not, the entire eye must be removed. I have seen many cases of this disease. But, I must warn you, extirpation, or removal of the eye, is a dangerous procedure with a high mortality rate."

"But I'm a sculptor. How can I work with one eye? Will the tumor grow in the other eye?"

"No, it should not affect in the other eye. You would have normal vision in the other. Your depth perception would be altered."

"Altered, what do you mean?"

"Your ability to judge the distance between objects would not be as good," said Dr. Desmarres.

"That's what a sculptor does, three-dimensional perspective is essential."

"I'm sorry, but that is my opinion. I wish it was better news."

"This is overwhelming. Are you certain?"

"You may wish to have someone else give you an opinion. I'll give you some drops which may ease your discomfort," said Dr. Desmarres.

"I will have to think about this before making any decision about surgery," said a shaken Crawford.

∽

Crawford had not told Jenny he visited an oculist, nor did he discuss what now preoccupied him. She thought he may have received some bad news about a commission. What else could explain his obvious bad mood?

They reached Rome the second week of October. As the carriage approached Villa Negroni, Crawford remembered it was the same time of year he came to Rome for the first time twenty-one years ago - the sky then, as now, was a clear and beautiful blue. Rome had not changed a bit, but his circumstances, compared to then, were so dissimilar. He loved this city and his home.

Jenny looked about in awe as they entered the grounds of the villa with its well-tended gardens and trees. The villa, larger than the impression she had from her brother's letters, seemed to bask in the late afternoon sunlight, which accentuated its grandeur. Her brother, never hesitant to promote himself, had surprised her this time. Certainly, anyone who lived in a villa this size must not be just good, but one of the best.

They were greeted with hugs and kisses by two pleasantly surprised servants, Teresa and Giusepe, a familiarity to which Jenny was not yet accustomed. The sincerity and warmth of this reunion touched Jenny. She was awestruck by the high elaborately decorated ceiling and the floor with its intricate pattern of different colored marble.

Leaving Teresa to show Jenny around the many rooms of the villa, Crawford headed for his studio. The workday was over, and all the assistants were gone. The peaceful studio was a welcome refuge for the bewildered Crawford. He just sat for a while and stared at the marble dust he had disturbed, now suspended in the late afternoon sun coming through the windows. This along with the familiar smells was his welcome home.

When he saw *Freedom*, which had been enlarged in clay to full size while he was gone, he smiled broadly. It was more than he had hoped for. More than three times his height, it overwhelmed him. The majesty and strength he wished to portray were unveiled by the size. All Crawford needed to do was go over the surfaces and make his final changes.

Moving further into the studio, he came to the panels of the first door. When he left for America, he had only done the rough clay sketches. They also were completed, and only his finishing touches would be required before they would be assembled to begin the outer, or framing, areas of the door. Once this was done, a final plaster could be made for the foundry.

The full size plaster casts of *History and Justice* sat in the center of the next area. Crawford wanted this work to be carved in Italian marble in his studio. He decided he would somehow persuade Meigs to have at least one of his works carved in Rome under his supervision.

Seeing all his work temporarily made him forget his eye, but when he sat down to admire it and all the progress made in his absence, the diagnosis and treatment suggested by Dr. Desmarres came back to haunt him. The doctor admitted he could not be 100 percent certain. Even a famous oculist could be wrong. As far as Crawford was concerned, only death would be worse than losing an eye.

෦෧

The next day Crawford returned to the studio and worked on *Freedom*. He struggled. Gustav Kaupert, his German chief assistant, detected a change. A few days later, the assistants could not help notice how slow and deliberate the maestro handled his tools and became easily irritated and impatient. Crawford, out of respect for his assistants and to maintain their respect for him and his work, had always kept what he considered a 'professional' distance from the others in the studio. Now, no one attempted to ask if he did not feel well or if something bothered him.

Jenny managed the household and tried her best to make her brother comfortable, but the change in the left eye soon became apparent to her. Noticing how he covered the eye when he wrote to Louisa, she finally found the courage to ask, "Thomas, what is wrong with your eye? I notice how you cover it when you write."

"Something is irritating it, I'm not sure what, but it should get better. An oculist in Paris gave me drops which help," answered Crawford.

"Have you seen a physician in Rome?"

"No, but I have used Dr. Smyth in the past and may go to see him."

"Soon I hope," said Jenny.

Crawford did visit Dr. Smyth who gave him more drops which provided him some comfort, but he admitted his limited knowledge of diseases of the eye and could offer no specific diagnosis or treatment. However, Smyth had heard a famous American surgeon was in town and suggested he might be of help.

In December, the touring physician, Dr. William Gibson from Philadelphia, agreed to examine the eye. Jenny arranged a table for the examination beside a window with the best light. After Crawford gave the physician a tour of his studio, Dr. Gibson, elderly, distinguished looking, and recently retired from the University of Pennsylvania as Professor Emeritus, was shown the area where he could perform his examination. Satisfied with the light, he began by asking Crawford, "Who examined your eye in Paris?"

"Dr. Desmarres, a famous oculist recommended to me by an oculist in London," said Crawford.

"And what was his diagnosis?"

Because Jenny was in the room, Crawford hesitated, but then he decided she might as well begin to understand the seriousness of his problem. Crawford began, "He felt there was what he called a possible tumor in the back of the eye." He saw Jenny cover her mouth to suppress a gasp. Not sure what a tumor meant, it nevertheless sounded serious to her.

"I see. Did he say anything more?" asked Dr. Gibson.

"He used a word I never heard before. I think he called it 'melanosis'."

"Interesting. Experts are not always right. Patients have come to me with diagnoses of other physicians which make no sense after I examine them. I understand he is a famous oculist, but sometimes the famous are looking for the unusual and because of that miss some of the more common problems."

"Well, I hope you have better news for me."

"What did he suggest for treatment?"

Crawford again looked toward Jenny and said softly, almost under his breath,

"Removal of the eye." He saw Jenny steady herself on a chair. He thought she was about to faint.

"I am not an oculist, but after 25 years of practice, I have seen just about everything." He then began to palpate the right and then the left eye. The pressure on the left eye did cause Crawford mild pain, but he gave no sign that the examination hurt.

"I have seen what we call 'cysts' or tiny bags filled with fluid around the eye, which can become large enough to push the eyeball one way or another and distort the vision. I would like to probe the area, and if there is a cyst, the fluid will drain out and relieve the pressure on the eyeball. Sometimes the solution can be quite simple," said Dr. Gibson.

Crawford, impressed by the man's confidence and desperate to try anything rather than lose the eye, consented.

❧

Dr. Gibson asked for some towels and a basin of water. Taking a small case from his pocket, he opened it and placed it on the table. In it were long needles of varying diameter. Crawford looked at the miniature tool chest filled with needles with some apprehension, but he was committed to the exam.

"This looks more painful than it will be. I move quickly, but gently. When I touch whatever is changing your eye and eyesight, I will make one last, quick thrust to enter the lesion"

Now Crawford knew Jenny was about to faint. He asked her if she wished to leave and if not, at least be seated. She chose to sit down and stay with her brother.

Dr. Gibson asked Crawford to close his eye. He then inserted his needle through the top of the upper eyelid and guided it along the surface of the bone of the roof or top of the orbit, never touching or puncturing the eyeball, but moving toward the area behind it. He moved quickly, but then he stopped abruptly, paused only a second, and just as quickly withdrew the needle. The expression on his face, which he tried to hide by turning away, was surprise. The entire procedure lasted less than ten-seconds, but to Crawford it seemed like minutes.[70]

The glimpse Crawford caught of Dr. Gibson's surprised expression told him Dr. Desmarres was right. There was no cyst. It was a tumor. He felt as though his entire being fell off a cliff into a bottomless black hole. He had never felt so helpless in his life.

Dr. Gibson applied some pressure to the area of the puncture to control the small amount of bleeding from the eyelid. He did not look at his patient and seemed to be searching for words.

Crawford broke the silence, for confirmation of what he already knew, "Did you find a cyst?"

"No, there was no cyst," replied Dr. Gibson.

"What do you think? Is Dr. Desmarres right?"

"I cannot answer that question with any confidence. I have never encountered a case such as this before," said Dr. Gibson, obviously uncomfortable.

The more Crawford questioned the doctor, the less clear his answers became. Crawford decided the doctor was either genuinely puzzled by what he found, or for some reason he could not bring himself to give him the worst possible news. He concluded, it was a combination of both.

Jenny and the servant Giusepe, helped Crawford to his bed where he fell into a deep sleep until the next morning.

Dr. Gibson's needle had found a solid mass in the back of the eye which frightened him. He realized this reinforced Dr. Desmarre's diagnosis of a tumor, but he did not have the extensive experience of the Parisian oculist and decided it best to say no more. However, he became more articulate with his American friends in Rome. With them, he did not hesitate to hint Crawford had a malignant condition and doubted he would survive more than a year.

In his letters, Crawford did not tell Louisa what the two doctors had found. The devastating gossip about Crawford's condition eventually worked its way from Rome to Louisa in America

~

The less time Crawford spent in his studio, the more his assistants wondered when or if he would return to work. This artist, the man who could change clay into something beautiful in minutes, no longer sketched new projects. His brief time in the studio was spent reviewing what had already been started. In the past, he always worked on new ideas, but now there were none coming from the hands of the maestro with the bad eye. The future of Rome's busiest and largest sculpture studio did not look promising, and most of the assistants were concerned about their jobs.

Villa Negroni no longer hosted parties and dinners for the American artists in Rome, further amplifying the gossip about Crawford's eye. His sister, Jenny, now wrote his letters, read to him in the evenings and at his request, politely told those who came to visit, he was receiving no visitors.

Meanwhile, Louisa was uncertain what to believe about Crawford's eye and decided to return to Rome, but without the children, who could come in spring when crossing the Atlantic would be safer. At the same time, Crawford, certain his eye was getting worse, planned to return to Paris for additional treatment.

Luther Terry, an American painter, and good friend of the Crawford's, persuaded Crawford he should accompany him to Paris. Jenny would stay in Rome. Terry knew Crawford required more assistance than he would admit for a long trip to Paris. Giuseppe would also make the trip.

On the train in France, Crawford suddenly began to shake mildly, and then his uncovered right eye rolled upward and he became unresponsive. The shaking did not last long, but frightened Terry and Giuseppe who did not know what to do except to make him comfortable.

Crawford remained unresponsive for at least twenty minutes. When he finally showed signs of regaining consciousness, he was confused. When his confusion persisted they left the train at Dijon and took him to the closest hotel.[71]

A local doctor contacted by the hotel, listened to their story and told them it sounded like a seizure. He said confusion and amnesia were common after a seizure, and the symptoms should disappear in about twenty-four hours. When he uncovered Crawford's eye, unnerved by what he saw, he suggested they continue the next day to Paris to have the eye treated.

The next morning Crawford was better but still slightly confused and insisted they continue on to Paris. In Paris Terry immediately took Crawford to see Dr. Desmarres who on seeing the eye asked, "Mr. Crawford, has anything been done to your eye? This redness and swelling are not typical of my original diagnosis of a tumor in the back of the eye."

"A doctor in Rome did explore the eye with a needle," answered Crawford.

"How long ago did he do this?"

"About two months ago."

"Have you noticed any other changes? Is your appetite the same? Do you have any trouble walking? Is anything different since you saw me last?"

"On the train here, they tell me I may have had a seizure. I can't remember, but they said I was shaking and lost consciousness. Is your diagnosis still the same?"

"Yes. It does sound like you had a seizure. Are you having pain?"

"Yes, for the first time. Can you give me something to stop the pain, so I can get some rest?"

"I can give you an opiate. That should relieve the pain."

Crawford, beginning to accept the fact his eye would not get better, asked, "I am at wit's end. I would even let you remove the eye. Anything to let me get back to work."

"That would be impossible now. The tumor is larger than before," said Dr. Desmarres.

Terry took Crawford to see three more oculists in Paris, but none would offer any chance of recovery. Any hope Crawford had for recovering vision in his eye vanished, and for the first time, he began to accept the reality of his predicament.

∿

Louisa reached Paris in mid February, 1857. When she found where her husband was staying, Luther Terry was reading in the room outside Crawford's bedroom. He told her Crawford had just taken a sedative, and it might not be possible to awaken him for several hours. Glad to see a friend after her long, difficult trip, she told Terry there were so many different reports about Crawford's condition, she did not know what to believe.

Terry, reluctant to be the one who delivered the grim news, said, "He is in some pain. The opiates sometimes leave him confused. So be patient with him."

"No one told me about the pain. I did not know he was suffering. How long has this been going on?" asked Louisa.

"It began in December, it was mild in the beginning, but I think he kept it to himself most of the time. When it bothered him throughout the day, he decided to come to Paris to see the best oculists."

"I was told Dr. Gibson operated on him in December. Is that true?"

"He did."

"What did he do with this operation?"

"I was not there, but Crawford told me it had something to do with a needle. He called it an exploration."

"Dr. Gibson never wrote to me, but he obviously informed others about my husband's condition. I am still upset about that and with Dr. Gibson. Everybody in Rome knew more than I did," said an angry Louisa.

"I am surprised he did not write to you."

"So am I. I will not forget it. What have the doctors here in Paris had to say?"

"I did not stay in the room during Crawford' different examinations, so you will have to let him tell you what they found."

"I heard something about a tumor. Is that true?"

"He can tell you what they found when he awakes."

"Luther, you are an old and dear friend. I can tell you are uncomfortable discussing this, which means the news can only be bad. I also need some sleep, but first I want to see him, even if he is asleep," said Louisa.

Louisa found Crawford sleeping deeply in the darkened room. She thought he looked thinner. She walked to the side of the bed, gave her husband a kiss on the right cheek, and paused a moment before she gently lifted the bandage covering the left eye. What she saw shocked her.

The eye, now protruded well beyond its socket. She gasped, then wept. He would never again see with that eye. What else did it mean? Terry helped her out of the room where she wept uncontrollably. She asked to be excused, went to her room, and, exhausted from the trip, cried herself to sleep.

∽

From this point forward, Crawford's condition only became worse. Whenever he felt comfortable enough, he brought Louisa up to date on the status of his unfinished works. They both decided Luther Terry should return to Rome immediately to take charge of the studio.

Word spread fast of Crawford's serious condition. One favor Crawford wished from Meigs was final approval to complete *History and Justice* in his Rome studio. Meigs granted him this favor. The director of the foundry in Munich realized there would be no American warship designated to bring the equestrian Washington to Richmond. He arranged for a Dutch company that was willing to modify the deck of one of their ships, to deliver the large crates. Louisa handled all these details and more.

Charles Sumner traveling in France in March, 1857, found the hotel where Louisa and Crawford were staying. Due to Crawford's serious condition and frailty, Louisa asked Sumner to spend only a few minutes with his talented friend. As he entered the room he found Crawford, dozing, his left eye covered with a bandage. Touching him, he said, "Thomas, it's Sumner. Louisa said I could spend a few minutes with you."

"Thank you for coming," answered Crawford. He could not see, and it took a moment for him to realize who his guest was. "How is the distinguished Senator? Have you fully recovered from the vicious attack in the Senate?" asked Crawford.

"I am well, thank you, but how are you?"

"Not well, as you can see. Charles, I think this is the end for me. None of the doctors give me any hope. I never gave any thought to dying. I loved my life, my work. I had so many more ideas and so many things to finish. That hurts more than the physical pain."

"I understand, but at the same time, I probably do not fully grasp the depth of your frustration. I saw George Greene and Henry Longfellow before I left America. They wanted me to be sure I saw you and let you know they are thinking of you."

"Such good friends. They helped me so much. Tell them I said thank you."

"Louisa and Luther Terry are working hard to keep the studio active," said Sumner.

"I will not finish my work, but you must finish yours. You have suffered physically and mentally for a just cause, the end of slavery. To stop now would be regrettable for you and your supporters. I never fully committed to the abolitionist movement, nor any movement. All I thought about was sculpture, and it served me well, but I know how you feel about slavery. Finish the job. Take advantage of your genius and position while you can. Then you will have no frustrations at the end."

"Thank you for your confidence in me."

"You were confident in me, something I never forgot," said Crawford.

Sumner could tell Crawford wanted to say no more. It was as though they silently consented to part, each knowing what they had to do, each accepting the past and future as part of one inscrutable design.

∾

The relentless progression of Crawford's illness took its toll on Louisa as she faced her husband's death. Her children would be fatherless. Their happy life in Rome would be over. She was angry.

As she thought about Crawford's eye and the events which brought him to this disastrous terminal illness, she could not understand the needle probing operation of Dr. Gibson. For her, after the needle exploration, Crawford's condition became worse. She believed a definite relationship existed between Dr. Gibson's operation and the rapid progress of whatever was destroying the eye.

In this state of mind, she wrote a letter to the Philadelphia Evening Bulletin, venting her frustration and anger with Dr. Gibson. For her, there had been no need to perform the exploration and because of it, her husband, the great American sculptor, was going blind and might die. They published the letter.[72]

When Dr. Gibson heard of this, he asked four famous oculists in Paris, including Dr. Desmarres, to give their opinions of the needle probing or exploration. All unanimously endorsed the practice as a way of confirming the diagnosis in a case such as Crawford's.[73] This, of course, would not change Louisa's mind.

Crawford's pain increased daily, and there were frequent seizures interspersed between periods of delirium. Friends of Louisa told her of an American physician, Dr. Fell, working in London and considered the best cancer surgeon in the city. None of the physicians in Paris had any new suggestions for treating the eye, so Louisa took Crawford to London in late April, 1857.

Dr. Fell told them if the tumor had not invaded the brain, removal of the eye with the tumor might cure him. Crawford and Louisa felt they had no other choice and agreed. He removed the eye the first week in May. The surgery relieved Crawford's pain and decreased his seizures, leaving him more comfortable, but Dr. Fell could not remove the tumor completely and no longer promised a cure.[74] As happens so often in such cases, the patient made a brief rally, but then, again became worse.

༄

Crawford and Louisa finally accepted the fact that he would not live much longer and began to make plans. Crawford had a will prepared. Louisa would have to supervise completion of the work for the Capitol and any other sculptures currently being carved in the studio. The advance from the Richmond monument committee for the additional figures for the monument would have to be adjusted. He wanted her to keep the studio open for tourists. They might be interested in marble copies of the many plasters accumulated over the years.

They did not return to Rome. Crawford died in London, October 10, 1857, at age 44, twenty-two years after coming to Rome.

A meeting of the artists in Rome, November, 1857 sent the following resolution to Louisa,

> *Resolved,* That we unite in expressing our heart-
> felt grief for the loss of our esteemed late associate,
> Thomas Crawford, our cherished and lasting regard

for his memory as a friend, our high estimation of his character as a man, and appreciation of his eminence as an artist...[75]

The following resolution was passed at a meeting of the National Academy of Design in New York:

> *Whereas,* We have received intelligence of the death of Thomas Crawford, a distinguished member of this body, whose brilliant genius has greatly contributed to elevate American sculpture to its present rank with the highest contemporary achievement, therefore -
>
> *Resolved,* that we mourn this afflicting event in profound sorrow, as the loss to the Academy of a much honored and beloved member, to our profession of one of its brightest ornaments, and to our country of an illustrious citizen.
>
> *Resolved,* that we will attend the funeral of our deceased friend, and wear the usual badge of mourning for thirty days, and that the artists generally of this city and vicinity be invited to unite with us in these marks of respect to his memory."[76]

The body arrived in New York in December. The funeral was held December 5, 1857, at St. John's Episcopal Church with the burial in Greenwood cemetery. The pallbearers included Charles Sumner and George Washington Greene.

৩

Before she returned to Rome, Louisa would represent her late husband at the dedication of the equestrian Washington in Richmond, February 22, 1858. The ceremony began in the morning and did not end until late that night. All the local and state politicians of Virginia attended, as well as governors of other states. The orations at the monument were delivered by Governor Henry Wise and Senator Robert M. T. Hunter. Along with their praise of Crawford's work, they touched upon the growing tension regarding the preservation of the Union over the issue of slavery.

In the evening, Edward Everett (who had recommended Crawford to Meigs) gave a speech in which he compared the work of Crawford to the work of the great Greek sculptor, Phidias. Everett also commented on the current fragility of the Union.[77]

After Richmond, Louisa stopped in Washington. On February 26, 1858,[78] at the home of mutual friends, she met Meigs who introduced himself, "I have heard so much about you." said Meigs. "It is my pleasure to finally meet you. I too have lost a friend. Your husband was a great artist."

"Thank you. He had the utmost respect for you and the job you are doing on the Capitol," said Louisa.

"The reviews of his sculptures for the Richmond monument have been excellent. I am glad they found a way to ship the horse from Munich. He was worried about that when we last met."

"You and I still have to work out details for finishing and shipping his work for the Capitol. When I return to Rome I can update you on the progress of his pieces for the Capitol. Luther Terry, Crawford's good friend and an artist, is supervising the work. He tells me it is going well, and the plaster of Freedom will be shipped in April," said Louisa.

"Crawford must have had a well-organized studio considering all the work he completed in such a short time. I am not concerned with the works he had begun and approved before his tragic illness. One piece does concern me, however: the second *American Revolution Door*, for the House of Representatives. My understanding is the modeling had not begun before Crawford ceased work. Only his drawings exist. We approved them, but other arrangements may have to be made for their completion."

"It would be important to his memory and to me to follow his plan," said Louisa.

"I have no intention of changing his story of the American Revolution depicted on the doors, but the drawings are quite rough. Anyone modeling them in clay would essentially be starting over."

"Let me ask for more information from Rome. I am certain they have begun modeling some of the panels," replied Louisa.

Louisa returned to her sister and the children in Newport, Rhode Island. Meigs' comments upset Louisa who felt the second door should be identified as her late husband's work. After receiving a photograph from Rome of a completed plaster panel based on one of Crawford's drawings for the second door, she wrote him from Newport, August 26, 1858:

...When I had the pleasure in Washington to speak with you on the subject you remarked, that were there no fuller sketches than those, you could not accept finished works made therefrom as Mr. Crawford's, that they would in such case be almost entirely re-creations. My best counsellors do not agree with you.

Looking on these originals, they find in them all the impress of genius, all the spirit that larger studies could possess, and deem them only wanting in detail of costume of likeness.[79]

Meigs' mind would not be changed.[80]

Part VII

ART AND POLITICS
DISSENSION

It had been six years since Clark Mills received the commission from Congress for the sculpture of *George Washington* (January, 1853). Since then, he had moved about three miles from the Capitol to the farm he bought on Bladensburg Road, which was also the site of his foundry. The contract specified completion of the sculpture in five years.

Business had been good. He continued to make life masks and busts, selling more than ten George Washington plaster busts cast from the mold he made at Mount Vernon from Houdon's original terra cotta. The second Andrew Jackson sculpture had been installed in New Orleans (he cast a third bronze for Nashville, Tennessee in 1885). In 1855, he patented a small, maquette-sized model of his Andrew Jackson for reproduction by another foundry, Cornelius and Baker, a manufacturer of lamps.

A wealthy man, he purchased more land and slaves. His first slave purchased in Charleston, South Carolina, Philip Reid, had become an important part of his foundry business. Reid participated in every casting done by Mills. He could bring the furnace to the proper temperature for melting the bronze, and Mills would not allow any pour to proceed without Reid either participating or supervising. Besides Reid, Mills owned five other adult slaves and their five children.

Congress became impatient and made Mills agree to complete the *George Washington* sculpture by July 4, 1859. He began the casting, and the dedication of the sculpture was planned for February 22, 1860. Deciding where to place the sculpture became a problem. Mills had one location in mind on Pennsylvania Avenue. Mills also had a more ambitious plan for the sculpture.

Reading the newspaper reports in 1858, of the dedication of the Richmond monument, he saw engravings of Crawford's *George Washington*, seated on its lofty pedestal. This made him think. His *George Washington* would be in the nation's Capitol, a far more prestigious location. It too, deserved a pedestal worthy of the work and Mills' reputation.

Mills designed a marble pedestal forty feet high. This pedestal would be divided into three sections with bronze reliefs depicting the story of America and Washington's victories at the different levels. He would not be outdone by another American sculptor, especially by one who lived in Rome. He began a campaign to have Congress appropriate additional funds for the pedestal.

Congress was in no mood to appropriate additional money for such an elaborate monument. They had contracted for an equestrian Washington, nothing more. The contract had stipulated the placement of the sculpture should be designated by the President. Since the contract had been drafted, Franklin Pierce had been succeeded by James Buchanan, elected President in 1857. Buchanan approved a site for the sculpture on Connecticut Avenue, and Congress approved funds for a pedestal the same size as Mills' Andrew Jackson.

■■

When President Buchanan took office, he appointed James B. Floyd, as Secretary of War to replace Jefferson Davis. Under President Pierce and Secretary Jefferson Davis, Meigs' authority over the construction of the Capitol never faltered in spite of his critics in Congress. His relations with the architect, Thomas Walter, were on less solid ground. As early as February 2, 1855, Meigs made this clear to Senator Pearce and entered the following in his journal:

> He [Senator Pearce] asked me, also, what were my relations with Walter to power. I told him that I had the power to dismiss him tomorrow if I thought it right, but that I had, by my own urgent representations, prevented his dismissal long ago by the Secretary, and that our personal relations were friendly, but that I did not depend upon any sincerity in Walter, who would desert me if he could thereby help himself. That he was a vain man and without proper strength

of character. That he said he lived upon praise, while
I did not and was satisfied with doing my duty. He
[Senator Pearce] said that was enough to show the sort
of man he was.[81]

Thomas Walter resented having a Captain in the Army as his superior,
which he considered inferior to his position as Architect of the Capitol. This
unhappy relationship was further emphasized in an entry in Meigs journal on
December 26, 1857:

> Knowing and expecting all this for 5 years, I still,
> believe him to be the best architect and faithful and
> industrious in his duty to the nation, though to me
> most untrue, kept him employed, and I trust will keep
> him. .... his talents and taste, which in architectural
> form and decoration are great.
>
> In all other branches of art, his taste is noth-
> ing. In painting and sculpture, which he hates as rival
> arts and taking, when used in building, the attention
> from the architect to the painter or sculptor, his taste
> is nothing. He says they are not arts, that architecture
> is the only art, and that Michelangelo was a humbug
> and no artist.[82]

Walter was no less critical of Meigs and wrote to a friend in Pennsylvania:

> I am under, the most tyrannical, despotic, vain,
> and unscrupulous man, viz Capt. M. C. Meigs - he
> seeks to rob me of every thing he can to pamper his
> own vanity; to check me in all my works because I will
> not allow him to have credit for what he had no more
> agency in producing than you had - He is a shallow
> brained pippenjohn with epaulets and brass buttons
> claiming to be architect, painter, sculptor, philosopher,
> and a thousand other things about which he is wholly
> ignorant... [83]

The struggle between the large egos of Meigs and Walter had reached a point of no return, and they would never again be capable of working amicably with one another.

⟶∾

Secretary Floyd believed in cronyism and it did not take long for Congress to suspect possible corruption when it came to granting contracts for construction of the Capitol. This clashed with the previous process of competitive bidding used by Meigs. Quickly, Floyd and Meigs disagreed, or perhaps more accurately described, quarreled. Thomas Walter knew it was only a matter of time before Secretary Floyd would find it necessary to eliminate Meigs from the business of awarding contracts. Walter would be happy to see Meigs gone.

Even the artists of America wanted Meigs gone, or at least prevented from choosing the artists for decorating the Capitol. One hundred twenty-seven artists signed a twenty-one page memorial (letter) to Congress, requesting the formation of a committee of distinguished artists (3) to be selected by the President. President Buchanan appointed the commission, and three artists on May 18, 1859.[84]

The animosity and mistrust between Meigs and Secretary Floyd, fueled by Walter, intensified daily. In September and October 1859, it peaked. While Meigs and Walter feuded over drawings, Secretary Floyd decided to take his case for the removal of Captain Meigs to the President, claiming Meigs had disobeyed an order. President Buchanan did not believe a military officer, particularly Meigs, was capable of disobeying an order from a superior, but he felt he must support a member of his Cabinet, especially one from a slave state.

Secretary Floyd contacted Captain William B. Franklin, another West Point graduate and an acquaintance of Meigs, asking him to assume Meigs' position. Meigs wrote in his journal, October 30, 1859:

> That I suppose he must now have made up his mind that one of us should retire. That I had for a long time held that one of the 3 - Walter, the Secretary or myself - must go, and that as they were together and I was of less importance to the administration than the Secretary, I felt that I would probably be the one to go.[85]

Franklin caught in the middle of the conundrum, would be replacing a friend but, on the other hand, the prestigious position would be the most challenging and interesting he might ever face. It did not matter, it would be an order.

On November 1, 1859, Meigs received the order:

> Sir,
>
> You are hereby relieved from duty as Engineer in charge of the construction of the Capitol and Post Office extensions and the new Dome.
>
> You will accordingly, turn over all the buildings, materials, tools, [books] papers and other public property connected with these works [complete?] with the funds remaining in your hands, to Captain William B. Franklin of the Typographical Engineers, who has been reassigned the duty of your stead.
>
> Very respectfully,
> Your obdt servt [sic]
> John B. Floyd[86]

The order did not include transferring Meigs to another city or fort. He was to remain in charge of the Washington aqueduct, the assignment which originally brought him to the city.

∽

Louisa and the children returned to Villa Negroni early November, 1858. Teresa and Giuseppe, welcomed them with tears and hugs. As Louisa moved from room to room, small, normally unnoticed objects would suddenly remind her of her husband, making the first weeks difficult for her and her children.

Luther Terry welcomed her in the studios. At first both found it difficult to talk, and their eyes filled with tears until Louisa said, "I have to get better control of myself. It is over a year now, but coming home to all this is difficult."

"I still miss him, too," said Terry.

"I never did see the enlarged plaster of *Freedom*. You wrote it had been shipped in April. Captain Meigs informed me there were some problems with the boat. Has it arrived in Washington?" said Louisa.

"No, that's a long story and getting longer. After the boat, the *Emily Taylor*, left Leghorn in April, it developed a leak and they stopped in Gibralter for repairs. The next I heard, the leak had returned, and the last report said the boat was in Bermuda. I have no other information."

"My God, did the plasters get soaked? That would be a disaster."

"It would be, but I know no more. We should hear something soon."

"What about the other works for the Capitol and Richmond?"

"The first door is ready to be put in plaster. The second needs more work. The panels are roughed out, but there is a great deal of detail remaining to be done."

"Let me see what it looks like," said Louisa.

Terry took Louisa to another room where both doors were modeled in clay. The first, as he mentioned was finished. The second, was well along, but incomplete.

"The second door is further along than Captain Meigs believes.[87] He has a rough sketch and thinks that is all Crawford had done. I wish he could see this. Because he has seen the photograph of the original rough sketch, he has decided it cannot be attributed to Crawford. Once he makes up his mind, he refuses to back down," said Louisa.

"Does that mean he will no longer accept the second door?" said Terry.

"No, he just wants someone else to complete it. I could not convince him otherwise."

"But it is Crawford's work."

"You and I know that, but he will not listen to me. Let's look at the other pieces."

As they moved through the studio, the workers would pause and look up from their work as she passed. By the look in their eyes Louisa could tell they were expressing the sympathy they felt for her loss as well as their own.

Satisfied with what she found, Louisa said to Terry, "You have everything under control. Thank you. Would you be willing to continue helping me finish his work?"

"I am enjoying this. Yes, I would like to continue helping in any way I can. These are important commissions, something you and your children and family will be proud of in the future."

Louisa commissioned William H. Rinehart, an American sculptor in Rome, to complete the second door. The carving of *History and Justice*, the two sculptures for above the first door, would be completed in Italian marble at the studio as Crawford wished. He had almost completed the clay figures of John Marshall and George Mason. Richmond commissioned Randolph Rogers, another American sculptor, to complete Crawford's figures and model the other two, Andrew Lewis and Thomas Nelson.

∾

The saga of the voyage of *Freedom* would cover the span of a year. After leaving Gibralter, the *Emily Taylor* again leaked, this time badly, and had to land in Bermuda where it was condemned. The crates with the five plaster sections of the sculpture did not get damaged or wet, and they finally arrived in Washington late March, 1859, one year after leaving Italy.

Senator Charles Sumner's physician again prescribed rest in southern France for his patient and in spring, 1859, feeling much improved, he returned to Italy. Happy to again be in Rome, where he had so many fond memories of his time with George Greene and Crawford, he visited Villa Negroni and Louisa.

After the studio assistants had left, Sumner walked through the studios alone. His thoughts drifted to the summer of 1839 when he first met the young Crawford. All the plaster models surrounding him testified to his genius, the genius Sumner had recognized and promoted. The monuments Crawford designed would last thousands of years, a permanent testimonial to the man. Even if a monument is buried in some natural catastrophe or by the sands of time, some archeologist will dig it up and write a book venerating it as the most important find since the last dig. Crawford's death at 44 was a cruel reminder of one's mortality. Sumner wondered what he had accomplished, if anything, that would survive as long as a sculptor's monument?

∾

Clark Mills' *George Washington* sculpture was dedicated by former President Franklin Pierce on February 22, 1860. The speech given by Clark Mills surprised everyone. Mills told the crowd:

> ....But permit me, in, justice to myself, to say that
> the statue was intended for a much higher elevation
> than it has now. It has been thus placed in consequence

of the appropriation being inadequate to carry out the
original design. The monument according to the original design, would have been forty feet in height, constructed of marble..... the pedestal divided into three
stories to represent the three great epochs in the history of the country......[88]

The apologia he delivered did little to stem the criticism of the sculpture which followed in the newspapers and periodicals. Different from the
reception of his Andrew Jackson, it began immediately. The horse received
the brunt of the bad reviews. Congress did appropriate the remainder of the
money originally approved for the sculpture ($50,000) and for a pedestal,
but one similar in size to the one he designed for his Andrew Jackson sculpture. This amounted to $8,270.07 bringing the total cost to $58,270.07.
Bloodied, but undeterred, Clark Mills still considered himself America's
foremost sculptor.[89]

Not one to back down from a fight, Meigs managed to continue annoy-
ing Secretary Floyd. He had many supporters in Congress, but Secretary Floyd
decided to get rid of this nuisance. He transferred Meigs to Fort Jefferson in the
Dry Tortugas west of Key West, as remote a station he could find.

Clark Mills noted this banishment of Meigs with interest. He knew Crawford's *Freedom* had arrived for casting in America. Meigs never contacted him to
bid on the casting and instead, spoke with the Chicopee Foundry in Ames, Massachusetts. Meigs had also considered the bid of $14,000 the Royal Foundry
in Munich Crawford obtained before his death. Captain Franklin had another
suggestion: why not use the bronze foundry Meigs had installed on the grounds
of the Capitol?

Mills understood Secretary Floyd's way of doing business. Secretary Davis
and Meigs kept all bidders at 'arm's length.' Franklin, cut from the same West
Point cloth, seemed no different. So Mills asked his influential southern friends
for their help in getting the contract for casting *Freedom* by bypassing Franklin
and contacting Secretary Floyd directly.

Mills' ties with Charleston and South Carolina continued to be as solid
as when he left in 1850. The congressional delegation from the state strongly
suggested to their fellow southerner, Secretary Floyd of Virginia, that Mills was
the obvious choice to cast the sculpture for the dome. His Andrew Jackson and
recently completed *George Washington* "were the most important sculptures in the

city," and his foundry was conveniently located just outside the city. There was no need to have it cast in Germany.

For Secretary Floyd, the benefit would be future support from the members of Congress from South Carolina for anything on his agenda, which by now was under scrutiny by Congress. On April 3, 1860, Secretary Floyd told Franklin to proceed with a contract.

Captain Franklin aware of the unorthodox and possibly corrupt business practices of Secretary Floyd by March, 1860, felt he too could be relieved of duty for quarreling with the Secretary. His opinion of Walter was no better than Meigs', and he wrote:

> Mr. Walter ... is a great sneak and liar, and is hand in glove with Floyd.[90]

No stranger to *Freedom*, Franklin made the final payment to the Italian plaster craftsmen hired by Meigs to reassemble the five sections and repair the minor damage incurred on the long trip. This took a year, but when they finished, everyone marveled at its size and grandeur.

Within a week of Secretary Floyd's letter to Franklin, Clark Mills sent him a letter offering to do the casting for $25,000 with $10,000 up front. Franklin, who had not yet met the man, asked Mills to come to his office to discuss his offer. Mills came to the meeting, confident he would just have to sign the written contract. He was not asking for a commission, he already had one from this man's superior. He felt he could dictate the terms. But, Franklin felt otherwise.

୭ঙ

When he arrived at the office, Franklin suggested they examine *Freedom*, now reassembled. As they stood before the plaster figure, Franklin said, "Do you have any concerns about the casting?"

"No. It will be difficult, but I can do it. There are some complicated areas with deep undercuts. They will cause problems," said Mills.

"Will you cast it in one piece?"

"That would be impossible. I plan to cast it in the same five sections in which it was received."

"I saw the sections when they were unpacked. When they put it back together they did such a good job, the lines or joints have disappeared."

"I will find them. I can already tell where they should be," said Mills.

"You said your price would be $25,000?" asked Franklin.

"Yes, the amount of bronze required will be substantial, and I already mentioned the complexity of the piece. No one in America has ever cast something this size," replied Mills.

"Crawford forwarded Meigs a bid of $14,000[91] from the Royal Foundry in Munich, delivered," said Franklin.

"That's a tough price to beat. What about the quality of their work," said Mills.

"Crawford used that foundry for his sculptures for the Richmond monument. His equestrian George Washington sits on a horse twenty-one feet tall, cast in one piece. Secretary Floyd was the Governor of Virginia when the final contract was signed with Crawford, so he knows his work well. I already have a contract with a company in Philadelphia to supply bronze for the foundry at the Capitol, and the government orders bronze for the foundry in the Naval Yard. I'm certain I can get a better price than you."

"So you would pay for the bronze?"

"Yes, why don't you think about another bid with that in mind? We can meet again in a week," said Franklin.

"I will do that," said a disappointed Mills.

Franklin, not interested in any new bid from Mills, used the week to convince Secretary Floyd $25,000 was too high a price for the job. For a change, they agreed. Franklin proposed a contract in which the government paid a flat monthly rate for the use of Mill's studio. The government would supply the bronze and extra tools needed from their foundries and pay the wages of his assistants and slaves. The final clause of the agreement would include:

> The work should be under the superintendence
> of a proper officer of the United States during its
> prosecution.[92]

That would allow Franklin to keep a close watch over the progress of the project. At their next meeting Mills, already warned by his influential friends that Secretary Floyd had agreed with Franklin's proposal, acquiesced to the terms and the work began in June, 1860. The monthly rent of the studio was set at $400.

☙

Much happier in Europe, Senator Charles Sumner reluctantly returned to the Senate Chamber in December, 1859. He found an even more divisive atmosphere between the slaveholding states and the free states. The raid by John Brown on Harper's Ferry, with arms supplied by abolitionists, alarmed the slaveholding states who now as a group openly discussed secession from the Union.

Another developing threat to the slaveholding states involved the nomination of candidates by the political parties for the presidential election of 1860. The Republican party nominated Abraham Lincoln; the Democrats split and the northern faction nominated Stephen O. Douglas and the southern faction, John C. Breckinridge. A third candidate, John Bell, was nominated by the Constitutional Union Party. This split in the Democratic Party made Lincoln a likely winner. Considered a moderate and known to be against slavery, the slaveholding states did not feel they could trust Lincoln.

Sumner's colleagues from South Carolina and Virginia took up where they left off after his attack in the Senate, ridiculing him for his absence of four years, claiming he suffered no physical damage from the attack, just fear and cowardice. Sumner followed the business of the Senate quietly until a bill came to the floor for the admission of Kansas as a Free State.

On June 4, 1860, he decided to take the floor and began a four-hour oration which he called *The Barbarism of Slavery*. If Sumner feared another beating, he showed no evidence. Besides the moral and ethical arguments he carefully developed, he again personally attacked even more Senators from slaveholding states then in the previous oration, which resulted in the disabling attack:

> The whole character of Slavery as a pretended form of civilization is put directly in issue, with a pertinacity and hardihood which banish all reserve on this side. In these assumptions, Senators from South Carolina naturally take the lead. Following Mr. Calhoun, who pronounced "Slavery the most safe and stable of institutions in the world," and Mr. McDuffe, who did not shrink from calling it "the corner-stone of the republican edifice," the Senator from South Carolina [Mr. Hammond] insists that "its forms of society are the best in the world;" and his colleague [Mr. Chestnut] takes up the strain. One Senator from Mississippi [Mr. Davis] adds, that Slavery "is but a form of civil

government for those who are not fit to govern themselves;" and his colleague [Mr. Brown] openly vaunts
that it "is a great moral, social, and political blessing -
a blessing to the slave and a blessing to the master."
One Senator from Virginia, [Mr. Hunter,] in a studied
vindication of what he is pleased to call "the social
system of the slaveholding States," exalts Slavery as
"the normal condition of human society;" "beneficial
to the non-slave holder as it is to the slave-owner;"
and, in enthusiastic advocacy, declares, "that the very
keystone of the mighty arch, which by its concentrated
strength is able to sustain our social superstructure,
consists in the black marble block of African Slavery.
Knock that out," he says, "and the mighty fabric, with
all that it upholds, topples and tumbles to its fall.....[93]

...Between Slavery and Civilization there is
an essential incompatibility. If you are for one, you
cannot be for the other.....[94]

He concluded with:

Thus, sir, speaking for Freedom in Kansas, I have
spoken for Freedom everywhere, and for Civilization;
and, as the less is contained in the greater, so are all
arts, all sciences, all economies, all refinements, all
charities, all delights of life, embodied in this cause.
You may reject it; but it will be only for today. The
sacred animosity between Freedom and Slavery can
end only with the triumph of Freedom."[95]

No cheers or applause filled the chamber when he sat down. Mr. Chestnut
of South Carolina responded as follows:

Mr. President: After the extraordinary though
characteristic speech just uttered to the Senate, it is
proper that I assign the reason for the position we are
now inclined to assume. After ranging over Europe,
crawling through the back door to whine at the feet of

the British aristocracy, craving pity, and reaping a rich harvest of contempt, the slanderer of States and men reappears in the Senate. We had hoped to be relieved from the outpourings of such vulgar malice. We had hoped that one who had felt, though ignominiously he failed to meet, the consequences of former insolence, would be wiser, if not better, by experience. In this I am disappointed, and I regret it...... It has been left for this day, for this country, for the Abolitionists of Massachusetts, *to deify the incarnation of malice, mendacity, and cowardice.* Sir, we do not intend to be guilty of aiding in the apotheosis of pusillanimity and meanness. We do not intend to contribute, by any conduct on our part, to increase the devotees at the shrine of this new idol. We know what is expected and what is desired. *We are not inclined again to send forth the recipient of* PUNISHMENT *howling through the world, yelping fresh cries of slander and malice. These are the reasons* which I feel it due to myself and others to give to the Senate and the country, why we have quietly listened to what has been said, and why we can take no other notice of the matter.[96]

Sumner received support from a few in the Senate, but most remained silent. All felt trapped in a political quicksand, dragging them deeper toward a major confrontation with the slaveholding states. No one had a solution.

౷

When Captain Meigs reached Key West, he found the forts in Key West (Fort Taylor) and the Dry Tortugas (Fort Jefferson) ill-prepared to defend the entrance to the Gulf of Mexico. Secretary of War Floyd ignored Meigs' requests for additional troops, arms, and ships to defend the forts. This led to pleas from congress for the removal of Secretary Floyd, and he resigned December 29, 1860. Postmaster John Holt, was temporarily appointed Secretary of War by outgoing President Buchanan until Lincoln took office and could choose his own Cabinet. Captain Meigs returned to Washington, February 20, 1861, and assumed he would return to his previous position of superintendent of construction of the Capitol.

Captain Franklin did not welcome the return of Meigs as did others in Washington. He wished to continue his position and so informed Meigs. The standoff between the two lasted one week, and Meigs prevailed, convincing Secretary Holt to transfer Franklin to supervise the current new construction at West Point. On February 28, Meigs returned to his office in the Capitol and resumed supervising the Capitol construction.

Meigs would again have full authority over the Capitol construction as he did under Jefferson Davis. Not being one to forgive and forget, he attempted to dismiss Thomas Walter and had the authority to do so. Lincoln's choice for Secretary of War, Simon Cameron, and others persuaded Meigs to concentrate on finishing the Dome which Walter designed and put their bickering to rest.

෴

The inauguration of Abraham Lincoln, winner of the Presidential election of November 6, 1860 was scheduled for March 4, 1861. Before Lincoln's inauguration, seven states from the deep south, led by South Carolina, would have seceded from the Union to form the Confederate States of America.

Meigs attended Lincoln's inauguration and entered in his journal, March 4, 1861:

> I stood in the crowd at the inauguration. So near that I heard much of the inaugural. Mr. Lincoln declares his intention to also occupy and possess the forts in possession of the United States. To be patient, lenient, and to endeavor by pacific policy to bring all misguided people to a proper sense of their duty.
>
> The general impression seems to be that we have at last found that we have a government. The troops were under arms in parts of the city, and the whole thing passed more quietly than usual.[97]

None of the attempts by Congress to bring about a compromise with the seceding states would be supported by Senator Charles Sumner. On April 12, 1861, Fort Sumter in South Carolina, was bombarded by the forces of the new Confederacy, and President Lincoln faced a civil war.

Part VIII

Topping the Dome

Clark Mills, unhappy with the final contract for casting Freedom, took his slave and unofficial foreman, Philip Reid, with him to determine how they would transport the large plaster to his foundry in Bladensburg. Seeing the plaster for the first time, Reid said, "This is bigger than I expected. We have never cast a piece this size. Have you decided where to cut it?"

"It was already divided into five sections before they shipped it. We should use the same lines they chose," said Mills.

Reid walked over to the plaster and ran his hand over the lower area hoping to feel where they had re-plastered or rejoined an area. After about ten minutes, he looked at Mills and said, "I cannot feel a seam. Whoever did this knew what they were doing and hid the seams perfectly."

"You keep looking, I know you can find them. Look higher, that may give you a clue to the other areas. I'll go see if I can find the plasterers who did the work."

When Mills found the men who reassembled *Freedom* he got a surprise. The Italian craftsmen showed no interest in helping him find the seams unless they were paid. They argued that since they were the ones who put the massive sculpture together, and did it so skillfully, only they should properly disassemble their work. This, they said, would take time and money.

In no mood to pay anyone after the disappointing contract he had negotiated with Franklin, he returned to see if Reid had solved the puzzle. He found him still searching the surfaces of the plaster and told him, "We will have to find the seams ourselves. Those Italians are impossible to deal with. They never move a muscle unless they get paid."

"We might have more luck if we could see the inside, but this piece is too big to tip and if we did, the weight might crush the bottom edge," replied Reid.

"We can't even move it until we find those seams. Just the problem of moving these plaster sections makes me nervous. The two lower sections are much wider than most wagons. The only good news is there are plenty of hoists available on the Capitol grounds."

"What would happen if we hoisted the piece?" asked Reid.

"I don't understand. It will just be lifted off the ground."

"Those seams have been recently plastered, so they are the weakest points in the piece."

"I still do not understand. What are you getting at?"

"The weight of the piece might put enough stress on the seams to make them separate, at least crack a little," said Reid.

Mills had to agree, that might work. And it did work.[98] When they gently hoisted the plaster by the head, they finally found the seams, and knew where to separate the five sections. Then they moved them to Mills' foundry. They began the casting June, 1860.

They decided to start with the head section and work down, leaving the largest section for the last. Reid and his crew, were now well-experienced in the casting process and trial and error was a thing of the past in Mills' foundry.

His crew had done well, but Mills did not think he was making enough money on the project. In May, 1861, Mills wrote to the recently-promoted Brigadier General Meigs that the casting of *Freedom* was two-thirds finished and he would like to change the contract.[99] He asked for $6000 to finish the casting, but rather than having the government pay his workers and purchase supplies he said he would be responsible. Meigs' recent promotion by President Lincoln also made him quartermaster general of the Union Army giving him little time to devote to the expansion of the Capitol. Meigs agreed to pay $5000 and Mills accepted.

Meigs, because of the war, had ordered a halt to all Capitol construction, but President Lincoln reversed the order later. The President felt stopping work on the Capitol would suggest the beginning of a weakening or collapse of the Union government. Because of the demands now facing the Department of War, Congress transferred the supervision of all Capitol construction to the Department of the Interior, with Thomas Walter assuming Meigs' position. Walter no longer had to report to a military officer.[100]

෨෨

The election of Lincoln and secession of the seven slaveholding states, quickly followed by the secession of four more, completely changed the composition of the Senate. His detractors gone, Charles Sumner now became a powerful force in the chamber. Discussions about the formation of Lincoln's cabinet included the possibility of Sumner for one of the positions. Sumner, as usual, denied he had any interest in becoming a cabinet member.

President Lincoln had other ideas and eventually appointed Sumner Chairman of the Committee on Foreign Relations. This suited Sumner, his interests, other than the abolition of slavery, had always been overseas. Sumner found President Lincoln difficult to fathom and questioned his ability to govern with so little formal education. In reality, Sumner questioned the intellectual ability of almost everyone in Congress.

❧

Clark Mills notified Thomas Walter he had completed casting *Freedom* in December, 1861. The final cost to the government was $23,796.82,[101] which included the $3,000 already paid to Thomas Crawford for the plaster model. Mills had done well and was financially secure, but even though no battles were being fought in Washington or on his farm in Bladenburg, the conflict would bring a major change to his life.

President Lincoln entered office hoping to reverse the secession movement by peaceful means, but the rapid developments leading to an all out civil war gave him no chance. The underlying issue, slavery, now hounded him. He made a choice, and the Senate and House passed *An Act for the release of certain Persons held to the Service or Labor in the District of Columbia*, signed into law by the President on April 16, 1862.[102] The Act freed the slaves in Washington, granted reimbursement to their owners and an offer of $100 to those freed who wished to emigrate to Liberia or some other country. Those freed could also, if qualified, enlist in the Union Army.[103]

With no other choice, Mills petitioned for reimbursement for his eleven slaves, five of which were children. He put 'values' varying from $50 to $1500 (Philip Reid) on his slaves, totaling $5250, but the final figure allowed was $300 per slave. His 'foreman' was now a free man.

Philip Reid, with Mills since Charleston, South Carolina, continued to work in the foundry, but now he received full wages, and any time away from work was his own. The District of Columbia Emancipation freed almost 3000 slaves. President Lincoln signed the Emancipation Proclamation for all states, January 1, 1863.

∾

Thomas Walter wanted to display the bronze *Freedom* before placing it on top the Capitol dome. He had Mills bring it to a site near the east side of the Capitol. Everyone came to see this symbol of freedom and found it impressive except for one detail, the headdress, which puzzled many, including members of Congress. The critics claimed the odd-looking eagle head covered with large feathers detracted from the overall appearance of the work.

In December, 1863, Thomas Walter was ready to have the final section of *Freedom* hoisted to the top of the Capitol dome. For him, this represented the culmination of his design of the Capitol extension and dome, but the country was fighting a war. It was no time for a celebration. The following is an excerpt from his letter of December 2, 1863 to Captain C. F. Thomas, now the super-intendent of construction of the dome under Walter:

> Sir: It is the wish of the Department that no demonstrations whatever be made, on our part, on the placing of the head on the statue of the Dome: and this expression of desire agrees precisely with my own taste; I have therefore to request that the head be put on as a matter of everyday work, that none of the persons on the Dome be permitted to make any noise whatever, or to wave their hats, and also that no attempt be made by anyone at speech making. And you are further directed to permit no one to get on the head after it is up. It is always dignified, when we do a good or great thing to appear to be unconscious of it ourselves; the raising of the American flag will be all that we shall have to do; the War Department will do the rest....[104]

The War Department sent the following order to the Twenty-second Army Corps December 1, 1863:

At 12 n. on the 2nd inst. [sic] the Statue of Freedom which crowns the dome of the National Capitol will be inaugurated. In commemoration of this event and as an expression due from the Department of respect for this material symbol of the principle from which our Government is based, it is ordered -

First, at the moment at which a flag is displayed from the statue a national salute of 35 guns will be fired from a field battery on Capitol Hill.

Second, that [the] last gun from the salute will be answered by a similar salute from Fort Stanton, which will be followed in succession from right to left by salutes from Forts Davis, Mahan, Lincoln, Bunker Hill, Totten, DeRussy, Reno, Cameron, Corcoran, Albany and Scott....[105]

At noon, December 2, 1863, Thomas Walter, Architect of the Capitol, could only feel vindicated as he watched the final section, the head of *Freedom*, hoisted to the top of the dome. It took a war to return him to the position which he felt should never have been taken from him.

Brigadier-General Montgomery C. Meigs reminisced about all he accomplished in building the Capitol extension and dome. The normally tough, unemotional Meigs, looking at *Freedom*, remembered his favorite artist and sculptor, Thomas Crawford, and quickly suppressed the tear which threatened to escape his eye.

Clark Mills knew it was his signature, which would forever be found on the lowest segment of the sculpture, not Thomas Crawford's.[106] Crawford and the others who traveled to Italy to study sculpture ignored and dismissed Mills' work as amateur, but there was no question in his mind his stamp would always be a part of the history of the nation's Capitol.

Senator Charles Sumner, pleased to see Crawford's *Freedom* on the dome, congratulated himself for recognizing the talent of the young genius.

One can only wonder what the former slave, Philip Reid, was thinking.

Epilogue

Crawford's figures for the Senate east pediment, as well as *History and Justice* above the east door of the north wing, were put in place in 1863. *History and Justice* had to be re-carved in 1974. Meigs predication regarding Italian marble proved correct; it degenerated quicker and more extensively than the Lee, Massachusetts marble. Crawford's first Revolutionary War Senate door was installed in 1868, the second, not until 1905. Crawford never saw any of his work for the Capitol completed and in place. His name is not on *Freedom* and it is unlikely the plaster of *Freedom* would have been shipped from his studio in Rome without his signature. However, Crawford is the only sculptor who has a bust in the Capitol.

Meigs sent the original plaster figures of the pediment to his alma mater, West Point. They have disappeared, and were apparently destroyed. The other plasters in Crawford's Rome studio were presented to the Park Commissioners of New York by Louisa Crawford in 1860, and displayed in the art gallery of Mount St. Vincent College in Central Park. A fire on January 2, 1881, destroyed the gallery and most of his plasters.[107] Besides the sculptures of Crawford at the Capitol, over forty of his other works, almost all in marble, can be found in America.

Louisa Crawford married Luther Terry in 1861, four years after her husband's death. The Crawford's had three daughters; Jeannie died in England at nineteen. Annie married a German Baron, and Mimoli married a British diplomat. After her husband's death she became a writer. The son, Francis Marion, became one of the most popular novelists of the late nineteenth century. Louisa Crawford died in 1897, and is buried in Rome.

Randolph Rogers was selected to complete the sculpture for the Richmond *George Washington* monument. He finished the sculptures of Marshall and Mason, which Crawford had begun, and modeled the two twelve-foot figures of Nelson and Lewis. He also did six allegorical figures, each six-feet high, placed below the famous Virginians. Because of the Civil War, the monument was not completed until 1869.[108]

Charles Sumner continued as Senator from Massachusetts until his death in 1874. Throughout his distinguished tenure he continued to fight for the rights of African Americans.

Quartermaster General Montgomery C. Meigs, played a major role in the success of the Union Army during the Civil War. After the war, he returned to supervising building projects in the District of Columbia.

The committee of artists formed by President Buchanan, a reaction to Meigs' control over art commissions for the Capitol, lasted one year. After criticizing the artwork already completed in the Capitol, the committee submitted a list of commissions they felt necessary for the building. Congress, after receiving the report, disbanded the committee.[109]

Clark Mills, with the help of his sons, continued to cast sculpture in his foundry, the first art foundry in America. He also maintained a studio in Washington and taught sculpture. Even though Mills had made a life mask of Lincoln, his eighteen year old student, Vinnie Ream, received the commission from Congress for the marble sculpture of Abraham Lincoln which stands in the Capitol. She followed in the footsteps of Crawford and completed the sculpture in Rome.[110]

Clark Mills completed over 100 face molds and busts of Native Americans at Fort Marion, St. Augustine, Florida and Hampton Institute, Hampton, Virginia for the Smithsonian Institution. His many other plasters of famous Americans included a bust of General Robert E. Lee. He completed his third Andrew Jackson sculpture for Nashville, Tennessee in 1880 and sold many smaller (24 inch) reproductions of his Andrew Jackson sculpture, which he had patented. He died in 1883.

During the time Thomas Walter had *Freedom* exhibited on the grounds of the Capitol many complained of the headdress on the sculpture. They admired the sculpture except for the bewildering eagle head and feathers. This objection to the headdress continued even after *Freedom* had been placed on the dome. Members of congress wanted it removed, but Thomas Walter, also admitting he did not like it, responded to the major critic, Congressman John H. Rice:

> ...In the third place you ask whether in my judge-
> ment "it is advisable to remove the crest." To this
> inquiry I may be permitted to say, that I always con-

sidered it a very objectionable feature of the figure; but that the removal of it alone would leave the statue imperfect as a work of art; the idea of leaving the head bare could not be entertained for a moment; the figure is so formed, and so draped, and so armed, that some kind of head ornament is absolutely necessary; to omit would subject us to severe criticism.[III]

Thomas Walter retired after 14 years as Architect of the Capitol in 1865. Louisa's sister, Julia Ward Howe and her husband, Samuel Gridley Howe had a turbulent marriage. Samuel, twenty years older, wanted her to stay home, raise the children (they had seven) and be seen but not heard. Her abolitionist husband raised funds for John Brown and his men for their infamous raids. Julia raised the children but was her own woman, an intellectual and poet. She outlived her husband by thirty-four years and championed women's rights and suffrage. Her poem *Battle Hymn of the Republic,* sung to the tune of *John Brown's Body,* is an American classic.

George Washington Greene did complete a three volume work on his famous grandfather, Major-General Nathanael Greene. A prolific and eclectic writer, he served on the faculties of Brown University and Cornell. He died in 1883.

On May 30, 1861, Jefferson Davis arrived in Richmond, Virginia as President of the Confederacy. The West Point graduate, former Governor of Mississippi, United States Senator, and Secretary of War would again be reunited with the sculptor he endorsed for so much work on the Capitol. The Executive Mansion or Confederate White House was less than a quarter of a mile from Thomas Crawford's equestrian monument of George Washington, on Richmond Capitol Square.

Persico's *Discovery of America* and Greenough's *Rescue Group,* originally on either side of the main steps of the east facade of the Capitol, had interesting histories. Persico's *Discovery* depicted a bold Columbus with a globe raised high in the right hand and an intimidated Indian maiden quivering beneath the triumphant intruder. Greenough's *Rescue Group* shows a settler defending his family from an Indian brave who is about to bring his tomahawk down on the settler's wife.

Over the years, Native Americans repeatedly objected to both works, calling them racist. In 1958, during another expansion of the Capitol, they were removed from the steps and placed in storage. In 1976, while Greenough's *Rescue Group* was being moved, the crane lifting the work dropped it. The pieces are now stored in the Smithsonian Institution. It has never been restored. This was the second work of Greenough removed from the Capitol (the first, his sculpture of *George Washington*).[112]

Bibliography

1. Allen, William C. *History of the United States Capitol.* Washington, D.C: United States Government Printing Office, 2001.
2. Allen, William C. *History of Slave Laborers in the Construction of the Capitol, Washington, D.C:* Office of the Architect of the Capitol, 2005.
3. Arnason, H. H. *The Sculptures of Houdon.* London, England: Phaidon Press Ltd, 1975.
4. Baker, Paul R. *The Fortunate Pilgrims.* Cambridge, MA: Harvard University Press, 1964.
5. Brumbaugh, Thomas B. "The Evolution of Crawford's Washington." *The Virginia Magazine of History and Biography,* v. 70, n.1, (1962): 2-29.
6. Crane, Sylvia E. *White Silence - Greenough, Powers and Crawford - American Sculptors in Rome.* Coral Gables, FL: University of Miami Press, 1972.
7. Dearinger, David B. "American Neoclassical Sculptors and their Private Patrons in Boston." *PhD Dissertation, The City University of New York,* 1993.
8. Dickinson, William C, Herrin, Dean A, and Kennon, Donald R. *Montgomery Meigs and the Building of the Capitol.* Athens, Ohio: Ohio University Press, 2001.
9. Dimmick, L. "An Alter Erected to Heroic Virtue Itself: Thomas Crawford and His Virginia Washington Monument." *American Art Journal,* v. 23, n. 2: 4-73.
10. Dimmick, L. "A Catalogue of the Portrait Busts and Ideal Works of Thomas Crawford (1813 - 1857) in Rome." *PhD dissertation, University of Pittsburgh,* 1968.
11. Dimmick, L. "Thomas Crawford's Orpheus: The American Apollo Belvidere." *American Art Journal,* v.19, n. 4, (1987): 46-84.
12. Fairman, Charles E. *Art and Artists of the Capitol of the United States.* Washington, D.C: United States Government Printing Office, 1927.
13. Foner, Eric. *The Fiery Trial - Abraham Lincoln and American Slavery.* New York and London: W.W. Norton & Company, 2010.

14. Fryd, Vivien G. "Two Sculptures for the Capitol: Horatio Greenough's Rescue and Luigi Persico's Discovery of America." *American Art Journal*, v. 19, n. 2 (1987): 16-39,

15. Gale, Robert. *Thomas Crawford American Sculptor.* Pittsburgh, PA: University of Pittsburgh Press, 1964.

16. Gardner, Albert T. G. *Yankee Stonecutters: The First American School of Sculptors.* New York, NY: Columbia University Press, 1945.

17. Gibson, Dr. William. "Domestic Intelligence - Mr. Crawford - the Sculptor's Case." *The Medical News and Library*, v. XV, n.176, (1857):134-139.

18. Gillespie, William M. *Rome as Seen by a New Yorker, 1843-1845.* New York and London: Wiley and Putnam, 1845.

19. Greenough, Frances B. *Letters of Horatio Greenough.* New York, NY: Kennedy, Inc. Da Capo Press, 1970.

20. Hicks, Thomas. *Thomas Crawford, His Career, Character, and Works.* New York, NY: D. Appelton & Company, 1858.

21. Hillard, George Stillman. *Six Months in Italy,* Cambridge, MA: Houghton, Mifflin and Company, The Riverside Press, 1853.

22. Hopkins, Rosemary Butler. "Clark Mills, the First American Sculptor." *MFA Thesis University of Maryland,* 1965.

23. Howard, Seymour. "Thomas Jefferson's Art Gallery for Monticello." *The Art Bulletin.* v. 59, n. 4 (1977): 583-600.

24. Johnston, Randolph W. "The Practice of Direct Art Casting." *Technical Studies (Fogg Art Museum)* v. VIII, n. 4 (1940).

25. Licht, Fred. *Canova.* New York, NY: Abbeville Press, 1983.

26. Maroon, F. J and Maroon, S. *The United States Capitol.* New York, NY: Stewart, Tabori and Chang, 1993.

27. Marraro, Howard R. "Unpublished Mazzei Letters to Jefferson." *The William and Mary Quarterly*, v. 2, n.1 (1945):71-100.

28. Palmer, Beverly W. *The Selected Letters of Charles Sumner.* Boston, MA: Northeastern University Press, 1990.

29. Rogers, Millard F. *Randolph Rogers American Sculptor in Rome.* Amherst, MA: The University of Massachusetts Press, 1971.

30. Scigliano, Eric. *Michelangelo's Mountain: The Quest for Perfection in the Marble Quarries of Carrara.* New York, London, and Sydney: Free Press, 2005.

31. Saint-Gaidens, Homer. *The American Artist and His Times.* New York, NY: Dodd, Mead & Company, 1941.

32. Shapiro, Michael E. *Bronze Casting and American Sculpture*: University of Delaware Press, 1984.

33. Sinha, Manisha. "The Caning of Charles Sumner: Slavery, Race, and Ideology in the Age of the Civil War." *Journal of the Early Republic,* v. 23, n. 2 (2003): 233-262.

34. Snell, Mark A. "Rascality in High Places - Captain William B. Franklin vs. the Secretary of War." *The Capitol Dome*, Fall, 2007: 2-8.

35. Sumner, Charles. *Freedom National; Slavery Sectional. Speech of the Hon. Charles Sumner of Massachusetts on His Motion to Repeal the Fugitive Slave Act*, Boston, MA: Ticknor, Reed, and Field, 1852.

36. Sumner, Charles. *The Crime Against Kansas; The Apologies for the Crime; The True Remedy; Speech of Hon. Charles Sumner.* Boston, MA: Jewett, Procter, & Worthington, 1856.

37. Sumner, Charles. *The Barbarism of Slavery; Speech of Hon. Charles Sumner.* Boston, MA: Thayer and Eldridge, 1860.

38. Thorp, Margaret, F. "Literary Sculptors of the Caffe Greco." *American Quarterly*, v.12, (Summer 1960): 160-174.

39. Vasari, Georgio. *Vasari on Technique.* New York: NY. Dover Publications, Inc. 1960.

40. Voss, Frederick S. *John Frazee 1790 - 1852 Sculptor.* National Portrait Gallery, Smithsonian Institution, and Boston Athenaeum. Boston, MA and Washington D.C. 1968.

41. Walton, Eugene. *The Biography of Philip Reed Historical Fiction*: Lexington, KY: Lulu, 2006.

42. Wolf, Wendy. *The Shorthand Journals of Montgomery C. Meigs* 1853-1859, 1861. Washington, D. C.: United States Government Printing Office, 2001.

43. Wunder, Richard P. *Hiram Powers, Vermont Sculptor.* Newark, London, and Toronto: University of Delaware Press, 1974.

44. Harrison, Frederick Charles, "The Early Letters of George Washington Greene, 1827-1846." *PhD Dissertation, University of Washington,* 1966.

Endnotes

Prologue

1. Fairman, 3.
2. ibid., 5.

Part I   The Mentor and Two Patrons

3. Letter from Thomas Crawford to Captain Montgomery C. Meigs December 13, 1854. In this letter Crawford goes into great detail to explain the technique used in Rome and in his studio for 'pointing' a plaster model to a marble block. Records of the Architect of the Capitol, Washington, D.C., Sculptors, Thomas Crawford, Correspondence.
4. Thorp, 160.
5. Licht, 18.
6. Gale, 18.
7. Harrison, 182.
8. Crane, 290.
9. Gale, 18.
10. Baker, 31.
11. Wunder, excellent two volume work on the life and works of Hiram Powers.
12. Arnason, 75.
13. Greenough, 87.
14. Fairman, 101.
15. Gale, 20.
16. Gale, 23.

Part II   An American Interlude

17. Burton's Gentleman's Magazine, October, 1839.
18. Fairman, 101.
19. Gale, 49.

20. Fairman, 66-68. Before the Statue of Thomas Jefferson was placed in the rotunda of the Capitol it was on display outside the White House for 35 years.

Part III   Outsider Art

21. Hopkins, 35.
22. ibid., 43.
23. ibid., 44.
24. Arnason, 53.
25. Hopkins, 44. Mills spent two weeks at Mount Vernon.
26. ibid., 46.
27. Shapiro, 38.

Part IV   Art and Politics: A Monument and Monumental Debate

28. Wolf, 136. Captain Montgomery C. Meigs comments in his journal, "His wife has about $6000 per year, and they live delightfully." This was reported to him by Kate Totten, who had recently visited the Crawford's in Rome.
29. Dimmick, *An Alter Erected...*, 8.
30. Brumbaugh, 11.
31. Dimmick, *An Alter Erected...*, 34.
32. Brumbaugh, 13.
33. Shapiro. 39.

Part V   A New Patron

34. Brumbaugh, 14.
35. ibid., 18.
36. Gale, 91.
37. Donald, 170.
38. ibid., 175.
39. ibid., 189.
40. Sumner, *Freedom National; Slavery Sectional*, 8.
41. ibid., 77.
42. Donald, 198.
43. Hopkins, 64.
44. ibid., 67.
45. ibid., 75.
46. ibid., 76.

47. Brumbaugh, 17.
48. Fairman, 143.
49. ibid., 143.
50. ibid., 144.
51. Wolf, 24.
52. ibid., 24.
53. Fairman, 152.
54. Gale, 135.
55. see endnote 3.
56. Wolf, 289.
57. ibid,, 332.
58. Fairman, 169-170.
59. Wolf, 392.
60. Sumner, *The Crime Against Kansas*, 3 & 5.
61. ibid., 9.
62. Donald, 240.
63. ibid., 240.
64. ibid., 246.
65. Sinha, 247.
66. Wolf, 412.
67. Fairman, 165.
68. Wolf, 419.

Part VI   Unforeseen Circumstances

69. Thomas Crawford's eye tumor was, almost certainly, a melanoma of the eye. The tumor originates in the choroid or ciliary body of the eye from the same brown pigment producing cell, the melanosome, which causes skin melanomas.
70. Gibson, 135. This description of the needle probing done is Dr. Gibson's own description as he related it in a prominent medical journal of the time. Insulted by the insinuation of Louisa Crawford that he was responsible for the rapid degeneration of Crawford's eye and condition, he comments in the article, "Crawford himself would never listen to the suggestion there was a danger."
71. Gale, 179.
72. Letter, April, 27, 1858, Philadelphia Evening Bulletin.

73. Gibson, 137. A malignant melanoma (called melanosis in the 1800's) of the eye can grow for quite a while before visual changes are noticed making the diagnosis delayed in many cases. The tumor metastasizes or spreads widely throughout the body, and besides the involvement of Crawford's eye, the tumor would have metastasized to the brain causing the seizures. Even today, the mortality rate five years after a diagnosis is 35%. The tumor rarely involves both eyes.

74. The Crayon, 219. July, 1857. Records of the Architect of the Capitol, Washington, D.C., Sculptors, Thomas Crawford.

75. The Crayon, 25. January, 1858. Records of the Architect of the Capitol, Washington, D.C., Sculptors, Thomas Crawford.

76. ibid.

77. Dimmick, *An Alter Erected...*, 58.

78. Wolf, 601.

79. Letter of Louisa Crawford to Captain M. Meigs, August 26, 1858. Records of the Architect of the Capitol, Washington, D.C., Sculptors, Thomas Crawford, Correspondence.

80. Wolf, 745. On October 19, 1859, over a year after Louisa's letter, Meigs enters in his Journal: "I had a visit this morning from Mr.[John G.] Chapman, the painter from Rome. He came to see me to tell me the condition of the works of Crawford upon the doors. He says that they were more than sketched, that they were massed out, and that his man, a German, can finish them, not as Crawford could, but better than any American now living can. That the artists of all countries in Rome are ready to give advice and labor to assist in the completing them. That the feeling in favor of Crawford is very strong in Rome. He was a man highly esteemed, both personally and as an artist, and his early death when in the beginning of success of his career excited great sympathy." The German referred to would be Gustav Kaupert who also worked on the clay enlargement of Freedom in Crawford's studio.

Part VII   Art and Politics: Dissension

81. Wolf, 217.

82. ibid., 567-568.

83. Allen, *History of the Capitol of the United States*, 278.

84. Fairman, 187.

85. Wolf, 750.

86. ibid., 753-753.

87. endnote 79.
88. Hopkins, 91-93.
89. ibid.
90. Snell, 5.
91. Wolf. 455.
92. Hopkins, 101.
93. Sumner, *The Barbarism of Slavery*, 9.
94. ibid., 13.
95. ibid., 115.
96. ibid., Appendix.
97. Wolf, 774.

Part VIII   Topping the Dome

98. Allen, 15-16. History of Slave Laborers in Construction of the Capitol.
99. Hopkins, Appendix B, Letter June 3, 1861, to Captain Meigs.
100. Fairman, 208.
101. Hopkins, 106.
102. United States Government; National Archives and Records Administration - Transcription; www.archives,gov/exhibits/featureddocuments
103. Foner, 199.
104. Fairman, 219.
105. Fairman, 219-220.
106. Personal communication May 10, 2011, from Dr. Barbara Wolanin, Curator for the Architect of the Capitol and the supervisor of the restoration of Freedom in 1993. "Clark Mills signed the bronze. ....and his name [Thomas Crawford] is NOT on the bronze..... There are names stamped on the bronze of Charles Thomas who erected the sections, at the bottom, Abraham Lincoln, and others in the government on the top of the feathers." Captain Charles Thomas is referred to in Thomas Walter's letter regarding the placement of the final section of the bronze head. He was on the dome when the head was screwed into place.

Epilogue

107. The New York Times, "Destruction in the Park; Buildings at Mount St. Vincent Ruined by Fire." January 3,1881. The article lists the plasters saved as well as destroyed, but most were lost in the fire.
108. Rogers, 72-73.

109. Fairman, 186-189.

110. Hopkins, 109.

111. Fairman, 226-228.

112. Fryd. The article also discusses the question of whether architect Robert Mills had the *Rescue Group* installed incorrectly. When it was placed next to the stairs, the mother and child are at the side of the settler and Indian. Greenough died before the sculpture was delivered but his brother said the mother and child should have been in front of the Indian. No change was made.

Acknowledgements

Thanks to Ray Paul who started me on this writing adventure. Sharon Brock gave me the early encouragement I needed, made some suggestions in the early part of the book, and read the first draft. Her wise comments also gave me the motivation I needed to continue and finish the book. Thanks to Janet McMahon, Library Specialist at the University of Illinois, Rockford Campus Crawford Library for her help in finding some of the more elusive references. Jan Neudeck's editing of the manuscript brought it all together for the final draft. Thanks to James Wolf for his practical advice, and Linda Hoffman for her computer expertise. Thanks to the office of the Curator for the Architect of the Capitol for their hospitality and help when I visited. The cover photo was taken by R. Novak.

I am certain my wife, Rose, who reads more books than anyone I know, read the manuscript more times then she cared to, but never refused my requests. That helped immeasurably.

About the Author

Richard F. Novak, a sculptor for 40 years, has works in both public spaces and private collections. This background gave him an appreciation of the genius of Thomas Crawford, and particularly the amount of excellent work he completed in his short life. His frequent trips to Italy allowed him to observe the culture of the ateliers and quarries in the marble areas of Pietrasanta and Carrara. He is also a Professor Emeritus (MD) at the University of Illinois College of Medicine, Rockford campus. For more, see toppingthedome.com.

Pictures

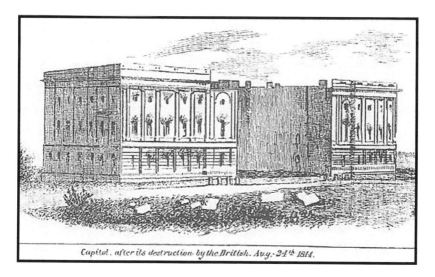

After the raid by the British, both wings of the Capitol were gutted. (Architect of the Capitol.)

Washington D. C. 1858. The construction of the Capitol dome has begun. (Architect of the Capitol.)

3 and 4. *War*, Luigi Persico. circa 1834 (both). Marble, H 11 feet. *Peace*, Luigi Persico. Marble, H 10 feet. East front portico, flanking the doors of the Capitol Rotunda. (Architect of the Capitol.)

The Genius of America, Luigi Persico. 1828. Sandstone, pediment L 81 feet 6 inches. Figures 9 feet tall. Left - Justice, Center - America, Right - Hope. "....the whole intended to convey that while we cultivate Justice we may hope for success." Charles Bulfinch, June 22, 1825. Fairman, Art and Artists of the Capitol, 48. (Architect of the Capitol.)

Discovery of America, Luigi Persico. 1844. Marble, H 15 feet 11 inches. Removed from the Capitol steps in 1958. (Architect of the Capitol.)

George Washington, Horatio Greenough. 1841. Marble, H 12 feet. (Photo circa 1899, Library of Congress Prints and Photographs Catalog.)

Thomas Crawford, Tomasso Gagliardi. Circa 1857. Marble, H 27 inches.
(U.S. Senate Collection)

Charles Sumner. Circa 1855, about 44 years old.
(Courtesy of the Boston Public Library.)

Clark Mills. (National Archives.)

Montgomery C. Meigs. Circa 1865, about age 49.
(Library of Congress Prints and Photographs Catalog.)

Andrew Jackson, Clark Mills. 1853. Bronze, H 14 feet. Washington, D.C.
(Photo by and courtesy of Fred Delventhal.)

George Washington, Clark Mills. Bronze, H 14 feet. Washington D.C.
(Photo by and courtesy of Todd Huebner.)

George Washington Monument, Richmond, Virginia, Thomas Crawford and Randolph Rogers.
1856-69. Patrick Henry and Thomas Jefferson are in the foreground beneath the
equestrian Washington. (Photo by and courtesy of Philip M. Riggan.)

The Capitol, January, 1859. (Library of Congress Prints and Photographs Catalog.)

The Progress of Civilization, Thomas Crawford. 1863. Marble, pediment L 80' H 12'
at the center. (Architect of the Capitol.)

The Progress of Civilization, detail, right side, *Early Days of America.* Woodsman, hunter, Indian chief, Indian Mother and child, and Indian grave. (Photo by R. Novak.)

The Progress of Civilization, detail, left side, *Diversity of Human Endeavor.* Soldier, merchant, two youths, the schoolmaster and child, and the mechanic. (Photo by R. Novak.)

The Progress of Civilization, detail, center. The figure of *America.* (Photo by R. Novak.)

Door, Senate Wing, Thomas Crawford. Bronze, H 14' 5" x 7" W 7' x 4". Put in place 1868.
(Architect of the Capitol.)

1. Laying of Cornerstone of Capitol
2. Inauguration of George Washington
3. Ovation for Washington at Trenton
4. Medallion - Peace and Agriculture

1. Battle of Bunker Hill
2. Battle of Monmouth
3. Battle of Yorktown
4. Medallion – War

Door, House Wing, Thomas Crawford and William H. Rinehart. 1868. Bronze, H 14' x 7" W 7' 4". Put in place 1905. (Architect of the Capitol.)

1. Wyoming, PA Massacre	1. Reading of Declaration of Independence
2. Battle of Lexington	2. Treaty of Paris
3. General Nathaneal Greene	3. Washington's Farewell
4. General Montgomery's Death	4. Benjamin Franklin in His Studio

Justice and History, Thomas Crawford. 1856. Marble, H 3' 10" W 11' 2". Located above the door of the Senate wing. (Architect of the Capitol.)

Statue of *Freedom,* ink and watercolor drawing by Thomas U. Walter, 1859. (Architect of the Capitol.)

Freedom, Thomas Crawford. Bronze, H 19 feet 6 inches. (Architect of the Capitol.)

Freedom. Inscription - E Pluribus Unum. (Architect of the Capitol.)

4552797R00125

Made in the USA
San Bernardino, CA
28 September 2013